How to back up your PC

How to back up your PC

Patrick Bultema

Mike Murach & Associates, Inc.
4697 West Jacquelyn Avenue, Fresno, California 93722-6427 (209) 275-3335

Editor
Cris Allen

Graphics designer
Steve Ehlers

Other books for PC users
The Only DOS Book You'll Ever Need by Patrick Bultema and Doug Lowe
The Least You Need to Know About DOS by Patrick Bultema
Get More from Word by Using Style Sheets by Tim Schaldach
The PC Mailing List Book: Everything you need to know to set up, use, and maintain your mailing lists on a PC by Patrick Bultema
Write Better with a PC: A publisher's guide to business and technical writing by Mike Murach

© 1992, Mike Murach & Associates, Inc.
All rights reserved.
Printed in the United States of America.

20 19 18 17 16 15 14 13 12 11 10 9 8 7 6 5 4 3 2 1

ISBN: 0-911625-63-1

Library of Congress Cataloging-in-Publication Data

Bultema, Patrick, 1959-
  How to back up your PC / Patrick Bultema.
    p. cm.
  Includes index.
  ISBN 0-911625-63-1 (alk. paper) :
  1. Electronic data processing--Backup processing alternatives.
2. Microcomputers. I. Title.
QA76.9.B32B86 1992
005.7--dc20
                                 92-4562
                                    CIP

Contents

Preface VII

Section 1 **Introductory backup concepts** 1

    Chapter 1   When and how to back up your hard disk   3

    Chapter 2   Ten guidelines for fast and effective backups   31

    Chapter 3   Backup considerations for network users   43

Section 2 **Three options for backing up a hard disk** 53

    Chapter 4   How to use DOS commands to back up a hard disk to diskettes   55

    Chapter 5   How to use a backup utility to back up a hard disk to diskettes   65
                     Utility 1: Central Point Backup   75
                     Utility 2: Norton Backup   99
                     Utility 3: PC-Fullbak+   131
                     Utility 4: FastBack Plus   157

    Chapter 6   How to use a tape drive to back up a hard disk   187

Index   198

Preface

In the last two years, I've talked with dozens of PC users who've lost one or more files from their hard disks. In every case, the person either didn't have a backup of the hard disk, or didn't have a backup that was current enough to be of any use. And in some cases, the loss was disastrous.

Over and over again, people have said to me, "I know I should be backing up my hard disk, but it just takes too long." Or, "Backups are too complicated." Or simply, "I don't know how to do backups." If one or more of these responses is yours as well, then this book is for you.

In this book, you'll learn how to do fast and effective backups of your hard disk. You'll learn how to select and use the right software and hardware for your backups. And you'll learn the concepts and techniques you need to know if you're going to come up with a sensible approach to backing up your system. In short, you'll be able to put together a backup plan that meets your requirements...one that's simple and fast.

How this book will help you

If you take a moment to look at the table of contents, you'll see that this book is divided into two sections. The first section presents the concepts and techniques that will help you make the right decisions on how to back up your system. In chapter 1 you'll learn about the software and hardware that you can use for backups. You'll also learn about the techniques that make for efficient backups. And you'll learn how to analyze your own backup requirements. So when you finish this chapter, you'll have a good idea of what subjects you need to know more about in order to create a sensible backup plan.

Based on what you need to know next, you can go to any chapter in the rest of the book. In chapter 2, for instance, you'll get some guidelines and practical advice that will help you streamline your backups, no matter what

hardware or software you're using. And if you're working on a PC network...
or if you're thinking about installing one...chapter 3 will tell you how networking may affect your backups.

In section 2, you can take an in-depth look at the software and hardware options you have for backing up your hard disk. If you're backing up to diskettes, chapters 4 and 5 will help you select the appropriate program for your backups and will teach you how to use that program for the most common backup tasks. To be specific, chapter 4 will teach you how to use the commands that DOS provides for backups, and chapter 5 will teach you how to use the four most popular backup utilities. But you don't have to read about all of these software options; you can just read about the ones that you think are appropriate for your needs...and chapter 1 will help you decide this. Chapter 1 will also help you decide if you should consider backing up to tape. If so, chapter 6 will tell you what you need to know about the various tape drives and backup programs that are available to you.

Who this book is for

This book is for anyone who uses a hard disk PC running under the DOS operating system (that includes PCs like the IBM XT, AT, or PS/2 and IBM-compatibles and clones). If you're responsible for your own backups, you're the primary person I wrote this book for. But even if you have someone else to set up a backup procedure for you, you need to know what's in this book. It will help you understand the procedure so you can follow it conscientiously.

This book assumes that you know how to enter simple DOS commands. For example, if you know how to use the DOS Copy command to copy a file from your hard disk to diskette, you probably understand enough about DOS commands to use this book. If you don't know how to enter simple commands, you need a little more background first. You can gain the knowledge you need by reading the first 5 chapters of my book, *The Least You Need to Know about DOS*. At that point, you'll be more than ready for this book.

Two DOS books you should know about

Backing up your hard disk regularly is just one aspect of being a competent, independent PC user. To help you quickly learn the other skills you need, we offer two DOS books. *The Least You Need to Know about DOS* is for the vast majority of users who want to use their PCs more effectively; *The Only DOS Book You'll Ever Need* is for people who provide PC support to less technical users or who just want in-depth knowledge of DOS.

As its title suggests, *The Least* covers the minimum set of DOS skills every PC user should have. To be specific, it teaches you how to manage directories and files, how to start application programs from DOS or a shell, how to transfer data between PCs using diskettes, the basics of doing backups, how to use the DOS 5.0 shell, and how to change the AUTOEXEC.BAT and CONFIG.SYS files (in case you don't like the way your PC starts up or operates). At the same time, this book gives you the hardware and software background you need to troubleshoot— or avoid— the PC problems that occur most often.

Since *The Only* is designed for more technical PC users, it covers much of the information that's in *The Least* but in more detail. In addition, it presents subjects that aren't in *The Least* at all: error recovery, performance considerations, utilities, the DOS 4.0 shell, and advanced subjects like how to partition and format a hard disk.

If you're interested in either of these books, you'll find more information about them at the back of this book.

Conclusion

Surveys show that the majority of PC users don't back up their hard disks. And yet, it's common knowledge that regular backups are the only way to protect the data on your hard disk. But how should you back up your hard disk? What software should you use? What hardware should you use? And how does a network affect backups? Those questions aren't so easy to answer.

That's why I wrote this book. I wrote it because there isn't another book that answers all these questions. I wrote it because I've seen too many disasters that could have been prevented by doing backups. And I wrote it because I believe you can learn how to do effective backups in just a couple of hours.

If you have any comments, questions, or criticisms, I would enjoy hearing from you. That's why there's a postage-paid comment form at the back of the book. And thank you for reading this book.

Patrick Bultema
Fresno, California
January 1, 1992

Section 1

Introductory backup concepts

Whether you use your PC a few minutes each day or a few hours, you don't want to lose the data you have on your system. To protect yourself from losing this information because of a hardware failure or user error, you need to back up your PC. Then, you have an extra copy of all the program files, data files, and operational information on your system. You can use this copy to restore any of this information to your hard disk when you need to. To back up effectively, though, you need to develop an efficient backup plan. That's why the goal of this section is to give you the information you need to develop a backup plan that fits your individual backup requirements.

In chapter 1, you'll learn about the hardware and software options that are available for backups. You'll also learn about the different types of back-ups you can use. Then, you'll learn how to put hardware, software, and backup type together to form a backup plan that fits your backup needs. In chapter 2, you'll find useful guidelines to help you refine your backup plan. If you're part of a network, you should also read chapter 3. It tells you how a being part of a network can affect your backup plan.

Chapter 1

When and how to back up your hard disk

Sooner or later, you're going to lose some or all of the files on your hard disk. It's as simple as that. Eventually, for example, the hard disk on your PC will fail, and all of the data on it will be lost. This can happen the first month you have the hard disk, or it can happen after five years of heavy use. You can also lose all the data on your hard disk if someone accidentally reformats drive C. Or you can lose all the data due to theft, fire, or vandalism.

Even if you manage to avoid one of these disasters, you'll probably lose at least one of the files on your hard disk because of a programming or operating error. If, for example, you're using your word processing program to create two proposals and you accidentally replace the first one with the second one, the first one is lost. Or, if you're using the DOS Delete command, you can accidentally delete all the files in the current directory when you meant to delete all the files on the diskette in the A drive. If this happens, you can lose dozens of files. Unfortunately, mistakes like these happen to even the most proficient PC users.

So think about it right now. Can you afford to lose all of the data on your hard disk? Can you afford to lose one of your largest and most important files? Can you afford the time it will take to recreate a file you've lost, assuming you can recreate it? If your answer is "no," you should protect yourself by backing up the data on your hard disk. Then, when a disaster happens, you can recover from it by restoring the backed-up data to your hard disk.

In this chapter, you'll learn the concepts you need for backing up the data on your hard disk. You'll also learn how software and hardware choices affect your backups. And you'll learn about several different backup techniques. Finally, you'll learn how to select the right software, hardware, and backup techniques for various backup requirements.

In short, after reading this chapter, you'll be able to create a backup plan that's best for you. As a result, you'll save time doing backups because you'll be doing them quickly and effectively. More importantly, your data will be protected because you'll be backing it up regularly according to your plan.

How backups work

When you back up a hard disk, you use a special program called a *backup program*. This program copies the files on your hard disk onto *removable storage*, like diskettes or tape cartridges. A backup program can also copy the directories and other system information on the hard disk to removable storage. In addition, a backup program uses a special format to copy data. With this format, large files that won't fit on one diskette can be stored across two or more diskettes.

Then, if one or more of the files on your hard disk is lost, you can use your backups to restore the files back to your hard disk. Because of the special operational characteristics of backup programs, you can't use the DOS Copy command to copy files from a backup. Instead, you must use the *restore function* of the backup program you used to create the backup. With this function, you can restore a single file to your hard disk, or you can restore all the files including directory and system information.

The types of hardware you can use to back up a hard disk

There are several types of hardware that you can use to back up a hard disk. Most PC users are familiar with diskettes and diskette drives. Many users are also familiar with tape drives. But there are other hardware options too, some that you may not be as familiar with.

When and how to back up your hard disk   5

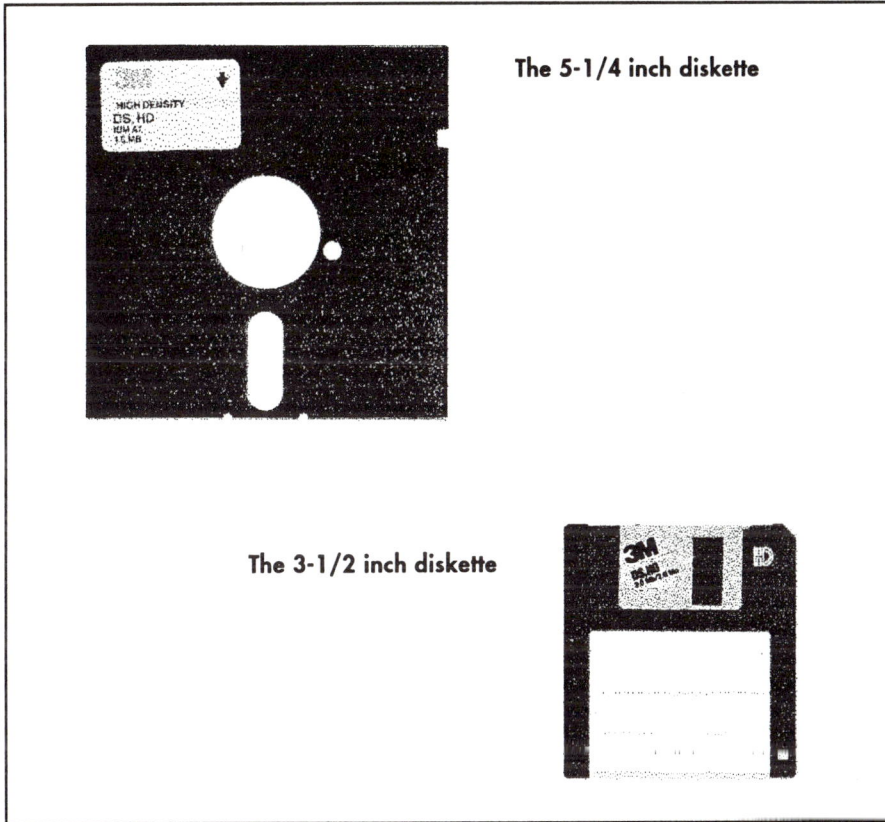

Figure 1-1   The two diskette sizes

Diskette drives   Today, *diskettes* are the most widely used storage medium for backups. That's largely because almost every PC already has at least one diskette drive. Since you should already have some experience working with diskettes, I won't tell you how to use them. Instead, I'll focus on the different types and capacities of diskettes and how this affects your backups.

Figure 1-1 shows the two sizes of diskettes that can be used with PCs. Originally, all PC, XT, and AT computers used 5-1/4 inch diskettes, and all PS/2 computers used the newer 3-1/2 inch diskettes. Today, however, you can install a diskette drive for either type of diskette on an XT, an AT, or a PS/2.

To complicate matters, both types of diskettes come in two storage capacities: *standard capacity* and *high capacity*. These capacities are measured in *bytes* of data. For practical purposes, you can think of one byte of data as one character of data, and you can think of a character as a letter, a number, or a special character such as #, %, or &. Thus, ten bytes of diskette storage are required to store the word *impossible*; four bytes are required to store the number *4188*; and two bytes are required to store *$9*.

For 5-1/4 inch diskettes, the standard capacity is 360,000 bytes, or 360KB (where *K* stands for 1,000, *B* stands for bytes, and *KB* stands for *kilobyte*, which is approximately one thousand bytes). In contrast, the high capacity is 1,200KB, or 1.2MB (where *M* stands for 1,000,000, *B* stands for byte, and *MB* stands for *megabyte*, which is approximately one million bytes). For 3-1/2 inch diskettes, the standard capacity is 720KB, and the high capacity is 1.44MB.

Figure 1-2 summarizes these diskette sizes and capacities. Because the labelling for diskettes is often confusing, this figure also lists the common labelling designations for each type of diskette. Notice, for example, that the standard capacity diskettes are called *double density* diskettes, and the high capacity diskettes are called *high density* diskettes.

Since most hard disks today have capacities of 20MB or more, it takes many diskettes to back them up. When you use diskettes for a backup, you insert and remove a series of them during the backup operation. As a result, high capacity diskettes are better than standard capacity diskettes because you don't have to insert and remove as many diskettes during the backup operation.

To use high capacity diskettes, though, you must have a high capacity diskette drive. If your PC doesn't have a high capacity drive, you can buy one for around $100. A high capacity drive can use either high capacity or standard capacity diskettes. In contrast, a standard capacity drive can only use standard capacity diskettes.

Backup tape drives   *Tape drives* are becoming more popular for backups. Like a diskette drive, the tape drive unit accepts a removable storage medium. But instead of using diskettes, the tape drive accepts a *tape*

Size	Capacity	Common labelling notation
5-1/4"	360KB standard capacity	5-1/4" Double-Sided Double-Density 5-1/4" DSDD
5-1/4"	1.2MB high capacity	5-1/4" Double-Sided High-Density 5-1/4" DSHD
3-1/2"	720KB standard capacity	3-1/2" Double-Sided Double-Density 3-1/2" 2DD 3-1/2" 1.0M formatted capacity
3-1/2"	1.44MB high capacity	3-1/2" Double-Sided High-Density 3-1/2" 2HD 3-1/2" 2.0M formatted capacity

Figure 1-2   A summary of diskette characteristics

cartridge. Often, the tape drive unit is installed in a PC just like a diskette drive. But some times, the tape drive unit is in a separate case that's attached to the PC by a cable.

Figure 1-3 shows two common sizes of tape cartridges. These cartridges can store much more information than a diskette. Currently, for example, most tape drives can store 40MB to 150MB on a single tape. And the highest capacity drives can store over 1,000MB on a single tape.

Figure 1-4 gives you some idea of the capacity, speed, and cost of various tape drives. For instance, you can get a 40MB tape drive for $250. This drive backs up 40MB in about 20 minutes. By comparison, a 500MB, high performance drive costs about $2,000. This drive backs up 40MB in about four minutes.

Generally, you should buy a tape drive with a capacity that's equal to or greater than the capacity of the largest hard disk you want to back up. Then, you can do a backup of the hard disk without having to change tapes. This allows you to do *unattended tape backups*.

The higher capacity tape drives (80MB or more) that are available today perform backups faster than diskette drives. But the inexpensive, lower capacity tape drives are actually a little slower than diskette drives. However, the slower speed isn't a consideration if you're doing unattended tape backups. The only drawback of a tape backup is the cost of adding the tape drive and backup tapes to your system.

Other hardware   Several other hardware options can be used for backups. Some PC users perform their backups using a special removable disk cartridge called a *bernoulli box*. Others use special hard disks that are removable. In either case, you need to have two drives. Generally, one drive is a non-removable hard disk and the other is a bernoulli or a removable hard disk. However, some bernoulli boxes come in a two drive configuration that allows you to use one drive as your working disk and the other as your backup disk.

Since removable hard disks are more expensive than the other backup options, most users don't get them just for backups. Instead, they get them because of other considerations. Business people who travel a lot, for instance, often use a removable hard disk because it makes it easier to transfer their working files to a PC at another location. And some businesses that need to protect secret information use bernoulli boxes so they can collect them and lock them in a safe at the end of each day.

Another hardware option that you've probably heard about is a *CD drive*. This type of drive uses an optical/laser technology to read data from a disk. But at this time, most of these drives can't write to a disk. Consequently, CD drives are typically used for reference databases like encyclopedias, dictionaries, atlases, and so on. But advances are currently being made that will allow optical technology drives to write as well as read data to a disk. These drives are generally called *optical drives* to distinguish them from the more common CD drives. When this technology is perfected, optical drives should become popular for backups as well as for database and reference use.

Two types of programs you can use to back up a hard disk

The two types of programs you can use to back up a hard disk are: the commands DOS provides, and commercial backup utilities. Since you use DOS, you already have the commands that DOS provides for backups. For many

When and how to back up your hard disk   9

The DC 2000 series tape

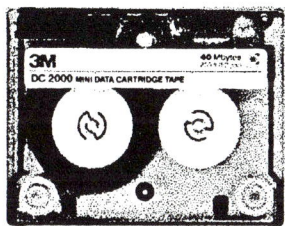

The DC 600 series tape

Figure 1-3   The two common sizes of backup tapes

Drive capacity	Typical backup speed	Cost
40MB-60MB	2MB/minute	$250-$400
80MB-150MB	4MB-6MB/minute	$400-$800
150MB-500MB	6MB-10MB/minute	$800-$2,000

Figure 1-4   The capacity, speed, and price of typical backup tape drives

---

A command that backs up hard drive C, including all directories, files, and system information.

    C:\>backup c:*.* a: /s

A command that backs up all the files on hard drive C that have been added or modified since the last backup.

    C:\>backup c:*.* a: /s/m/a

Figure 1-5 Two typical DOS Backup commands

people, though, these commands are not adequate. That's why backup utilities are so popular.

The DOS commands DOS provides two commands you can use for backups called *Backup* and *Restore*. As you might expect, you use the Backup command to back up the data on your hard disk to diskettes. Similarly, you use the Restore command to restore data from your backup diskettes to your hard disk.

One way to use these commands is to enter them at the DOS command prompt using the correct format for each command. To illustrate, figure 1-5 shows two typical Backup commands. The first command backs up all the files and directories on hard drive C to diskettes in drive A. The second command backs up only the files that have been added or modified since the last backup. You'll learn more about these two types of backups in a moment.

As you can see, the command format you use for the Backup command is complicated, which makes the command hard to use. In addition, the DOS Backup command is by far the slowest backup option. Furthermore, these commands can only back up data to and restore data from a diskette drive. You can't use them with a tape drive or other types of hardware. For these reasons, you may want to consider getting a backup utility even though you already have the DOS Backup command.

When and how to back up your hard disk

> *Central Point Backup* (included with *PC Tools Deluxe*)
>
> *Norton Backup*
>
> *PC-Fullbak+*
>
> *FastBack Plus*

Figure 1-6 The four most popular commercial backup utilities

Commercial backup utilities Figure 1-6 lists the four most popular *commercial backup utilities*. Each of these utilities is presented in detail in chapter 5 of this book. All of these utilities provide the same basic functions as the DOS Backup and Restore commands. But unlike the DOS commands, these utilities can back up to tape as well as to diskettes. In addition, all of these utilities are much faster than the DOS Backup command. They're also easier to use because you use menus to select different backup options instead of entering complicated command formats.

To illustrate, figure 1-7 shows a screen of a typical backup utility, *FastBack Plus* version 2.10. Here, the Backup menu has been activated. As you can see, the menu offers you several options. To specify the diskette drive you want to use for the backup, you select the Destination option as shown here. To specify the hard drive you want to back up, you select the hard disk option from this menu. And so on.

Figure 1-8 gives you some idea of the speed gains you can expect from a backup utility. This chart summarizes the data from an informal test on a typical system, but the message is clear. If a backup takes you 15 minutes when you use the DOS Backup command, you can probably save 10 minutes or more each time you back up by using a backup utility. The more data you have on your hard disk, the more valuable a backup utility becomes because of the time you'll save.

At a price of about $100, you can figure out how soon a backup utility will pay for itself. But the most important benefit of a backup utility is not

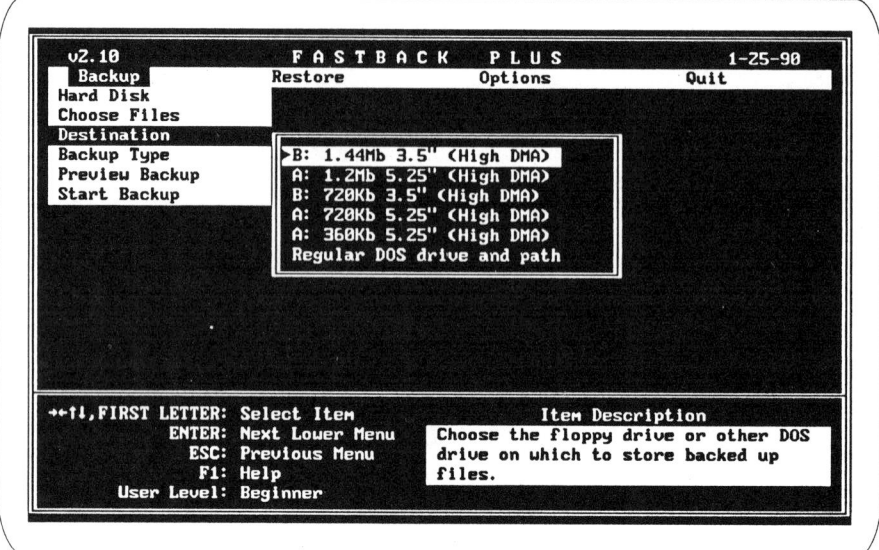

Figure 1-7   The *FastBack Plus* screen with the Backup menu activated

the time you save by using one. It's the fact that you're far more likely to do regular backups because they take less time and are easier to do.

Two types of backups

One of the keys to efficient backups is realizing that there are two types of backups. These are illustrated in figure 1-9. Here, the hard disk is backed up on Monday using a full backup. On the other days of the week, the hard disk is backed up using an incremental backup.

Full backups   A *full backup* is a backup of all the information on a hard disk. That includes program and command files as well as data files. It also includes directory and other system information. A full backup is illustrated in figure 1-9 by the procedure for Monday. When a hard disk fails, the full backup is the starting point for recovery.

When and how to back up your hard disk 13

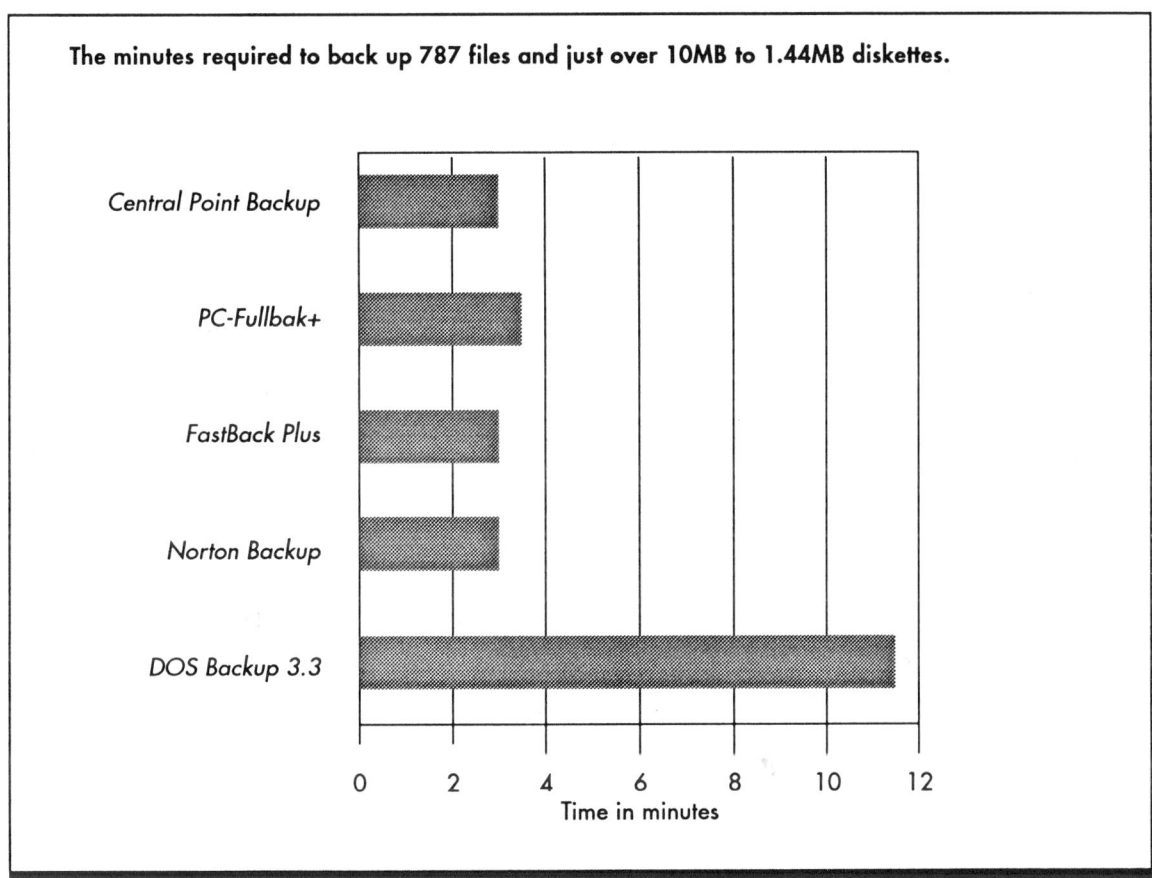

Figure 1-8 Relative backup times required for the DOS backup command and four backup utilities

Unfortunately, full backups can be time consuming. If, for example, you have 20MB of data on a hard disk, it can take 30 minutes to do a full backup. As a result, you're less likely to do them regularly.

Incremental backups An *incremental backup* is a backup of just the files that you've created or changed since your last backup. This is illustrated in figure 1-9 by the procedures for Tuesday through Friday. Even if you have hundreds of files on your hard disk, you probably use only a few files each day. Since fewer files are backed up when you do an incremental backup, the backup operation is much faster than a full backup. On my PC, for example, I do an incremental backup each day before I leave the office, and this backup operation takes less than 30 seconds.

Generally, speed is only a consideration when you're backing up to diskettes. After all, you have to sit at your PC and insert diskettes as the program asks you for them. This is not the case when you're backing up to a tape, however. If you're backing up to a tape, you can run your backups unattended so you usually don't need to use incremental backups.

To make the most efficient use of diskettes, most backup programs add the files to the last diskette in the backup set. When files are added this way, it's called an *appended incremental backup*. Then, when the last diskette is filled by an appended incremental backup, the backup program asks for the next diskette.

Older versions of DOS (before 3.3) and some of the older backup utilities don't provide for appended incremental backups. Instead, they provide for *separate incremental backups*. In other words, you have to use a separate diskette each time you run an incremental backup. Then, if each incremental backup requires more than one diskette, you end up with several new diskettes each time you back up. Not only do you end up using more diskettes, but it's hard to keep track of the individual sets of backup diskettes that are created. So if you have a program that doesn't provide for appended incremental backups, you may want to upgrade to a backup program that does provide for them.

If you're wondering how incremental backups are possible, they work because the information that's stored with each file on a DOS system has an *archive bit*. This bit indicates whether or not the file needs to be backed up. When you create or change a file, this bit is set so the backup program knows that the file should be backed up during an incremental backup. Then, when you run the incremental backup, the backup operation resets all of the archive bits. As a result, these files won't be backed up in the next incremental backup unless you change them again.

When and how to back up your hard disk

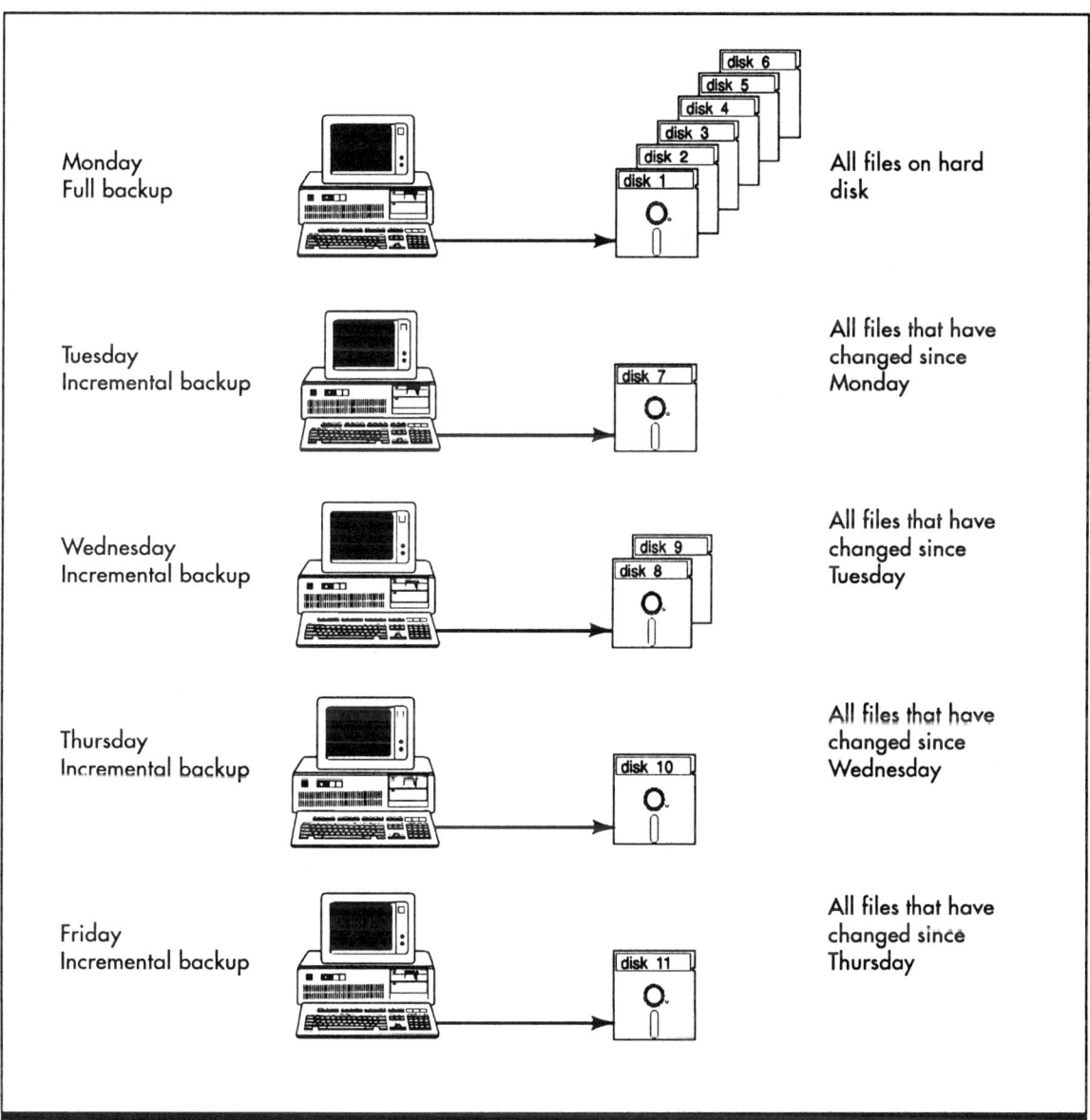

Figure 1-9 A weekly schedule of full and incremental backups

How the drives, directories and files on your hard disk affect backups

You should already know that DOS uses drives, directories, and file names to identify data that's stored on a PC. To back up the data on a hard disk, for instance, you have to enter a specification that identifies the drive, directories, and files you want to back up. Often, you'll see this specification referred to as a *file specification*, or *file spec* for short. Figure 1-10 shows the parts of a typical file specification. Since you need to understand these parts to identify the data you want to back up, I'll take a few moments to review them.

Disk and diskette drives   DOS identifies hard disk drives and diskette drives by using letters. To specify a drive you want to use, you often have to use the DOS convention. When that's the case, you type the drive letter followed by a colon. For example, you type *A:* for diskette drive A, *C:* for hard drive C, and so on.

In general, the first diskette drive on every system is drive A, and the second diskette drive is drive B. If a system has two diskette drives with one drive on the left and the other on the right, the one on the left is usually the A drive. If a system has two diskettes with one on top of the other, the one on the top is usually the A drive.

The hard disk, or at least the first portion of it, is always identified as drive C. However, one hard disk can be divided into more than one drive, as shown in figure 1-11. To use the DOS terminology, the hard disk is divided into *partitions*. Then, the first drive is drive C; the second is drive D; and so on. Today, a 40MB drive is often divided into drives C and D, while a 120MB drive is often divided into several drives, like C, D, E, and F.

In PC and DOS literature, the drives are often referred to as *logical drives* to distinguish them from the hard disk, or physical disk drive. Thus, one physical drive is divided into two or more logical drives. From a practical point of view, though, you can think of each logical drive as a physical drive. As a result, I won't distinguish between the two in the remainder of this book. I'll simply refer to disk drives by letter as in "the C drive" or "the D drive."

When and how to back up your hard disk 17

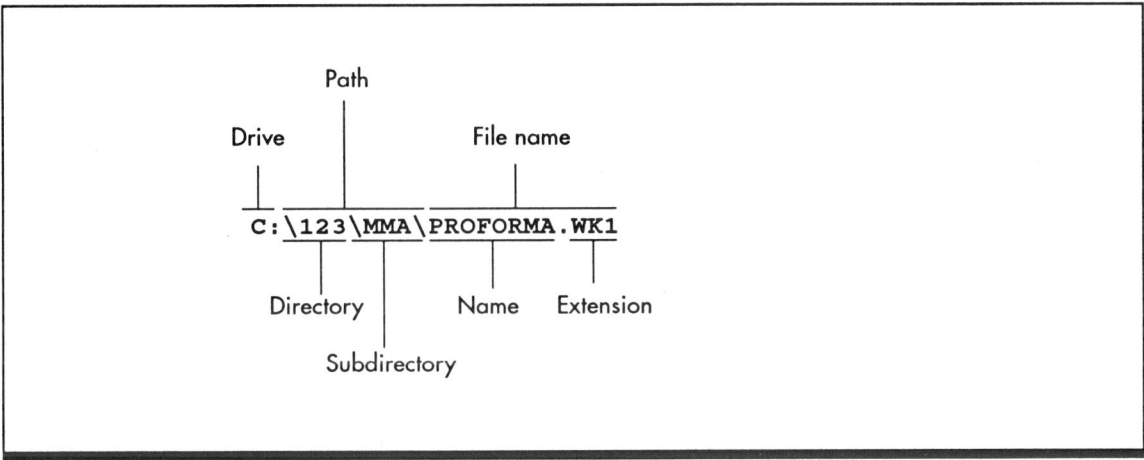

Figure 1-10 The parts of a typical file specification

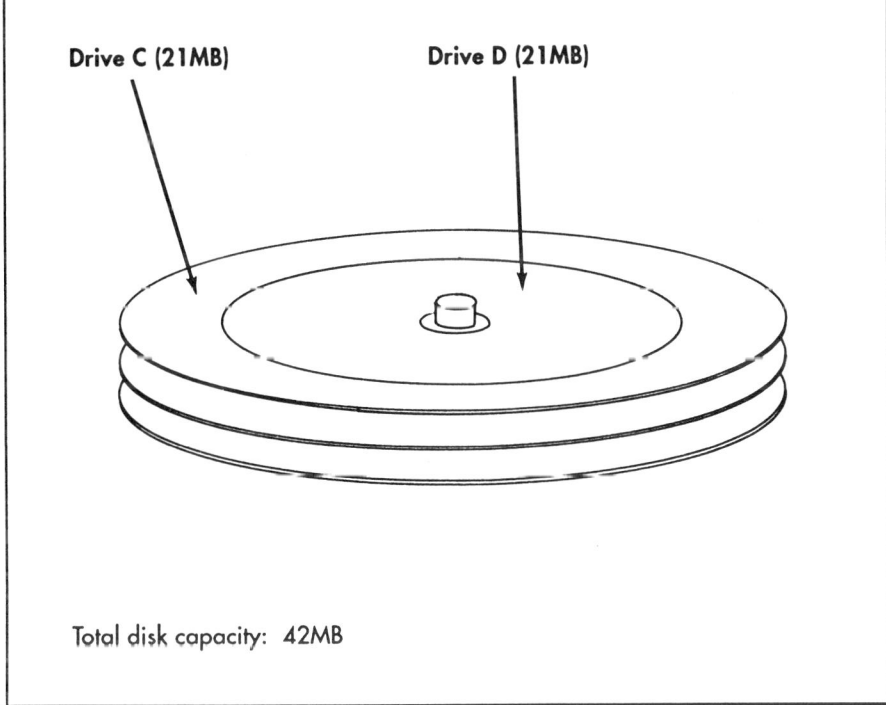

Figure 1-11 Two drives on one hard disk

Often, the logical drives are defined on a PC before you get it. But you should know that you can partition your hard disk with logical drives using a program provided by DOS called *Fdisk*. To use this program, first you back up all the data on your hard disk. This is critical because Fdisk destroys all the data on the disk. Next, you use Fdisk to redefine the partitions and logical drives on the hard disk. Then, you reformat the disks and restore your backups. Since this is a time-consuming job, you should have a good reason for doing it. In addition, you must know how to do each of the steps that are required to redefine the partitions of a hard disk.

Frankly, redefining the partitions on your hard disk is a complex task that's beyond the scope of this book. But I mention it because having more than one drive on your hard disk often improves your backup procedures. In a moment, you'll be able to decide if your backup procedures will improve enough to warrant redefining the partitions on your hard disk. Then, if you do decide to re-partition your disk, you can learn how by referring to your DOS manual or to *The Only DOS Book You'll Ever Need* that's mentioned in the preface.

Directories and subdirectories   DOS lets you organize or group files into *directories*. On my system, for example, there are 1,368 files organized into 39 different directories. These directories are just a special type of file that DOS uses to keep track of the names and locations of the files that are stored on a disk. In fact, every file on a DOS system is stored in a directory.

Figure 1-12 illustrates a typical directory structure for a hard disk. For each hard disk or diskette, the top-level directory is always called the *root directory*. In this figure, the root directory contains references to five other directories named DOS, UTIL, WP50, 123, and QA. These directories contain the files for DOS, for some utility programs, for *WordPerfect*, for *Lotus 1-2-3*, and for *Q&A*.

Because one directory can contain entries for other directories, the subordinate directories are called *subdirectories*. In figure 1-12, for instance, the WP50 directory has two subdirectories named MMA and PROJ1, and the 123 directory has two subdirectories named MMA and SALES. These subdirectories are just like any other directory; they're just subordinate to a higher-level directory. As a result, subdirectories can also be referred to as directories.

When and how to back up your hard disk   **19**

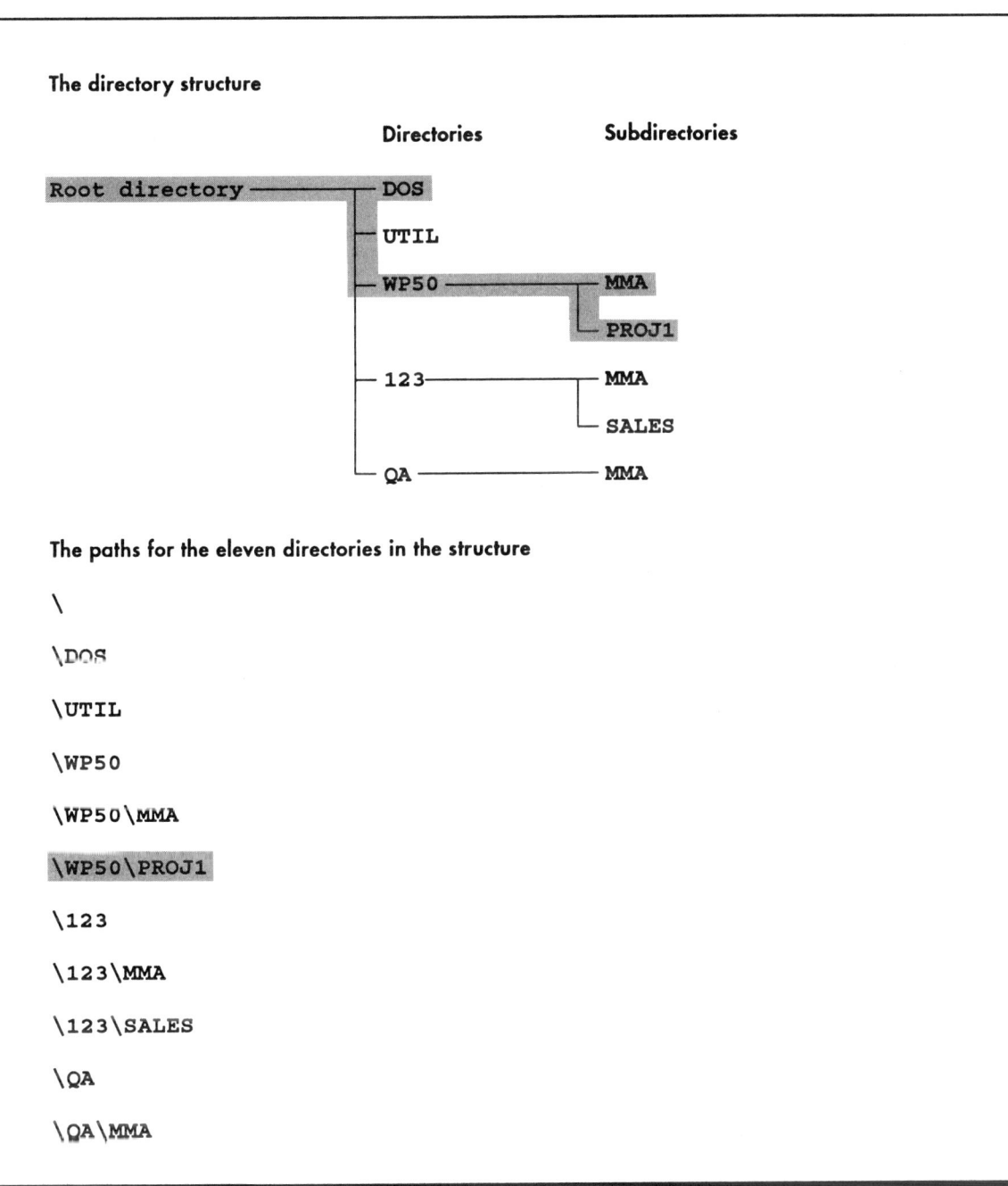

Figure 1-12   The paths for the directories of a hard disk

The *path* of a file specification identifies the directory for the file. More specifically, the path tells DOS how to get from the root directory to the directory that contains the entry for the file you want. In the directory structure in figure 1-12, the shaded path goes from the root directory to the WP50 directory to the PROJ1 directory.

Below the directory structure in figure 1-12, you can see the path specifications for the eleven directories shown in the structure. The first backslash (\) represents the root directory. A backslash followed by a directory name as in \DOS, \UTIL, \WP50, \123, and \QA represents a level-1 directory. To represent a level-2 directory, or subdirectory, you use a backslash, a level-1 directory name, another backslash, and the level-2 directory name as in \WP50\MMA and \WP50\PROJ1.

Note in figure 1-12 that \PROJ1 isn't a valid path. To be valid, it must be preceded by its level-1 directory as in this path: \WP50\PROJ1. Note also that the same subdirectory name can be used within more than one directory. Thus, there are several MMA directories. One is subordinate to the WP50 directory, a second is subordinate to the 123 directory, and a third is subordinate to the QA directory. For DOS to tell them apart, they must be referred to as \WP50\MMA, \123\MMA, and \QA\MMA.

For most backup operations, you enter the root directory as the path specification because you want the backup operation to start with this directory and include all the files and directories that are subordinate to the root directory. If, however, you want to back up or restore a single directory on a hard disk, you specify the directory you want by entering the path for the directory. Similarly, if you want to back up or restore a single file, you must include the path in the file specification.

File names   Whenever you save a file on a hard disk or diskette, you assign it a *file name*. If you look back at figure 1-10, you can see that a file name is separated into two parts by a period. The part before the period is required. I'll refer to this part as the *name* portion of the file name. The part after the period is optional and is called the *extension*.

Figure 1-13 gives the rules for forming valid file names. If you use just letters and numbers in your file names, you don't have to worry about the special characters listed in rule 3. Then, you use from one to eight characters for the name, and from one to three characters for the extension. Note also in

When and how to back up your hard disk   21

The rules for forming file names

1. The name must consist of from one to eight characters.

2. The extensión is optional. If you have one, it must be from one to three characters, and it must be separated from the name by a period as in this example:

    MONTHSUM.JAN

3. You can use any character in the name or the extension except for the space and any of these characters:

    . , ? / : ; " ' [ ] | \ + = *

4. You can use either lowercase or uppercase letters in the name or the extension of a file name, but they are treated the same. As a result, the two names that follow are the same:

    MONTHSUM.JAN   and   monthsum.jan

Valid file names

JAN90.WK1

letter.doc

5-16-90.doc

FEB90RPT

ltr10-21

Invalid file names

JANUARY90.WK1   (The name is more than 8 characters.)

JAN:90.WK1   (The colon is an invalid character.)

JAN90.TEXT   (The extension is more than 3 characters.)

Figure 1-13   The rules for forming file names

rule 4 that it doesn't matter if you use upper- or lowercase letters when you specify a file name.

By using a special feature that DOS provides called *wildcards*, you can identify more than one file at a time. DOS provides two wildcards: the * *wildcard* (asterisk wildcard), and the *? wildcard* (question mark wildcard). Since the * wildcard is the one that's useful for backups, it's the one I'll show you how to use.

The * wildcard represents one or more characters of any kind. By using it in the file specification, you can include more than one file in a backup operation. Some simple forms of file names that use this wildcard are illustrated in figure 1-14. As you can see, *.* refers to files with any name before the period and any extension. As a result, it refers to all the files in a directory. If you specify the root directory as the starting directory and include all subordinate directories, this wildcard will cause all the files on a hard disk to be backed up. This is what you want to do for most backup operations. In the other examples in figure 1-14, you can see how the * wildcard is used to represent all files with the extension of COM, all files with no extensions, and so on.

How to do separate program and data backups

The program files on a hard disk rarely, if ever, change. So why back them up every day? After all, it's the data files that you create and modify daily. That's why you should consider using logical drives or directories to separate your data files from your program files so you can back them up separately. By doing this, you can reduce the time required each month for backups.

How to use drives to do separate program and data backups On my PC, I store all the program files on drive C and all the data files on drive D. Once a month, I do a full backup of drive C (I don't do daily incremental backups for this drive). In contrast, I do a full backup of drive D on every Monday. And I do an incremental backup of this drive on the other days of the week. By using separate backup procedures for the program drive and the data drive, my total backup time for the month is less than 30 minutes.

If you buy a new PC or install a new hard disk, you can easily set up the drives so you can use this method of backup. However, as I mentioned ear-

Wildcard examples	Meaning
.	All files (any name, any extension)
*.com	All files with COM as the extension
*.	All files that don't have extensions
C1.*	All files named C1 no matter what the extensions are
C*.*	All files with names that start with the letter C no matter what the extensions are

Figure 1-14   Common uses of the * wildcard

lier, it's time consuming to set up separate drives in this way after you've used a PC for a while. You have to spend several hours backing up the hard disk, re-partitioning it, reformatting it, and restoring the old files to the correct drives. So even though separate drives are the easiest way to do separate program and data backups, you may want to consider using directories instead.

How to use directories to do separate program and data backups   To set up your directories so you can do separate data backups, you must have all of your data directories subordinate to one directory. In figure 1-15, for example, all of the data directories are subordinate to a directory named \DATA. Then, you can enter a specification to back up all the files and directories under the \DATA directory. On Monday, you can do a full backup of the data directories. The other days of the week you can do an incremental backup of the data directories. And once a month, you can do a full backup of the entire drive.

This approach does have two disadvantages, though. First, your program backup is less efficient because it includes the data files. Only a few backup programs let you easily exclude the data directories from the program

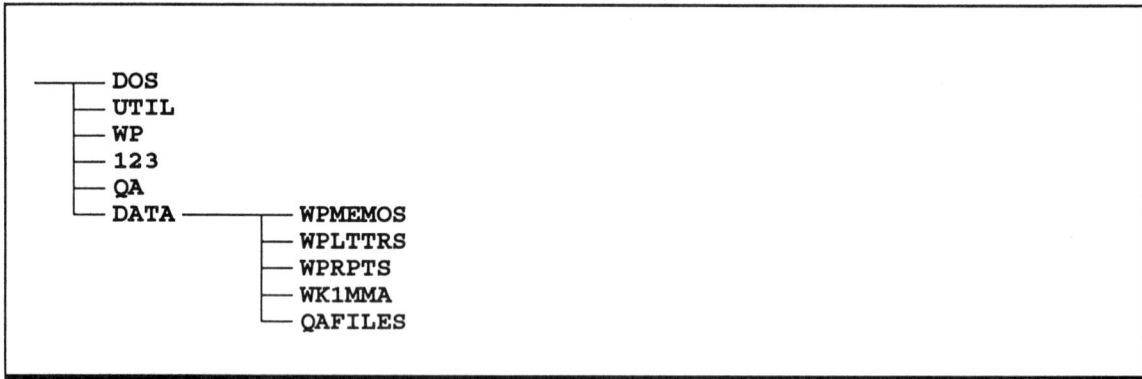

Figure 1-15 A directory structure with all data directories subordinate to the DATA directory

backup. Second, this approach makes your directory structure a little harder to use because every time you want to use a data file you must type \DATA as part of the path specification. Given the directory structure in figure 1-15, you have to include two directories in every data file specification. To retrieve a file in the \WPLTTRS directory, for example, you must precede the file name with \DATA\WPLTTRS\.

How to use a backup to transfer files to another PC

You should know that protecting your data isn't the only use for backups. You can also use a backup to transfer files from one PC to another. Occasionally, you might need to use a backup to transfer a single file from one PC to another because the file is too large to fit on one diskette. Similarly, you might want to use a backup to transfer many directories and files because the backup program requires fewer diskettes to store the data than the Copy command does. Or you might want to transfer all the directories and files to a new PC so you don't have to install all the programs on the new hard disk.

But before you use a backup to transfer data, you need to consider whether the backup program and the storage medium you're using are compatible with the system you want to transfer the data to. For instance, if you back up using 5-1/4 inch, high capacity diskettes, the PC you're restoring the data to must also have a 5-1/4 inch, high capacity drive. If it doesn't, you need to use standard capacity diskettes for the transfer. Furthermore, if you use a backup utility like *PC-Fullbak+* version 2.02 to back up the data, you have to use the same program to restore it. You can't restore the data using the DOS Backup command or *Norton Backup*. Often, you must restore it using the same version of the utility. In other words, if you used version 2.02 to back up, you might not be able to use version 1.0 to restore.

How to select the right software, hardware, and backup techniques for your backups

Aside from a few operational details, you now know all of the software concepts, hardware concepts, and backup techniques that you need for doing effective backups. However, if you select the wrong software, hardware, or backup techniques for your backups, you won't end up with a backup plan you can live with; your backups will either take too long, or be too complicated to be practical. As a result, you still won't back up your hard disk as often as you should.

That's why the primary purpose of this book is to help you put together an effective plan for your backups. To make sure you make the right selections for your plan, you should start by analyzing your backup requirements. Then, you should review the backup options presented in this chapter. As part of the review, you may need to read several more chapters of this book to learn more about certain software or hardware options. But once you've done this, you shouldn't have much trouble deciding on a backup plan that's right for you.

Analyze your backup requirements   The most obvious backup requirement is the number of megabytes that you need to back up. So to start off, you need to find out how much data is already stored on your hard disk. The easiest way to do that is to use the DOS Check-disk command. You do this by typing *chkdsk* at the command prompt for each drive on your hard disk to get the total number of bytes used to store data.

Next, you should consider the files that will be added to your hard disk. On many PCs, the amount of data storage on the hard disk stays about the same because files are deleted as new ones are added. But on other PCs, the total number of megabytes used for storage increases dramatically over time.

It all depends on how the PC is used. So ask yourself, "Will the amount of data on my hard disk increase dramatically, or will it stay about the same as it is now?"

However, the amount of data on your hard disk isn't the only consideration. You should also think about the value of the data. In other words, what would happen if you lost a day, a week, or even a month's worth of data from your hard disk? Would it paralyze your business? Or would it just be an inconvenience? If the data on your hard disk is critical, you may need to select more advanced software, hardware, and backup techniques than might otherwise be indicated.

Finally, you should consider any other factors that affect your backup plan. Are you technically inclined? If you aren't, by all means make sure your backup plan is as simple as possible. Similarly, how valuable is your time? If every minute of your day is at a premium, you should consider spending more money on software and hardware so your backups are as fast as possible.

Review the backup options Figure 1-16 lists the software and hardware options along with the backup techniques presented in this chapter. As you look at this list, start by ruling out the options and techniques that are obviously not appropriate for your needs. If, for example, you have more than 10MB to back up, you should probably rule out the DOS Backup command and choose a backup utility instead. Similarly, if you have 40MB or more to back up, you should probably do full and incremental backups in combination with separate program and data backups. Or maybe you should use a backup tape drive instead.

After you have identified the range of backup options that you think you should consider, you're ready to investigate them further. If you want to review backup utilities, you should turn to chapter 5 of this book because it shows you how to use the most popular backup programs for the most common backup tasks. If you're considering a backup tape drive, you should read chapter 6 on tape backups. Also, to refine your backup techniques, you should read chapter 2.

Decide on a backup plan As you formulate your backup plan, keep in mind that the goal is to come up with a plan that balances two factors: speed

Software options

   DOS Backup
   Commercial backup utility

Hardware options

   Standard capacity diskette drive
   High capacity diskette drive
   Tape backup drive
   Other removable media

Techniques

   Full backups
   Full and incremental backups
   Separate program and data backups using drives
   Separate program and data backups using directories

Figure 1-16   The backup options presented in this chapter

and simplicity. You want to make your backups fast enough so that you do them regularly. But you don't want to make them so complicated that the task is overwhelming technically. In short, try to select the simplest backup plan that's fast enough for you.

Figure 1-17 presents three typical backup plans. The first one is a plan that you might use if you're an occasional PC user with less than 5MB to back up. The second one is a plan you might use if you have 10MB to 40MB to back up. And the third one is a plan you might use if you have over 40MB of critical data to back up.

After you've used your backup plan for awhile, you may find that your backups are too slow or too complicated. If so, don't be afraid to modify your plan. What do you have to lose? If you decide to use the DOS Backup command, but later decide this program is too slow, you can always buy a

---

Backup plan 1: Occasional PC user with less than 5MB of programs and data

    Software: DOS Backup command
    Hardware: Standard or high capacity diskette drive
    Technique: Full backup once a week.

Backup plan 2: Regular PC user with between 10MB and 40MB of programs and data

    Software: Commercial backup utility
    Hardware: High capacity diskette drive
    Technique: For the data drive, combination of a full backup one day of the week with incremental backups the rest of the week. Full backup of the program drive once a month.

Backup plan 3: Daily PC user with 40MB of critical operational data

    Software: Commercial backup utility
    Hardware: Tape backup drive
    Technique: Full backup daily of the data drive. Full backup once a month of the program drive.

Figure 1-17   Three typical backup plans

commercial backup utility. Since you already had DOS, you didn't waste any money using it. Or, if you decide to do full and incremental backups to diskettes along with separate program and data backups, but later find this approach is too complicated, you can add a tape drive to your PC to simplify your backups. Again, since you didn't need to add hardware for diskette backups, you didn't lose any money backing up to diskettes.

How to use the rest of this book to your advantage

Now that you've finished this chapter, you can continue with any chapter in this book. If you have already formulated a backup plan, you can continue with the next chapter. It presents ten guidelines that will help you make your backups faster and more efficient.

If your PC is attached to a network, you should probably read chapter 3 next. It explains how networks affect backups. With some types of networks, you don't need to do individual backups at all. But with other types, the network has little or no effect on backups so you are still responsible for backing up the programs and data on your PC.

In section 2 of this book, you'll learn more about the software and hardware options that I introduced in this chapter. In chapter 4, you'll learn how to use the DOS Backup and Restore commands. In chapter 5, you'll learn how to use the four most popular commercial backup utilities. If you've already bought a backup utility or if your company has already adopted a standard backup utility, chances are good that it's one of these. Finally, in chapter 6, you'll learn how to acquire and use a backup tape drive.

Just remember that you don't have to read all of these chapters, and you don't have to read them in sequence. Instead, you can concentrate on the chapters that apply to your backup requirements and your backup plan.

Terms

backup program
removable storage
restore function
diskettes
standard capacity
high capacity
byte
kilobyte (KB)
megabyte (MB)
double density diskettes
high density diskettes
tape drive
tape cartridge
unattended tape backup
bernoulli box

CD drive
optical drive
DOS Backup command
DOS Restore command
commercial backup utility
full backup
incremental backup
appended incremental backup
separate incremental backup
archive bit
file specification
file spec
partition
logical drive
DOS Fdisk program

directory
root directory
subdirectory
path
file name
extension
wildcard
* wildcard
? wildcard

Chapter 2

Ten guidelines for fast and effective backups

In chapter 1, you learned about the software, hardware, and backup techniques that you need to back up a hard disk. As a result, you should now be able to identify all of the major elements of your backup plan.

In this chapter, I'll present guidelines that will help you refine your backup plan. In particular, these guidelines will help you do your backups quickly and easily, no matter what software or hardware you're using. In addition, these guidelines will help you make your backups as effective and reliable as possible.

Five guidelines for fast and easy backups

As I mentioned in the last chapter, a good backup plan should balance two factors. First, the plan should allow you to do your backups as quickly as possible. Second, the plan should be easy to carry out. Although these two factors sometimes conflict with each other, the five guidelines presented here should help you refine your backup plan so that it's both fast and easy. These guidelines are summarized in figure 2-1.

Set a schedule for your backups   Because backing up a hard disk takes time away from your other activities, it's always tempting to skip your backup procedure for a day, a week, or a month. Even if you're doing

1. Set a schedule for your backups.
2. Use batch files or the features provided by your backup utility to automate your backups.
3. Delete unnecessary files before you do a full backup.
4. Keep your backup media organized.
5. Keep a log of your backups.

Figure 2-1 Five guidelines for fast and easy backups

incremental backups that take less than a minute each, it's tempting to skip them. Before long, you won't even remember the last time you did a backup.

That's why it's important that you set a schedule for your backups. How often should you do them? That depends on how much you use your system. If, for example, you use your system more than four hours a day, you should probably do daily backups. If you use your system just an hour or two a day, you can perhaps get by with weekly backups, but you're going to be better off with daily backups. In short, schedule your backups so you'll never lose more work than you can afford to lose when a disk failure occurs. Then, stick to your schedule.

In chapter 1, you learned how to do separate backups of your program files and your data files. If you do that, you should set a schedule for each backup procedure. You can, for example, schedule program backups on the first Monday of every month. Then, you can schedule data backups daily.

You also learned about two types of backups: full and incremental backups. You can use these two types of backups independently or in combination with separate program and data backups. If you decide to do full and incremental backups, you can schedule the full backups for a day like the first day of each month, week, or whenever. Just schedule your full backups on days that usually provide the free time you need for this task. Then, schedule incremental backups on the other days.

Ten guidelines for fast and effective backups 33

```
BACKFULL.BAT

    backup c:\*.* a: /s

BACKINC.BAT

    backup c:\*.* a: /s/m/a
```

Figure 2-2   Batch files that use the DOS Backup command to do a full and an incremental backup of drive C

Use batch files or the features provided by your backup program to automate your backups   Once you've planned and scheduled your backups, you should use the features provided by your backup program to automate your backups. If you're using the DOS Backup command, that means you should put the commands for each of your backups in a *batch file*. A batch file is a special type of file that you can use to store a series of commands. When you enter the batch file name at the command prompt, DOS executes the commands in the file. As a result, you can execute a series of commands with a single command entry, and you don't have to remember the details for entering the commands because they are stored in the batch file.

To illustrate, figure 2-2 shows two batch files. The first batch file does a full backup of the C drive. The second one does an appended incremental backup of the C drive. If you don't know how to create or use batch files like these, you'll need to refer to your DOS manual, or to one of my DOS books mentioned in the preface.

Most commercial backup utilities provide *setup files* that you can use to store the options you need for a particular backup operation. When you load the setup file, it sets the backup options. This makes the backup easier because you don't have to remember all the options that are required for a backup, and you don't have to use the menus to set all the options.

To illustrate, figure 2-3 show the Setup-file panel that's displayed when you select the Load-setup-file option from one of the *Norton Backup* menus. As you can see, five setup files have been created. Each one provides for a

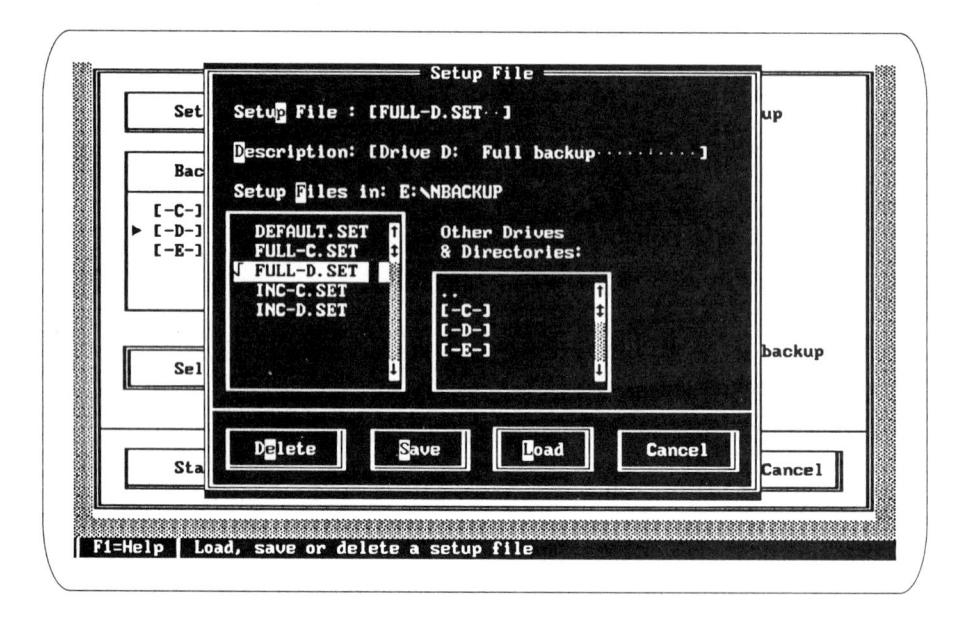

Figure 2-3   Five setup files created using *Norton Backup*

specific automated backup. The DEFAULT.SET file creates a backup based on the utility's default backup options. The FULL-C.SET creates a full backup of the C drive. The FULL-D.SET creates a full backup of the D drive. The INC-C.SET creates an appended incremental backup of the C drive. And the INC-D.SET creates an appended incremental backup of the D drive.

With most backup utilities, you can carry this one step further by creating a batch file that uses the setup file to run the backup. In the batch file, you include commands that set the appropriate drive and directory, that start the backup utility, and that start the appropriate setup file. With some backup utilities, the batch file actually starts the backup operation. With others like *Norton Backup*, however, you must still select an option from a menu to start the actual backup operation. You'll learn more about this in chapter 5.

To illustrate, figure 2-4 shows four batch files that start *Norton Backup* and that use setup files to run four separate backup operations. In each example, the first two command lines set the current drive and directory to the program directory. The third command line starts the backup utility and

```
FULLC.BAT

    c:
    cd \nbackup
    nbackup full-c.set

INCC.BAT

    c:
    cd \nbackup
    nbackup inc-c.set

FULLD.BAT

    c:
    cd \nbackup
    nbackup full-d.set

INCD.BAT

    c:
    cd \nbackup
    nbackup inc-d.set
```

Figure 2-4 Four batch files that start *Norton Backup* and load setup files for different backup operations

one of the setup files I mentioned earlier. The first batch file, for example, starts *Norton Backup* and loads the FULL-C.SET file. Then, to execute the full backup operation, you would select the Start-backup option from the menu that appears.

Delete unnecessary files before you do a full backup   Often, it's quicker to delete unnecessary files than it is to back them up. So before you start a full backup, it's worth taking a few minutes to see if your hard disk has any directories or files that you no longer need. If you find some and delete them, your backups will run more quickly. In addition, your directories and files will be more manageable.

Keep your backup media organized   This is obvious, but I think it's worth mentioning. Also, it applies whether you're using tape cartridges or diskettes as your *backup media*. If you're using tape cartridges, your *backup set* should include only one tape cartridge. As a result, you can just put a simple label on the tape to identify the backup. This label should indicate the drive or directory that was backed up, and it should indicate the name of the backup program (including the version number) you used.

By comparison, if you're using diskettes as your backup media, your backup set may contain ten or more diskettes. As a result, you should keep your diskettes organized by labelling them and numbering your backup diskettes and your diskette boxes. That way, you'll be able to run your backups as efficiently as possible. Also, when you need to restore data, you'll be able to insert the diskettes in the proper sequence so the restore operation will work the way you want it to.

In general, the label for each backup diskette should indicate the drive or directory that the backup is for. It should also give the sequence number of the diskette within the backup procedure. In addition, you should include the name of the backup program on the first diskette of the set. However, a diskette label shouldn't indicate whether it's for a full or incremental backup. If, for example, the full backup ended with diskette 6 and the first incremental backup started with diskette 7, you shouldn't indicate this on the diskette labels. Also, you shouldn't write the date of the backup on the labels. Instead, you should keep this information in a backup log.

Keep a log of your backups   When you use more than one type of backup, you can easily lose track of which backup procedure you should be doing and which diskette you should start with. That's why you should keep a *backup log* for your backup procedures. You don't need anything elaborate for this; a simple form like the one in figure 2-5 will do.

In this log, you can see that the PC user does a full backup of the D drive (the data drive) on the first day of each week. On the other days of the week, the user does an incremental backup of the D drive. Although it's not shown here, the user also keeps a separate log for the backups of the C drive (the

Ten guidelines for fast and effective backups

Backup Log			
Date	Drive	Backup Type	Last disk
6/3	D	Full	4
6/4	D	Incremental	4
6/5	D	"	5
6/6	D	"	5
6/7	D	"	6
6/10	D	Full	4
6/11	"	Inc.	4
6/12	"	"	5
6/13	"	"	6
6/14	"	"	6
6/17	D	Full	5
6/18	"	Inc.	5
6/19	"	"	6
6/20	"	"	6
6/21	"	"	7
6/24	D	Full	5
6/25	"	Inc.	5
6/26	"	"	6
6/27	"	"	6
6/28	"	"	6

Figure 2-5   A simple backup log

program drive). The user does a full backup of this drive once a month. By using separate procedures for backing up each drive, the user can keep backup time to a minimum and never be in danger of losing more than a day's work. However, without backup logs, a backup plan like this can get out of control.

Five guidelines for effective and reliable backups

When you back up your hard disk, you assume that the backup has been done without error. You also assume that the backup set will be available when you need it. Then, when a problem occurs, you can restore the files to your hard disk. But if a backup procedure hasn't worked correctly, the restore procedure won't work correctly either. And if the backup set isn't available, you can't even start the restore procedure. That's why it's important that you do what you can to make sure that your backups are reliable.

The main reason backup procedures don't work correctly is that the diskettes and tapes that you use for a backup set can be unreliable. That's particularly true for 5-1/4 inch diskettes, but it can also be true for 3-1/2 inch diskettes and tape cartridges. As diskettes and tapes age, the likelihood of a problem increases.

Unfortunately, backup utilities don't always detect diskette or tape problems. Sometimes it appears as though a backup procedure has run without error when it hasn't. In fact, some backup utilities will appear to run correctly even after you punch a hole in one of the 5-1/4 inch diskettes you use for the backup set. If a diskette has an error, the restore procedure often can't continue. Then, the backed up data on the remaining diskettes can't be restored either.

What steps should you take to make sure that your backups are reliable? That's up to you and the value that you place on your data. If you work on small files that get passed on daily or weekly to other people and other systems, backup isn't as essential for you. Consequently, the reliability of your backups isn't either. But if you work on large files that hold essential data that has taken you years to accumulate, you need to do everything you can to make sure that your backups are reliable. In other words, if you can't afford to lose your data, you must do everything you can to save it.

Ten guidelines for fast and effective backups

1. Use the error-checking features of your backup utility.
2. Use the compare features of your backup utility.
3. Store your backups in a safe place.
4. Keep two sets of backups.
5. Create a boot diskette with your backup utility on it.

Figure 2-6 Five guidelines for effective and reliable backups

With that in mind, here are five guidelines for making your backups more reliable. These guidelines are summarized in figure 2-6. In general, backup utilities are more reliable than the DOS backup command. Thus, you improve the reliability of your backups as soon as you get a backup utility. In fact, you can apply the first two guidelines only if you use a backup utility because the DOS Backup command doesn't support them.

Use the error-checking features of your backup utility Although backup utilities provide more sophisticated error-checking routines than the DOS command, these routines don't improve reliability unless you activate them. So when you install a backup utility, be sure to turn on all of the error-checking features that are recommended by the manufacturer.

Most utilities provide a *Verify function* that checks the integrity of the diskettes whenever it formats them. Also, most utilities provide an *Error-correction function*. This function increases the chance for recovering data, even if the backup media is damaged. Usually, these two functions are always on. However, you should check to make sure that they are. In addition, you should learn about any other error-checking features your utility provides and decide whether or not you should use them.

Use the compare features of your backup utility In addition to the basic Backup and Restore functions, most utilities provide a *Compare function*. When you run this function, the utility asks you to insert the backup set just as you would for a Restore function. However, the utility doesn't restore the files. Instead, it compares the data on the hard disk with the data on the backup set. If the Compare function doesn't detect any errors, you know that the backup utility has worked correctly.

Because the Compare function takes extra time, you won't want to run it each time you do a full backup. But you should run this function often enough to assure yourself that your backups are reliable. If you're an occasional PC user, that means you should run the Compare function once every six months. But if you use your system more than four hours each day, you should probably run the Compare function once every month.

Store your backups in a safe place   If you keep your backup set next to your PC, you have a potential backup problem. If your PC is destroyed by fire, theft, or vandalism, it's likely that your backup set will be destroyed also. To keep your backups safe, you should keep your backup set in a fireproof safe, or you should take it home with you.

Keep two sets of backups   If one backup set is destroyed, a second set can help you avoid a disaster. With that in mind, you should consider keeping two backup sets for each drive on your hard disk. Then, you alternate the sets each time you do a backup. If, for example, you do full backups weekly and incremental backups daily, you use a different backup set each week.

When you keep two backup sets, it's okay to keep one set in a drawer next to your PC. But you should keep the other set in a fireproof safe or at another location. Then, when your hard disk fails and something is wrong with the backup set at your desk, you have another backup set as security.

When you run the Compare function for some backups and not for others, you should keep one backup set for the compared backups and one set for the backups that aren't compared. Also, you should keep the compared set in a safe or at another location. Then, if the Restore function doesn't work when you use the backup set that wasn't compared, you can fall back on the compared set knowing that it's going to be reliable and that your data is safe.

Create a boot diskette with your backup program on it   Occasionally, you need to restore all the files from your backup sets because your hard disk has failed. But if that's the case, you obviously can't run your backup program from your hard disk. In fact, you may not even be able to start up your PC without using a boot diskette in the A drive. A *boot diskette*, or *system diskette*, is a diskette that contains the files that DOS needs for getting itself started.

That's why you should create a DOS boot diskette and install your backup program on it. If you're using the DOS Backup and Restore commands, you can just copy them to this diskette. If you're using a commercial backup utility, you should follow the manufacturer's instructions for installing it on a diskette. Then, if your hard disk fails and you have to reformat it or replace it, you can just use the boot diskette that you created to start your PC. And you can start your backup utility from the boot diskette to run the restore operation.

A final perspective on formulating a backup plan

As I mentioned at the beginning of this chapter, the ten guidelines presented here can help you refine your backup plan. But that doesn't mean you will necessarily use all of them. Instead, incorporate only those guidelines that add the speed, the simplicity, and the reliability that are required for your backup needs. Finally, if your needs change, don't be afraid to change your backup plan.

Terms

batch file
setup file
backup media
backup set
Verify function
Error-correction function
Compare function
boot diskette
system diskette

Ten guidelines for fast and effective backups 41

gram from your hard disk. In fact, you may not even be able to start up your PC without using a boot diskette in the A drive. A *boot diskette*, or *system diskette*, is a diskette that contains the files that DOS needs for getting itself started.

That's why you should create a DOS boot diskette and install your backup program on it. If you're using the DOS Backup and Restore commands, you can just copy them to this diskette. If you're using a commercial backup utility, you should follow the manufacturer's instructions for installing it on a diskette. Then, if your hard disk fails and you have to reformat it or replace it, you can just use the boot diskette that you created to start your PC. And you can start your backup utility from the boot diskette to run the restore operation.

A final perspective on formulating a backup plan

As I mentioned at the beginning of this chapter, the ten guidelines presented here can help you refine your backup plan. But that doesn't mean you will necessarily use all of them. Instead, incorporate only those guidelines that add the speed, the simplicity, and the reliability that are required for your backup needs. Finally, if your needs change, don't be afraid to change your backup plan.

Terms

batch file
setup file
backup media
backup set
Verify function
Error-correction function
Compare function
boot diskette
system diskette

Chapter 3

Backup considerations for network users

Today, more and more PCs are being linked together through *networks*. Often, these networks are referred to as *local area networks*, or *LANs*. Networking makes it possible for PC users at individual PCs or workstations to share files, programs, printers, and other resources that are part of the network.

Whether your PC is currently hooked up to a network, or whether you are thinking about setting up a network, you need to know how a network affects your backups. For instance, the network may be set up so all your files are backed up by the person who manages the network. This eliminates the need for individual backups. Often, though, the network is set up so that you still have to back up some or all of your files. Either way, you need to know how the network affects backups so you can be sure that all of your files are getting backed up regularly.

In this chapter, you'll learn about the two types of networks and how each type affects your backup procedures. Then, you'll learn how to make sure your files are getting backed up. Finally, you'll learn how to take advantage of your network for running backups.

Two types of networks

Two types of networks are in use today: file-server networks and peer networks. To make sure your files are getting backed up, you need to know which type of network you're using, and you need to have a basic understanding of how your network operates.

Before I tell you more about the two types of networks, though, I want you to know that the information presented here doesn't have anything to do with how a particular network is cabled. The figures and information presented in this section are intended to help you understand how these two types of networks operate at a conceptual level. So don't worry about the type of cable that's used with your network. And don't worry about how those cables are routed.

File-server networks   Figure 3-1 represents a *file-server network*. Here, a single computer called a *file server* provides the *network resources* to all of the PCs on the network. Because all of the network resources are part of the file server, this type of network can also be referred to as a *dedicated file-server network*.

In a file-server network, one or more network printers can be attached to the file server. In addition, the hard disk in the file server has all of the programs and data files used by the network. As a result, when you start an application program, it is loaded from the hard disk on the file server. Similarly, when you save a data file, it is saved to the hard disk on the file server.

Generally, the PCs that are hooked up to this type of network don't have hard disks. Occasionally, they don't even have diskette drives. Because of this, they are often called *diskless workstations*.

If a PC on the network has its own hard disk, the hard disk isn't used by the network. It's just used by the individual PC, and it's commonly referred to as a *local resource* or *local hard disk*. As a result, it's not uncommon for people who have hard disks to use their PCs without *logging on* to the network. Using a PC in this way is often refereed to as *running stand-alone*. Then, you run programs from your own hard disk and store files on it without accessing the network file server.

The most common networking program that lets you set up a file-server network is called *Netware*, and it's sold by a company called *Novell*. The

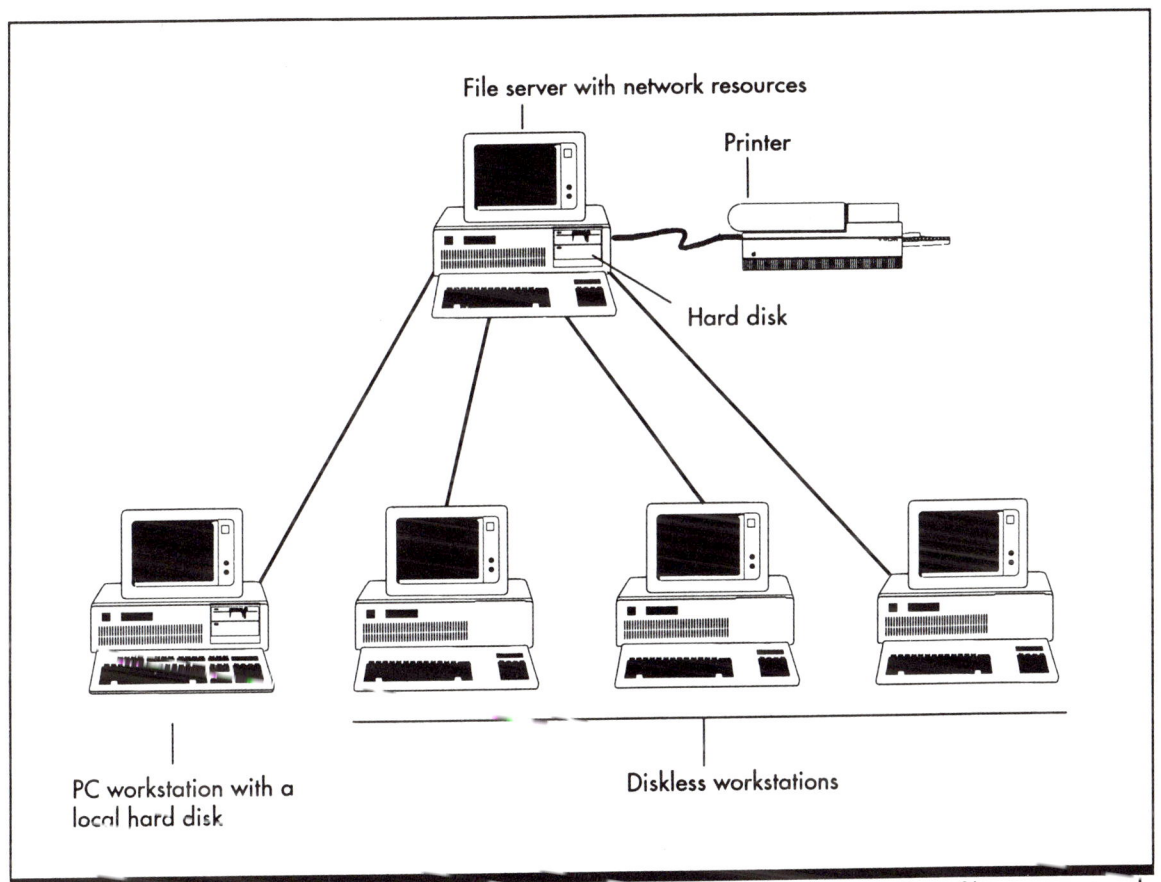

Figure 3-1 A typical arrangement of network resources and workstations for a file-server network

primary advantage of this product and this type of network is that it's fast. As a result, there is little delay when you access a network resource, like a hard disk or a printer. In addition, a file-server network allows the person in charge of the network, often called the *network administrator,* to control how people are using the network and its resources.

A file-server network, however, does have some disadvantages. First, this type of network is hard to set up. Second, it's a lot of work to maintain and administer a file-server network. As a result, you generally have to assign a specific person to the job of network administrator. And third, it's more expensive to set up a file-server network than a peer network in terms of hardware and software costs.

Peer networks Figure 3-2 represents a peer network. Here, every PC can access and use the resources of every other PC on the network. As a result, you don't have to dedicate a computer to the role of file server when you set up a peer network. This type of network can also be referred to as a *peer-to-peer network*.

With this type of network, you can access and use the hard disk on someone else's PC. You can also use a printer that's attached to another PC. As a result, it's not uncommon for many or all of the PCs on a peer network to have hard disks, printers, and so on. You should know, however, that it is fairly common to have a primary computer on a peer network that's roughly the equivalent of a file server. You just aren't forced to use this computer to access network resources.

Many networking programs are available today that support peer networks. *Lantastic* from *Artisoft* is currently the best selling program. The primary advantage of this product and this type of network is that it's easy to set up and use. It's also flexible. As a result, people can use the network in the most efficient manner. In addition, it's less expensive to set up a peer network than a file-server network. In part, that's because you don't need to have a special file-server computer; you can just use the computers you already have.

This type of network also has disadvantages, though. First, it isn't as fast as a file-server network. As a result, a peer network can be too slow for larger networking requirements. Second, because peer networks are so flexible, it can be hard to insure that they are being used appropriately. For instance, you can't always be sure that people are storing their files on the appropriate hard disk.

How backups work on a network

Now that you understand the difference between file-server and peer networks, you can see how they can affect your backups. If, for instance, you're using a file-server network, backups are probably being taken care of for you by the network administrator because your files are all on the file server. In

Backup considerations for network users   47

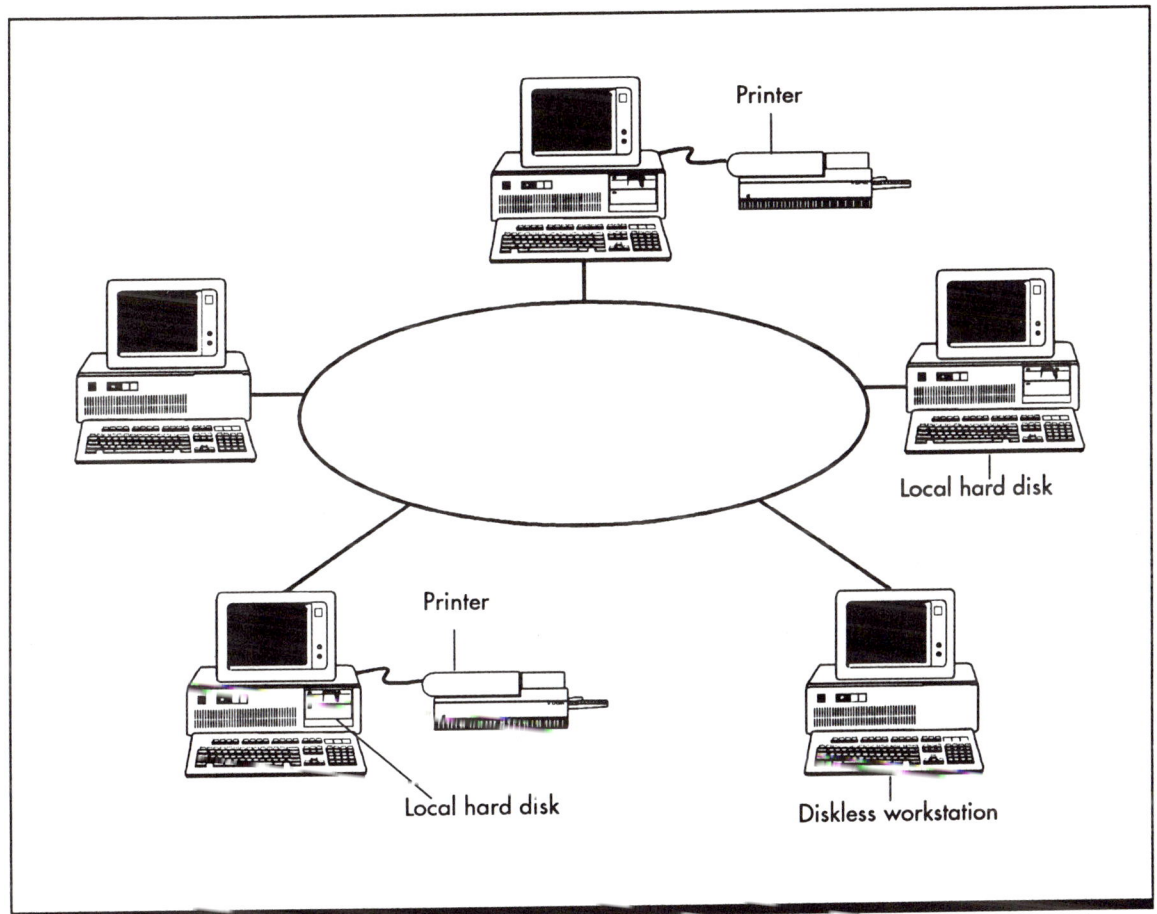

Figure 3-2 A typical arrangement of network resources and workstations for a peer network

contrast, if you're using a peer network, you're probably going to have to do your own backups or make arrangements otherwise. However, these generalizations can be greatly affected by how your network is set up and being used, and by how you are using your PC. As a result, there are several backup options for each type of network.

Backups on a file-server network   Figure 3-3 presents the two most common backup options on a file-server network. With most file-server networks, you just use the first backup option listed here. Since all of your files

1. The network administrator backs up your files stored on the file server.
2. You back up your files stored on your PC's hard disk.

Figure 3-3   The two most common backup options on a file-server network

are stored on the file server, you don't have to back them up as an individual network user.

However, you'll want to make sure that someone is backing up the file server. If you're on a larger network with 20 or more users, your company has probably already designated a network administrator who takes care of backups. If, on the other hand, you're on a smaller network that's administered rather informally, backups could be getting neglected. So it never hurts to ask.

If your PC has a hard disk, you're probably using it when you aren't logged onto the network. When you run stand-alone like this, you don't have to wait for network resources. But when you use your PC like this, you save your files on your hard disk instead of on the file server. As a result, you must take the responsibility for backing up the hard disk on your PC.

Backups on a peer network   Figure 3-4 presents three backup options on a peer network. The first two options listed here are the most common ones. If you have a hard disk on your PC, you probably use it for many if not all of your data files. As a result, you must back it up. In this case, the peer network has no effect on your backup requirements, and you must decide on your own backup plan.

On the other hand, if your PC doesn't have a hard disk, you probably store all your data files on one of the hard disks that's available through the network. Even if your PC has a hard disk, you may store files on a network for reasons of efficiency. One PC on the network, for example, may have all of the programs and data files for your accounting system on it. Several people can then access and use these files via the network.

If you store files on someone else's hard disk, that person generally backs up the files. Usually, you know which PC this hard disk is on so you can check with the person who uses it to make sure your files are being

Backup considerations for network users

1. You back up your files stored on your PC's hard disk.

2. Someone else backs up your files stored on their PC's hard disk.

3. You back up your files using a network resource (like a tape drive) that's located on someone else's PC.

Figure 3-4　The three common backup options on a peer network

backed up. In some cases, though, you might not even know the location of the hard disk that you use for storing files. As a result, you must first find out which hard disk you are using so you can make sure your files are being backed up. In short, you can't just store your files on a network hard disk and assume they are being backed up.

On some peer networks, you can use the third option listed in figure 3-4; you can use a resource on the network to back up your hard disk. If, for example, someone on the network has a backup tape drive, you may be able to use it to back up your hard disk. Of course, this isn't as convenient as having your own tape drive because you must go to the other PC and insert your tape into the drive before you can start the operation. In addition, the backup operation will be slower if you use the tape drive over the network. Still, it may be more convenient than doing diskette backups, particularly if you have a lot of data to back up.

How to take advantage of a network for backups

If you're using a file-server network like *Novell Netware*, chances are good that you're already taking advantage of the network for backups. You're probably storing all of your data files on the file server. And the person who manages the network should be backing them up regularly.

If you have a local hard disk and occasionally run stand-alone, you may want to copy your data files to a directory that's been assigned to you on the file server. That way, you can benefit from the speed and convenience of stand-alone operation, and you can make sure your data files are being backed up on the file server. Then, you can just do an occasional full backup of your hard disk to protect the time invested in installing and setting up your local programs.

If, on the hand, you're using a peer network, you can save your important files to a network hard disk that is backed up regularly. If, for example, you have one PC that has your accounting system on it, it should be getting backed up daily. And chances are, your company is using a tape drive to back up this PC. To take advantage of these daily backups, you can save your important work files on this PC. Then, you can just do a full backup every month or so to protect the time you have invested in installing and setting up the programs on your hard disk.

Of course, before you save your work files to another PC, you should work out the details with the person who uses that PC. That way, you can verify that there is enough storage available on the hard disk, that there is a directory set up for your files, and that your files won't be deleted by someone who doesn't think they are important.

Some perspective on networks and backup

One of the many reasons used to justify installing a network is that it can be used for backups. After all, it's clear that you can use a network to improve your backup procedures. However, you should know that a network isn't always the best solution. In most cases, installing a network costs more per PC than buying a tape drive for every computer. In addition, a network adds another layer of complexity to backups. As a result, people may be confused and think their files are being backed up, when in fact, they aren't.

For these reasons, I don't recommend that you install a network just to improve your backups. The main considerations should be the need to share files, programs, and other resources. But of course, if you decide to install a network, you should do everything you can to take advantage of it for backups.

Terms

network
local area network

LAN
file-server network
file server
network resource
dedicated file-server network
diskless workstation
local resource
local hard disk
logging on
running stand-alone
Novell Netware
network administrator
peer-to-peer network
Artisoft Lantastic

Section 2

Three options for backing up a hard disk

In section 1, you learned about backup concepts and about the software and hardware options available for doing backups. In this section, you'll learn how to use the options that you're interested in, and you can read about them in any order you choose. If you want to learn how to use the DOS commands for your backups, for example, you can read chapter 4. If you're interested in using a commercial backup utility for your backups, you can read chapter 5. Then, you can continue with chapter 5 to learn how to use any one of the four most popular commercial utilities. Or if you're interested in using a tape drive for your backups, you can read chapter 6 to find out if a tape drive is the right option for your backup requirements.

Chapter 4

How to use DOS commands to back up a hard disk

As you learned in chapter 1, DOS provides two commands for backing up and restoring data on a hard disk. Although the Backup and Restore commands are slower and less reliable than commercial backup utilities, they are appropriate for the backup needs of many users. Also, because they are a part of DOS, they are a backup resource that you already have. They are also a resource that you can use to transfer files from one PC to another.

In this chapter, you'll learn how to use the Backup command to back up all the files on a disk, only those that have changed since your last backup, only those in a single directory, or just the one file you want. Similarly, you'll learn how to use the Restore command to restore all the files you've backed up, or just the ones you need. Finally, you'll learn why you should consider getting a commercial backup program.

How to use the Backup command

If you study the format of the Backup command in figure 4-1, you can see that the command backs up the files indicated by the *source specification* to the *target specification*. When you use this command, the source specification indicates the drive, directory, and file specifications for data on the hard disk. And the target specification indicates the diskette drive. When you execute the command, it backs up the files in the source specification to the diskette in the diskette drive.

One of the keys to using any DOS command is understanding how *switches* work. Switches let you control various aspects of how the command is processed. They can be used alone or in combination with each other. It's the combination of these switches that allows the Backup command to perform different types of backups. If you look at figure 4-1 again, you can see that the /S switch lets you include subdirectories in your backups; the /M switch lets you do incremental backups; the /A switch lets you do appended incremental backups; and so on.

The most important switch for the Backup command is the /S switch. When you use this switch, the Backup command backs up the files in the source directory and all the files in directories that are subordinate to the source directory. If, for example, the source directory is the root directory of the drive, all the files on that drive are backed up because all the directories are subordinate to the root directory.

To execute the Backup command, you enter the command at the DOS command prompt. Then, you press the Enter key. If you make a mistake entering the command, you can just backspace and correct it. If you press the Enter key before you realize that you made a mistake, you can cancel the command with either of these keystroke combinations:

```
Ctrl+Pause or Ctrl+C
```

You can cancel the backup operation at anytime without harming your data.

After you execute the Backup command, DOS displays messages that tell you which diskette to insert into the target drive. For instance, when the backup operation is ready for diskette number 3, DOS displays this message:

```
Insert backup target diskette 3 in drive A:
Strike any key when ready
```

As you can see, you need to keep your backup diskettes organized and labelled so you can insert the diskettes of your backup set in the right order.

As I mentioned in chapter 1, the Backup command doesn't work at all like the DOS Copy command. To see what I mean, you can use the DOS Directory command to display the root directory of a backup diskette. In-

---

The format of the Backup command

```
BACKUP source-spec target-spec [switches]
```

Switch meanings

/s   Includes files that are in the subdirectories of the specified directory.

/m   Backs up only those files that have been modified since the last backup.

/a   Adds the new files to the files that are already on the backup diskette (DOS 3.3 or later).

/l   Creates a log file named BACKUP.LOG in the root directory of the source disk.

/f   Formats a backup diskette before using it if it isn't already formatted (DOS 3.3, but not 4.0 or 5.0 because under these versions the format is done automatically).

Figure 4-1   The format of the Backup command

stead of one entry for each file that has been backed up, you'll find just two directory entries for an entire backup diskette. One entry is for a file named BACKUP; the other is for a file named CONTROL. The first file contains all the files that have been backed up to the diskette, and the second one contains control information that is required for the proper operation of the Backup and Restore commands.

How to use the Backup command to do a full backup   The first command in figure 4-2 shows you how to use the Backup command to do a full backup of all the files on drive C. As you can see, this command uses the * wildcard. Since the * represents one or more characters of any kind, the *.* file specification includes all the files in the backup, regardless of their name or extension. Then, the /S switch includes the files in all of the subdirectories of the source specification. If you don't use the /S switch, only the files in the root directory will be backed up.

How to back up all the files on a drive (a full backup)

```
C:\>backup c:\*.* a: /s
```

How to back up all the files on a drive using unformatted diskettes (DOS 3.3)

```
C:\>backup c:\*.* a: /s/f
```

How to back up all the files on a drive and create a log file

```
C:\>backup c:\*.* a: /s/l
```

Figure 4-2   How to use the Backup command to do a full backup

Although the /S switch is the one you'll use most often for full backups, there are two other switches you may occasionally need. The second command in figure 4-2 shows you how to do a full backup to unformatted diskettes using DOS 3.3 and the /F switch. This switch causes DOS to format the diskettes as it backs up data to them. Although you can use the /F switch for either a full or an incremental backup, generally you only need it when you do a full backup to a set of new of diskettes. If you're using DOS 4.0 or 5.0, however, you don't need to use this switch because the Backup command for these versions automatically formats unformatted diskettes during the backup operation.

The third command in figure 4-2 shows you how to use the /L switch to create a *log file*. This file contains the name of every file that is backed up along with the number of the diskette that the file is on. Then, if you have to restore one or more files, you can use the DOS Type or Print command to display or print the log file.

When you use the /L switch, the command creates a log file named BACKUP.LOG that's stored in the root directory of the source drive. If BACKUP.LOG already exists when you issue the Backup command, a new log is added to the end of the old log. Usually, this is not what you want. So

How to use DOS commands to back up a hard disk   59

How to back up only those files that have been changed since the last backup (an incremental backup)

    C:\>backup c:*.* a: /s/m

How to do an appended incremental backup (DOS 3.3 or later)

    C:\>backup c:*.* a: /s/m/a

Figure 4-3   How to use the Backup command to do an incremental backup

you should delete the old BACKUP.LOG file before you start the Backup command.

How to use the Backup command to do an incremental backup   Figure 4-3 shows you how to use the Backup command to do an incremental backup of the files on drive C. In the first command, the /S switch causes the subdirectories to be included in the backup. And the /M switch causes DOS to do an incremental backup. When you use just these switches, the backed up files will be directed to a new diskette instead of being added to your last backup diskette.

The second command in figure 4-3 shows you how to use the /A switch to do an appended incremental backup. When you use this switch, the command adds the backed up files to your last backup diskette. Since this saves diskettes, you will probably want to use this switch for incremental backups. Note, however, that you can only do appended backups if you're using DOS version 3.3 or later.

How to use the Backup command to do a partial backup   Sometimes, you want to back up just one file or all the files in just one directory. This is called a *partial backup*. To do this kind of backup, you use the file specification to include only those files that you want backed up. In figure 4-4, for example, the first command uses wildcards in the file specification to back up all the files in the \123\WK1 directory. As you can see, partial backups

---

How to back up all the files in one data directory

    C:\>backup c:\123\wk1*.* a:

How to back up a single file

    C:\>backup c:\dbase\data\customer.dbf a:

Figure 4-4 How to use the Backup command to do a partial backup

are useful when you regularly work on one file or just the files in only one directory.

This kind of backup is also useful when you want to transfer these files to another PC. Generally, the Backup command works better than the DOS Copy command when you need to transfer many files because the Backup command will use as many diskettes as are needed for the backup operation. In contrast, the Copy command stops as soon as the first diskette is full. Then, you have to determine which files didn't get copied, and you have to run the Copy command again for those files. This is time consuming and often frustrating, especially when you have to run the Copy command several times.

The second command in figure 4-4 shows how to back up a single file. Here, a complete file specification, including the file name, is used to identify the file you want to back up. Again, this method is useful for transferring data when a file is too large to fit on one diskette. If, for example, the database file named CUSTOMER.DBF is too large to fit on one diskette, you can use the Backup command shown here to back up the file to diskettes. Then, you can use the backup diskettes to transfer the file to another PC.

How to use the Restore command

You use the Restore command to transfer the data from your backup set to your hard disk. Because of the special format used by the Backup command, you must use the Restore command to restore files that have been backed up; you can't use the DOS Copy command.

Whether you're restoring all of your files or just one, the Restore command has you insert each diskette from your backup set in the order it was created. Like the Backup command, DOS displays a message telling you which diskette to insert. As a result, if you're restoring only one file (and you don't have a backup log to tell which diskette that file is on) you may spend several minutes inserting diskettes before you get to the one that has the file you want restored. Then, if you've done incremental backups, you must continue through your set of backup diskettes to make sure that you restore the most recent version of the file. However, if you want to restore an earlier version, you can stop when you've restored that version.

Even if it takes several minutes to restore a file, you'll be delighted to discover that the file has been restored and you haven't lost all the hard work that went into it. If you ever have to restore hundreds of files, you'll be thankful indeed that you took the time to do an effective job of backing up your hard disk.

How to use the Restore command to do a full restore Figure 4-5 shows the command format of the Restore command. This figure also shows you how to use the Restore command to restore all of the files from a backup of drive C. Because you're restoring all the files, you can refer to this as a *full restore*. When you do a full restore, make sure that you use the /S switch as shown in this example. Otherwise, you won't restore any of the files that are in directories that are subordinate to the root directory.

During a full restore, you insert all of the diskettes that make up your backup set. You don't distinguish between diskettes based on whether you ran a full or incremental backup on them. You just insert them in the order they were created. This way, the Restore command restores the latest version of all the files contained in your backup.

How to use the Restore command to do a partial restore Figure 4-6 shows you how to use the Restore command to do a *partial restore*. In the target specification, you identify the file or files you want restored. To identify the file or files, you must include the path for the file and the name of the file. The command uses this information to identify the directory on the hard disk that it will restore the files to. Because of the way this command works, it won't let you restore the files to a directory other than the one they were backed up from. So you can't use a partial restore to move files from one directory to another.

The first command in figure 4-6 restores all the files from just one directory on drive C. You can use a command like this to restore some of the files from a full backup. Or you can use it to restore from a partial backup. This command, for example, restores the files from the first backup command in figure 4-4.

The second command in figure 4-6 restores just one file from a backup. Here, a complete file specification is used to identify the file. You can use a command like this to restore one file from either a full or partial backup. This command, for example, restores the one file from the second backup command in figure 4-4.

If your backup procedure creates a log file, you can use the log to find out which backup diskette contains the file you want to restore. Then, you can speed up the restore operation by inserting just that diskette. But it takes time to create and maintain a log file, and you probably won't need to restore a single file that often. As a result, it may not be worth keeping a log file as part of your backup plan.

Why you should consider buying a backup utility

If your backup requirements are simple, the DOS Backup and Restore commands may be all that you need. For most PC users, though, a backup utility will pay for itself in less than a year. In general, backup utilities are much faster than the DOS commands. On my system, for instance, it took me almost 12 minutes to back up 10MB of data to diskettes using the DOS Backup command. In contrast, it took me only 3 minutes to back up the same amount of data using a backup utility. Aside from running backups faster, utilities are also easier to use. As a result, you're far more likely to do regular backups.

If you're ready to consider a backup utility, read the first part of chapter 5 and select one of the backup programs for review. Then, you'll have more facts to help you decide whether you should get a backup utility for your PC.

How to use DOS commands to back up a hard disk

The format of the Restore command

```
RESTORE source-spec target-spec [switch]
```

Switch meaning

/s   Restores the files in all subdirectories.

How to restore all of the files from a full backup

```
C:\>restore a: c:\*.* /s
```

Figure 4-5   How to use the Restore command to do a full restore

How to restore all of the files in the \123\WK1\ directory from a backup

```
C:\>restore a: c:\123\wk1\*.*
```

How to restore a single file from a backup

```
C:\>restore a: c:\dbase\data\customer.dbf
```

Figure 4-6   How to use the Restore command to do a partial restore

If you decide to use a backup utility but you don't already have one available to you, you can read the descriptions of the other backup utilities in chapter 5. That way, you can compare the four most popular backup utilities without having to buy them. When you're done, you should be able to select the utility that's best for you.

Chapter 4

Terms

source specification
target specification
switch
log file
partial backup
full restore
partial restore

Chapter 5

How to use a backup utility to back up a hard disk

The DOS Backup command is hard to use and it's slow. That's why backup utilities have become popular. These utilities back up your hard disk in a fraction of the time it takes the DOS Backup command. These utilities are also easier to use than the Backup command. Furthermore, the backups they do are more reliable than those done by the Backup command.

The most important benefit of a backup utility, though, is not the time you save. Instead, it's the fact that you're more likely to do regular backups when they take only a minute or two a day. Then, when you lose just one file, all the files in a directory, or all the files on your hard disk, it won't be a disaster because you'll be able to restore all the files you've lost.

In this chapter, you'll learn about the four types of backups that most utilities are able to perform. You'll also be introduced to four of the most widely used backup utilities. Then, you'll learn how to back up and restore files using each of these utility programs.

The features of a backup utility

Figure 5-1 summarizes the features of four of the most popular backup utilities: *Central Point Backup* (or *CP Backup*), *Norton Backup*, *PC-Fullbak+*, and *FastBack Plus*. All of these utilities provide improved speed, ease of use, and file compression capabilities.

Central Point Backup version 7 (comes with *PC Tools Deluxe*)

    Full, appended incremental, differential, and date-selected backups
    Standard DOS or high-speed DMA performance
    Setup files for saved backup configurations
    User interface consistent with the other utilities of *PC Tools Deluxe*
    File compression
    Scheduled backups

Norton Backup version 1.1

    Full, separate incremental, differential, and date-selected backups
    Standard DOS or high-speed DMA performance
    Setup files for saved backup configurations
    File compression
    Macros

PC-Fullbak+ version 2.02

    Full, appended incremental, differential, and date-selected backups
    Standard DOS or high-speed DMA performance
    File compression
    Simplified menu system for the most common functions

FastBack Plus version 3.0

    Full, appended incremental, differential, and date-selected backups
    Standard DOS or high-speed DMA performance
    Setup files for saved backup configurations
    File compression
    Macros

Figure 5-1   The features of the four most popular backup utilities

Speed   Figure 5-2 gives you some idea of how the four backup utilities can improve on the speed of the DOS Backup command. Although this chart just summarizes the data from an informal test on a typical system, I think the message is clear. A backup utility can reduce the time you take for backups by 70 percent or more. This means a backup that takes 15 minutes when

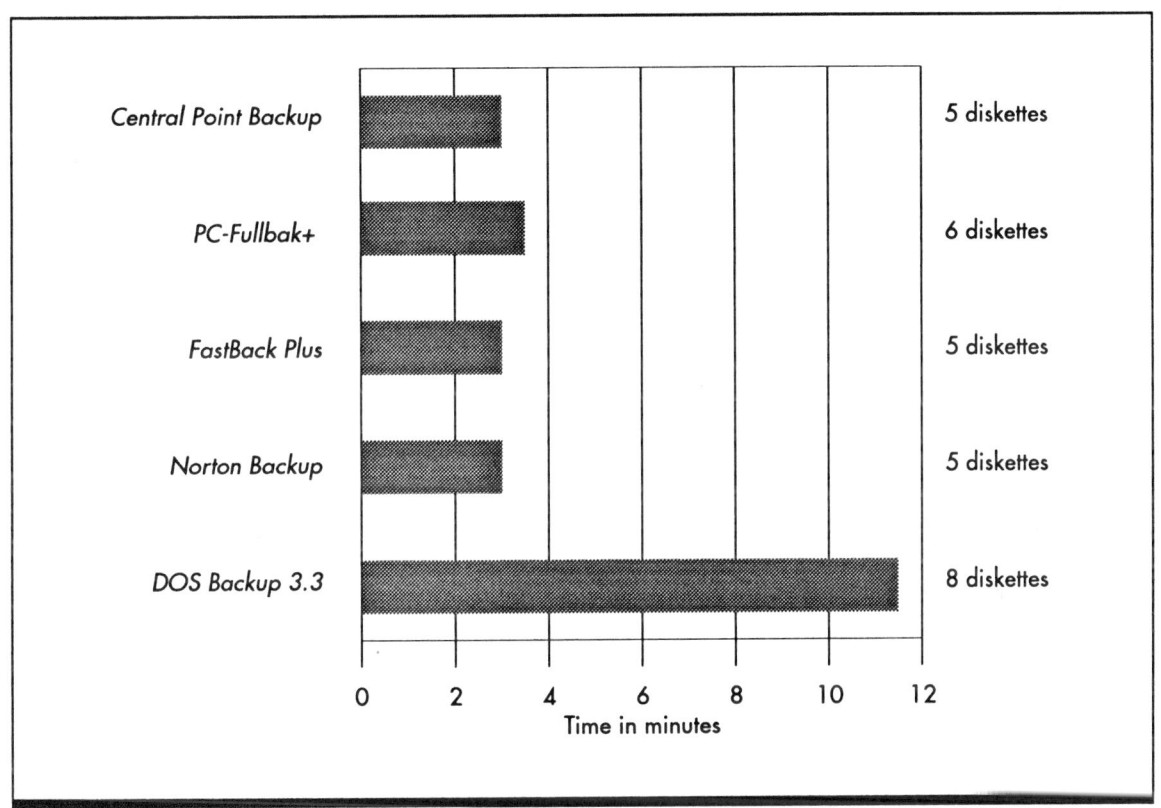

How to use a backup utility to back up a hard disk   67

Utility	Time	Diskettes
Central Point Backup	~3 min	5 diskettes
PC-Fullbak+	~3 min	6 diskettes
FastBack Plus	~3 min	5 diskettes
Norton Backup	~3 min	5 diskettes
DOS Backup 3.3	~11.5 min	8 diskettes

Figure 5-2 The relative backup times and number of diskettes required for the DOS Backup command and four backup utilities

you use the DOS Backup command will probably take less than 5 minutes when you use a backup utility.

To operate at maximum speed, a backup utility uses a hardware feature called *DMA*, or *Direct Memory Access*. Although most PCs support this feature, not all do. If your PC doesn't, you won't get the speed improvements promised by the chart in figure 5-2, but the backup utility will still improve upon the speed of the DOS Backup command. In figure 5-1, you can see that all four utilities provide for DMA performance as well as for standard DOS performance.

Ease of use As you learned in chapter 4, the command format of the DOS Backup command makes it difficult to use. In contrast, the backup utilities provide features that make them easy to use. All four programs, for example, have menu systems that make it easy to do the most common backup operations. Three of these programs also provide *setup files* for saved backup configurations. That means you can save the specifications for a backup procedure after you get the utility set up the way you want it. Then, you can run the backup procedure the next time just by loading the setup file.

In the place of setup files, *PC-Fullbak+* provides a simplified menu interface to make it easier for occasional users. *FastBack Plus* and *Norton Backup* also provide *macro* capabilities that you can use to simplify backups. Because the *Central Point Backup* program that comes with *PC Tools Deluxe* uses the same types of screens and menus that the *PC Tools Deluxe* shell uses, it's easy to use the backup program if you know how to use the shell.

A backup utility also makes it easier to restore files from backup diskettes. When you use *CP Backup*, for instance, you can select the directories and files that you want to restore the same way you select directories and files when you use the shell. You'll see this illustrated later on in this chapter.

File compression Backup utilities compress the data in the files that they back up. This means the files take up less space on the diskettes than they do on the hard disk. On the right side of the chart in figure 5-2, you can compare the number of diskettes each of the utilities requires to back up the same amount of data.

Although *file compression* isn't an essential feature of a backup utility, it can increase backup speed because it reduces the amount of data that has to be written on the backup diskettes. Also, it provides a minor savings in diskette costs. Because data files can be compressed more than program files, this feature is most advantageous when you're backing up data files. In general, the more data you have on your hard disk, the more useful this feature becomes.

Four types of backups

In chapter 1, I introduced you to the two major types of backups: full and incremental. Now, I'll quickly review these types of backups, and I'll introduce two more types. If you look again at figure 5-1, you can see the types of backups each utility supports.

Full backups   A *full backup* is a backup of every file on a hard disk starting with the root directory. That means it includes program and command files as well as data files. And it includes files that have been created or changed since the last backup as well as files that haven't been. Whether you need to recover one file or many, the full backup is the starting point for recovery.

Incremental backups   An *incremental backup* is a backup of just the files that have been created or changed since the last backup. Because you work mainly with an application program's data files, not its program files, incremental backups usually include only data files.

When you do a *separate incremental backup*, the backup starts with a new diskette. In contrast, an *appended incremental backup* starts at the end of the previous backup diskette rather than with a new diskette. This is illustrated by figure 5-3. Here, the full backup on Monday ended in the middle of diskette 6. As a result, the appended incremental backup on Tuesday starts with diskette 6. Then, each subsequent backup starts with the last diskette of the previous backup set.

If your backup utility supports appended incremental backups, you'll probably want to use them for two reasons. First, they reduce the number of diskettes you must keep track of. If you do a full backup on the first day of each month and incremental backups on all of the other days of the month, you'll use many fewer diskettes if you use appended backups.

Second, every time you run a separate incremental backup, you create a new backup set. Then, if each incremental backup requires more than one diskette, you end up with several new diskettes each time you back up. This makes it harder to keep track of the individual backup sets. On the other hand, if you keep the backup diskettes in a safe or at another location, it may be easier to do separate incremental backups.

Differential backups   In chapter 1, you learned that incremental backups are possible because each file has an *archive bit* that can be turned on when a file is created or changed and turned off when the file is backed up. Unlike an incremental backup, however, the archive bit isn't turned off during a *differential backup*. As a result, a differential backup is a backup up of all the files that have been created or changed since the last full backup, even if they have been backed up in a previous differential backup. You can't do this type of backup with the DOS Backup command because it doesn't provide this function.

To illustrate how you can use differential backups, figure 5-4 shows a weekly schedule of one full and four differential backups. As you can see, each differential backup requires only diskette 7. Since the diskettes for a differential backup include only one version of each backed up file, a schedule of differential backups is likely to require fewer diskettes than a schedule of separate incremental backups. However, the differential backups will take longer on the average than the incremental backups.

If you generally work on the same files every day, you may want to use differential backups because they will be just as fast as incremental backups, and they won't require as many diskettes. But if you tend to work on different files each day, you should probably use appended incremental backups because they will be faster than differential backups.

Date-selected backups   When you do a *date-selected backup*, you provide a date for each backup run. Then, the backup utility backs up all of the files that have been created or changed since that date. If, for example, you do a full backup on January 1, 1992, you can back up only the files that have been created or changed after that date.

Some backup utilities let you be even more specific. They let you specify a time in addition to a date. For instance, you can back up only the files that have been created or changed after 10:00 A.M. on January 1, 1992. The DOS Backup command also provides for date-selected backups with the /D and /T switches.

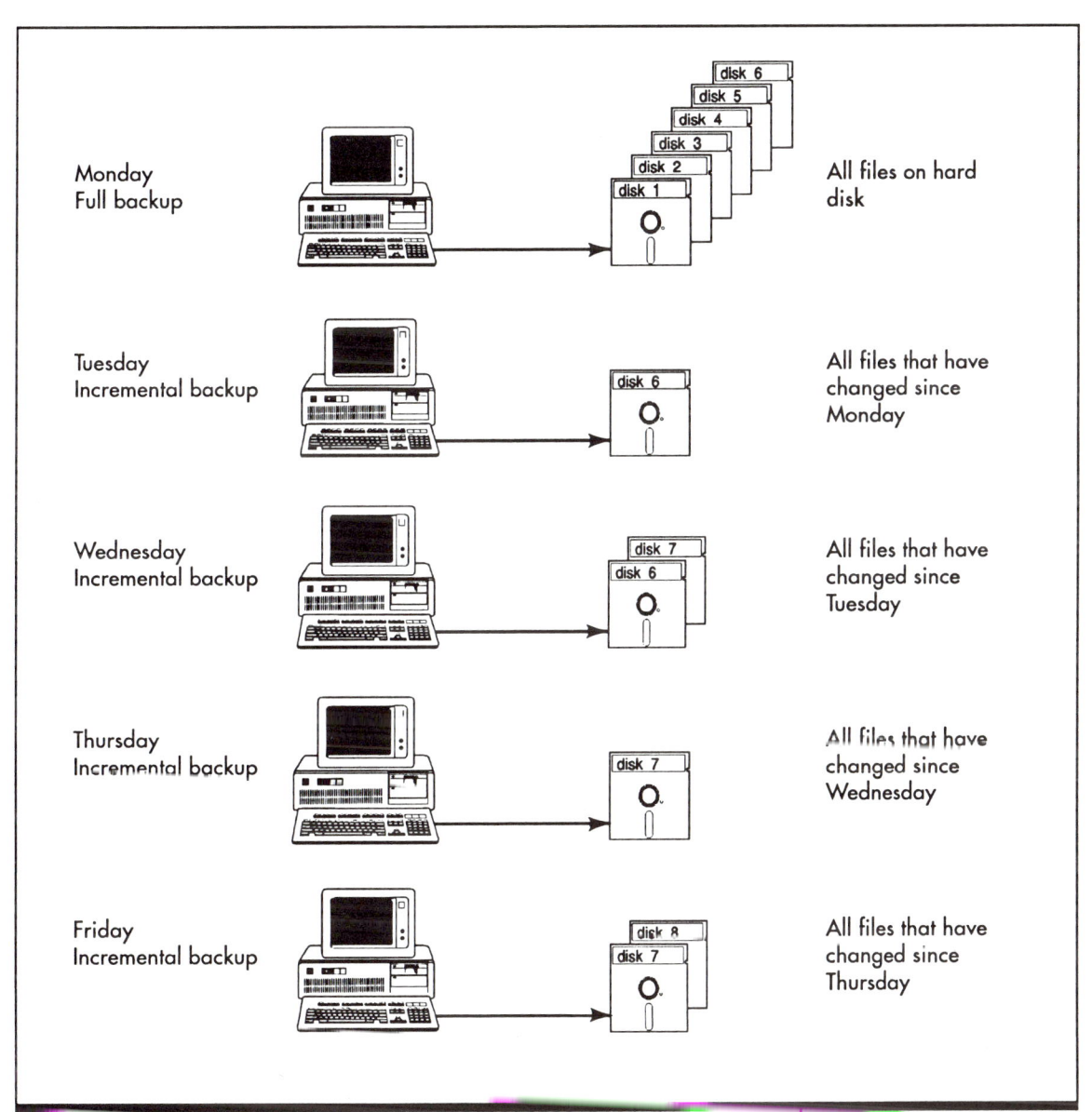

How to use a backup utility to back up a hard disk 71

Monday Full backup		disks 1-6	All files on hard disk
Tuesday Incremental backup		disk 6	All files that have changed since Monday
Wednesday Incremental backup		disks 6-7	All files that have changed since Tuesday
Thursday Incremental backup		disk 7	All files that have changed since Wednesday
Friday Incremental backup		disks 7-8	All files that have changed since Thursday

Figure 5-3   A weekly schedule of full and appended incremental backups

In general, though, incremental or differential backups are easier to manage than date-selected backups. When you use them, you don't have to specify the date or time, consequently there's less room for error. That's why you probably won't use date-selected backups. Nevertheless, most backup utilities provide for them.

How to use the rest of this chapter

The rest of this chapter shows you how to use the four most popular backup utilities. If you already own a backup utility or if your company has a standard backup utility, it's probably one of these four utilities. Then, you can use this chapter instead of the utility's manual to learn how to use that utility. That way, you won't have to wade through a lot of technical information that doesn't apply to your backup plan anyway.

If you don't already own a backup utility and you're not sure which one you want to buy, you can use this chapter to read about the ones you're interested in. That way, you can comparison shop without actually buying the programs. Then, when you buy one, you can re-read the material to learn how to use the program.

In case you're interested in my evaluations, figure 5-5 shows how I rank the four most popular backup utilities: (1) *Central Point Backup*; (2) *Norton Backup*; (3) *PC-Fullbak+*; and (4) *FastBack Plus*. In my opinion, *Central Point Backup* (the program that comes with *PC Tools Deluxe*) has the rare quality of being both powerful and easy to use. As a result, it's appropriate for both advanced and novice PC users. *Norton Backup* is a good utility for advanced users, but it is also good for novices who have someone to help them set up the utility. *PC Fullbak+* is a good utility for novices as long as their backup requirements are fairly simple. It has a simplified menu system that makes it especially easy to use for the most common backup operations. When compared to the other three utilities, *FastBack Plus* is capable, but it's expensive and hard to use. As a result, I find it ironic that this utility is the most widely used utility.

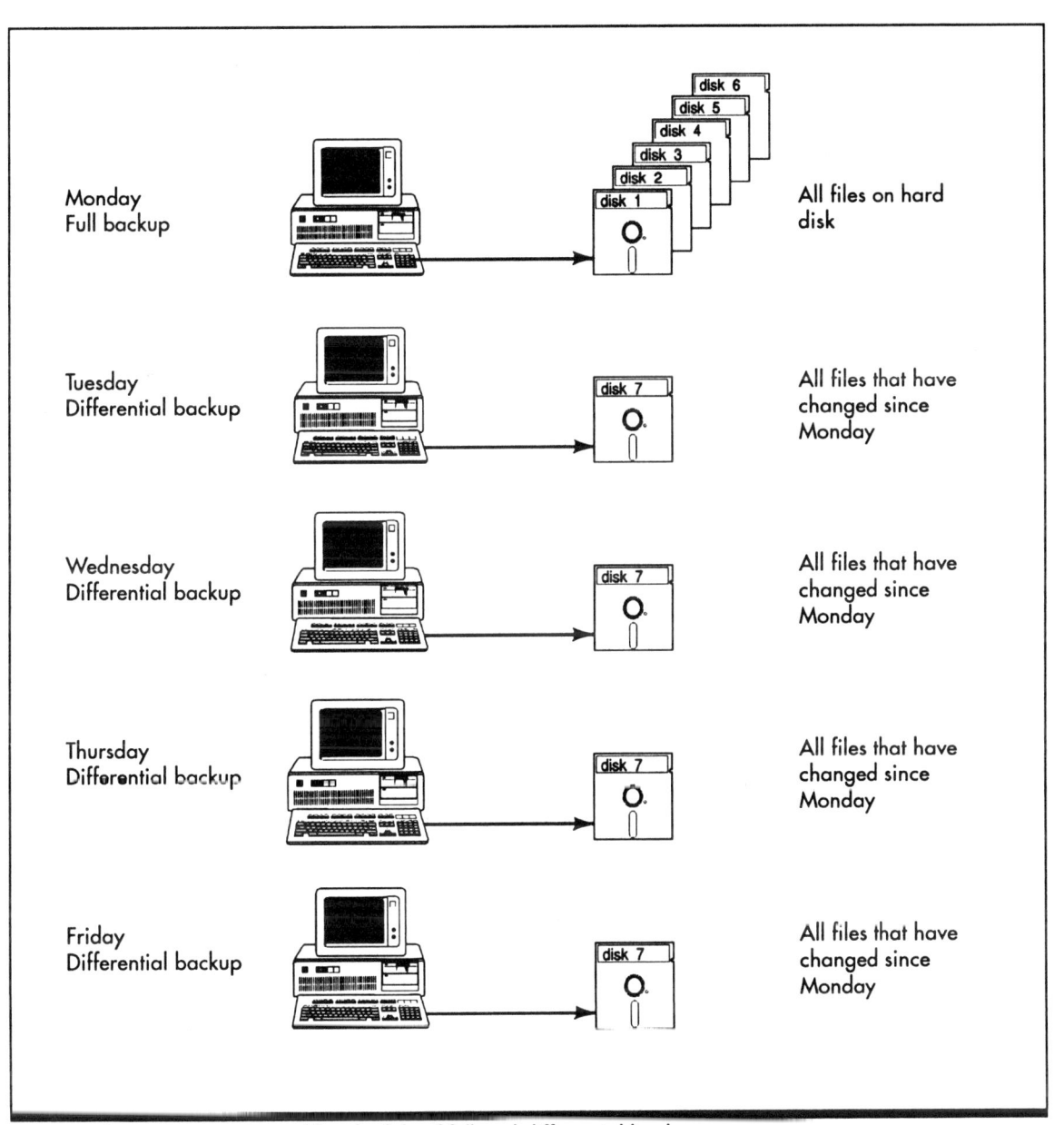

How to use a backup utility to back up a hard disk 73

Monday Full backup		disk 1, disk 2, disk 3, disk 4, disk 5, disk 6	All files on hard disk
Tuesday Differential backup		disk 7	All files that have changed since Monday
Wednesday Differential backup		disk 7	All files that have changed since Monday
Thursday Differential backup		disk 7	All files that have changed since Monday
Friday Differential backup		disk 7	All files that have changed since Monday

Figure 5-4 A weekly schedule of full and differential backups

Utility	Current list price	Reason for ranking
1. *Central Point Backup 7*	$ 85.00	A powerful and easy to use program that's appropriate for both novice and advanced users.
2. *Norton Backup 1.1*	105.00	A good utility that's best for advanced users.
3. *PC-Fullbak+ 2.02*	50.00	A great utility for novice users with simple backup needs.
4. *FastBack Plus 3.0*	120.00	A capable utility that's more expensive and harder to use than the others, even though it's the most popular of the 4 listed here.

Figure 5-5 How the author ranks the four most popular commercial backup utilities

Terms

direct memory access
DMA
setup file
macros
file compression
full backup
incremental backup
archive bit
separate incremental backup
appended incremental backup
differential backup
date-selected backup

Utility 1: Central Point Backup

Central Point Backup version 7 is an excellent backup utility. Not only is it fast, but it's also easy to use. And it offers at least as many features as any other backup utility.

You can buy *CP Backup* as a separate program for about $85. But many people get it as part of *PC Tools Deluxe*. This utility package also includes a DOS shell, an advanced disk utility, and much more, all for a price of about $115. Since *PC Tools* is an excellent utility package and it costs only $30 more than *CP Backup* alone, you may want to buy *PC Tools Deluxe*.

If you have *PC Tools* on your system, you can start *CP Backup* by selecting it from the *PC Tools* main menu. Otherwise, you can start it from the DOS command prompt. To do that, you change to the appropriate drive and directory. Then, you type in the following command at the prompt and press the Enter key:

    cpbackup

Figure CP-1 shows the screen that's displayed when you start *CP Backup*. Here, the Backup option starts the backup function, the Restore option starts the restore function, and the Compare option starts the compare function. To select one of these functions using a mouse, you move the mouse cursor to the function you want and click the left mouse button.

To select one of these functions using a keyboard, you can use two different techniques. You can press the Tab key until the function you want is highlighted and then press the Enter key. Or you can press the letter of the function that appears in a different color or intensity.

If at any point you need help, you can press the F1 key. *Central Point Backup* then displays a Help screen with information on the function you're using. To exit the Help screen, you press the Esc key once, or you can select the Exit function from the bottom of the Help screen.

75

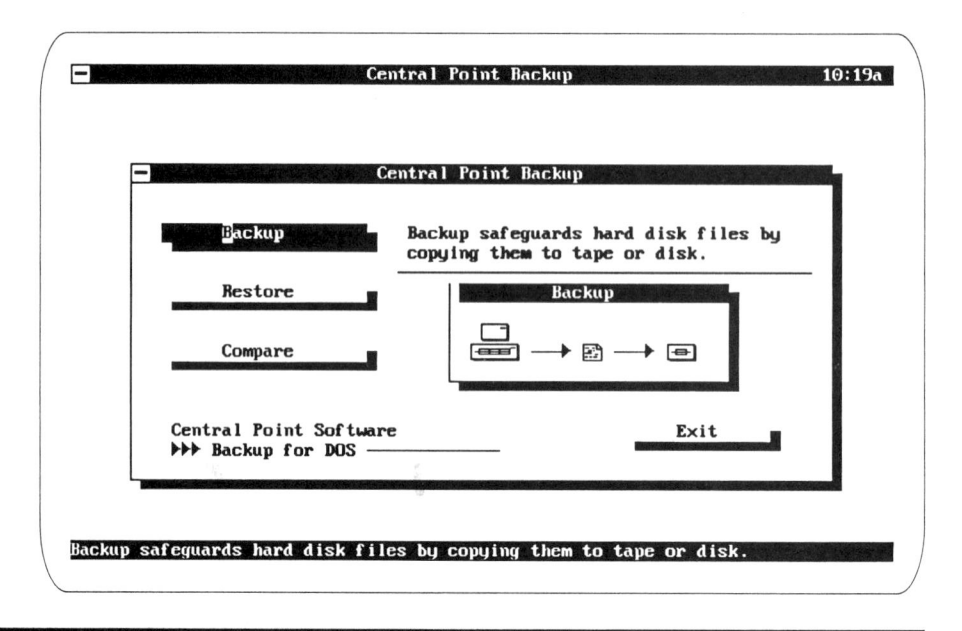

Figure CP-1 The opening screen of *Central Point Backup* version 7

If you have *PC Tools Deluxe* version 5.5 or 6.0, you should know that the backup utility that came with these versions provides the same basic features as *CP Backup* version 7. However, version 7 has a simplified menu system so you may have to look through a couple of menus to find a function if you're using an earlier version. Of course, you may also decide to upgrade to the new version so you can benefit from the improved menu system.

How to set up *CP Backup*

The first time you start *CP Backup*, it runs a special setup operation. This operation asks you to identify the drives on your PC. It also asks you to specify the drive and type of medium you want to use for backups. Then, it performs a trial backup to see if your PC can back up using direct memory access (DMA) for maximum speed. After it completes these operations, it displays the opening screen shown in figure CP-1.

Utility 1: Central Point Backup   77

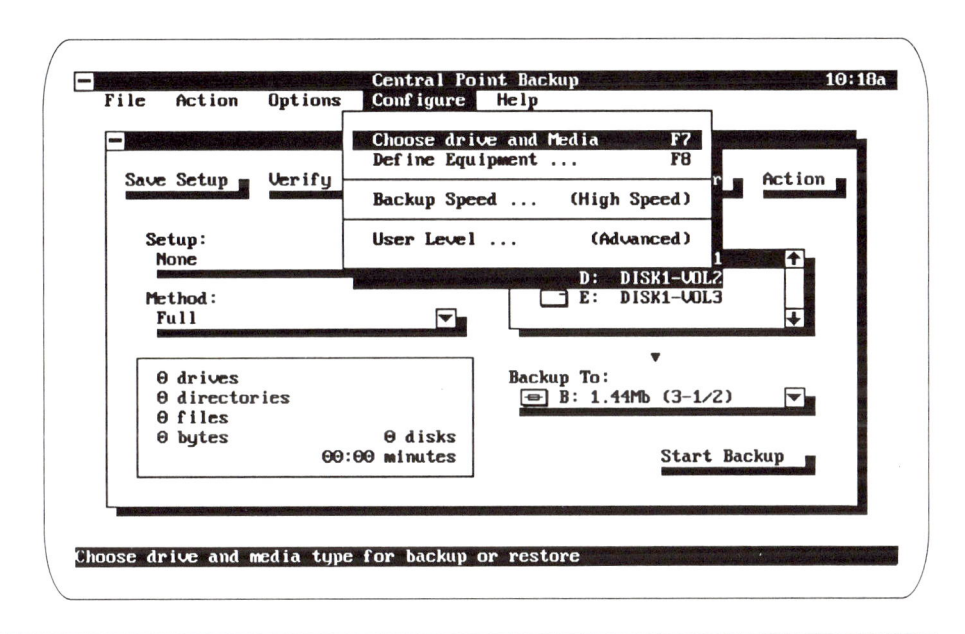

Figure CP-2   The Configure menu

Before you use the utility, however, you'll probably want to set several other options. Or you may want to change some of the options later on. That's why I'll show you how to use the Configure and Options menus. After you select the Backup function from the opening screen in figure CP-1, you can access these menus at the Backup screen that's displayed.

The Configure menu   Figure CP-2 shows the Configure menu selected from the Backup screen. The first three functions on this menu set the same options as the special setup operation does the first time you start *CP Backup*. The Choose-drive-and-media function, for example, lets you specify the drive and medium you want to use for backups. When you select this function, the *dialog box* shown in figure CP-3 is displayed.

The second function in figure CP-2 is the Define-equipment function. If you add a new diskette drive or tape drive to your PC, you must run this function again. When you run it, *CP Backup* checks to find out what hardware components your PC has. Then, the program displays several dialog boxes that let you verify that the program has detected the components correctly. If

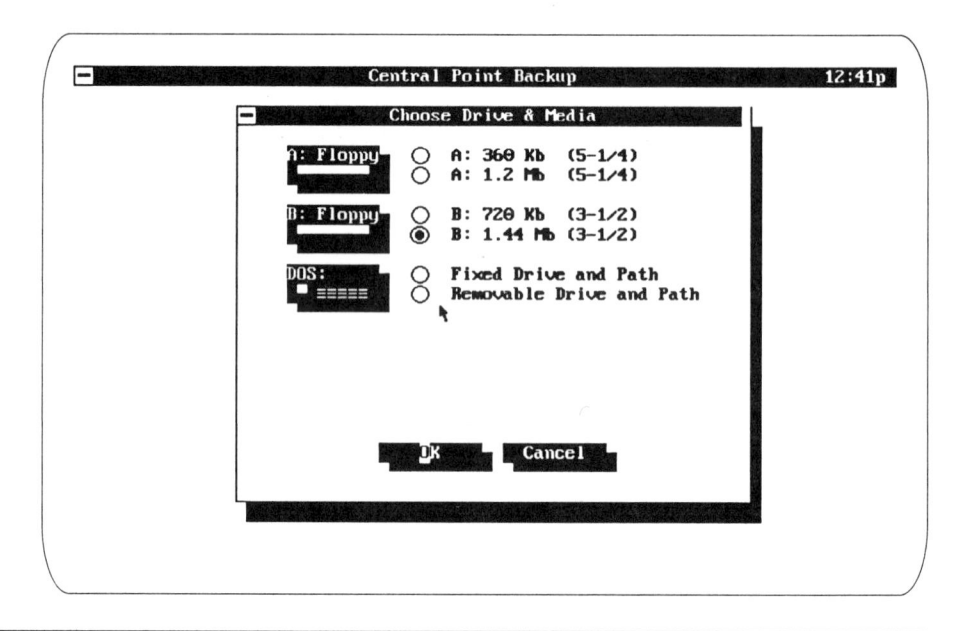

Figure CP-3 The dialog box you use to chose the drive and medium for your backups

it hasn't, you can make corrections. If you don't run this function after you add new equipment, *CP Backup* won't know that the new equipment exits. As a result, you won't be able to use it for backups.

The last two functions in figure CP-2 are the Backup-speed and User-level functions. The Backup-speed function lets you set the memory access method that's used. Since the special setup operation runs a test and sets this to the appropriate setting, you shouldn't need to change it. The User-level function lets you set the user level to beginner, intermediate, or advanced. These levels control the number of functions that are displayed on some of the menus. By default, *CP Backup* sets the user level to advanced so all of the functions are displayed. There is little reason to change the user level because you rarely need to use the menus that are affected by this function. Thus, changing the user level to beginner or intermediate doesn't make the program easier to use.

The Options menu   Figure CP-4 shows the Options menu. Before you run your first backup procedure, you should set the functions on this menu as

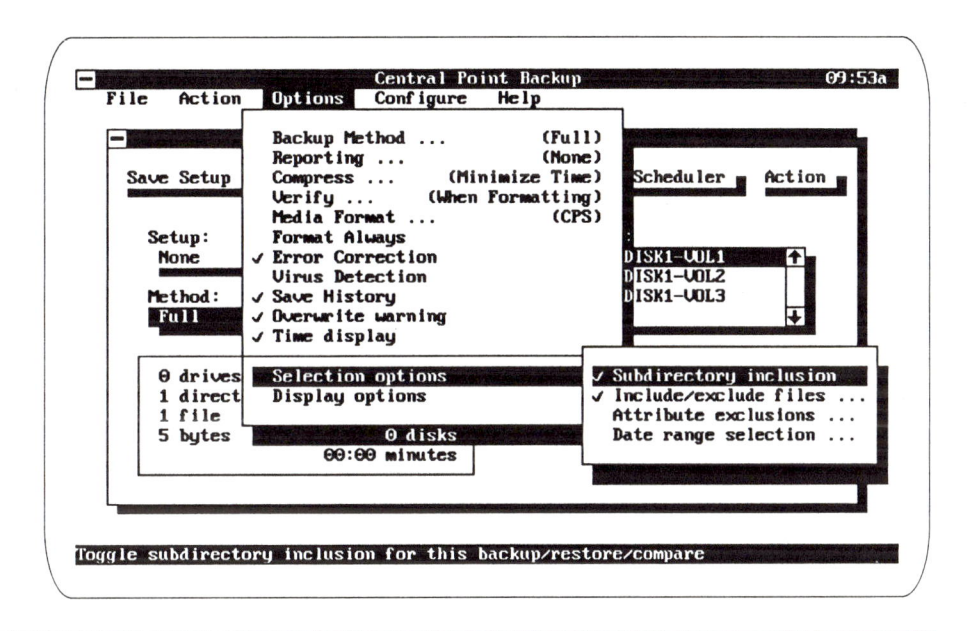

Figure CP-4   The Options menu

shown here. Generally, you'll set these functions just once and use them for all backup and restore procedures. The only function you're likely to change from one procedure to the next is the Backup-method function. But you'll use another menu to change it during your backup procedures.

Since all but one of these functions are the default settings, you shouldn't have to change them. Here, the Compress function is set to minimize the time required for a backup, not to minimize the number of diskettes that are used. The Verify function is set so it's on only when your backup medium is being formatted since that's when errors are most likely to occur. If you change this function so it's always on, it nearly doubles the time required for a backup, which is not what you want.

By default, the Media-format function is set to the standard DOS format. But this format doesn't store as much data on a diskette as the CPS format shown here. The DOS format also makes your backups run a bit slower. So I recommend that you select this function and change it to the CPS format setting.

As you can see in figure CP-4, the Format-always function is off. When it's off, *CP Backup* formats diskettes only if they haven't already been formatted during an earlier backup operation. If this function is on, you waste time formatting diskettes unnecessarily. And your backups take about three times longer.

To improve the reliability of a backup, the Error-correction function is on. Similarly, the Save-history, and Overwrite-warning, and Time-display functions are on. The Save-history function stores the directory information for all the backed-up files. It stores this information on both the hard disk and the last diskette in the backup set. This makes it easier to restore a file when you need to. The Overwrite-warning function protects you from losing data. When it's on, *CP Backup* warns you if the diskette you have inserted for a backup operation contains data. This function also warns you if the file you're restoring already exists on the hard disk. The Time-display is useful because it displays the estimated time required for a backup and the actual time that's required as the backup progresses.

When you select the Selection-options function, *CP Backup* displays the additional menu as shown in figure CP-4. The Subdirectory-inclusion function is on so that all the subdirectories are included in a backup, which is usually what you want. When the Include/Exclude-files function is on, you can provide a list of wildcard specifications that include or exclude files from the backup. If, for example, you want to exclude files with an extension of BK1, you use a specification like this:

`-*.BK1`

Here, the minus sign indicates that the files that match the specification should be excluded. Similarly, you can select the Attribute-exclusions function if you want to exclude files with attribute bits that indicate they are hidden files, system files, or read-only files. Or you can select the Date-range-selection function to do a date-selected backup.

After you set the functions for the backup procedures the way you want them, you need to save them as the default settings. To do this, you activate the File menu that's on the Backup screen. Then, you select the Save-as-default function from the File menu.

Utility 1: Central Point Backup   **81**

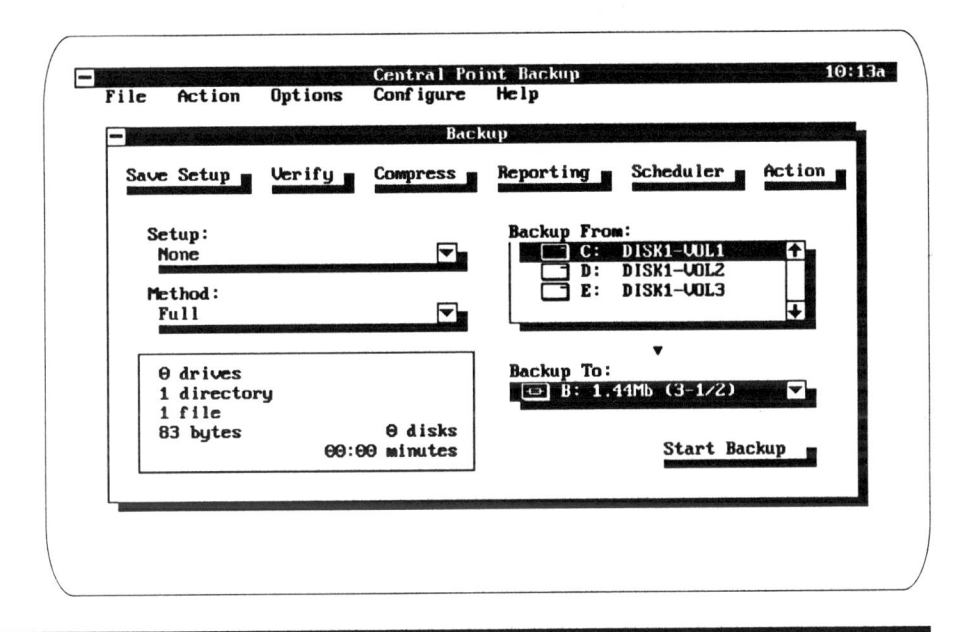

Figure CP-5   The Backup screen

How to do a backup

To do a backup, first you select the Backup function from the opening screen shown in figure CP-1. *CP Backup* then displays the screen shown in figure CP-5. At this screen, you can select the type of backup you want, the hard drive you want to back up, and the drive you want to back up to. In other words, you make selections at this screen to perform the most common backup procedures.

How to do a full backup   In figure CP-6, the functions have been set to do a full backup of drive C. Since you previously set up the program to default to full backups, you shouldn't have to set the Method function. Similarly, you shouldn't have to set the Backup-to function because you already set it using the Configure menu. All you have to do is select the hard drive you want to back up.

To do that, you click the mouse on the drive you want to back up. If you don't have a mouse, you press the Tab key to activate the Backup-from

Chapter 5

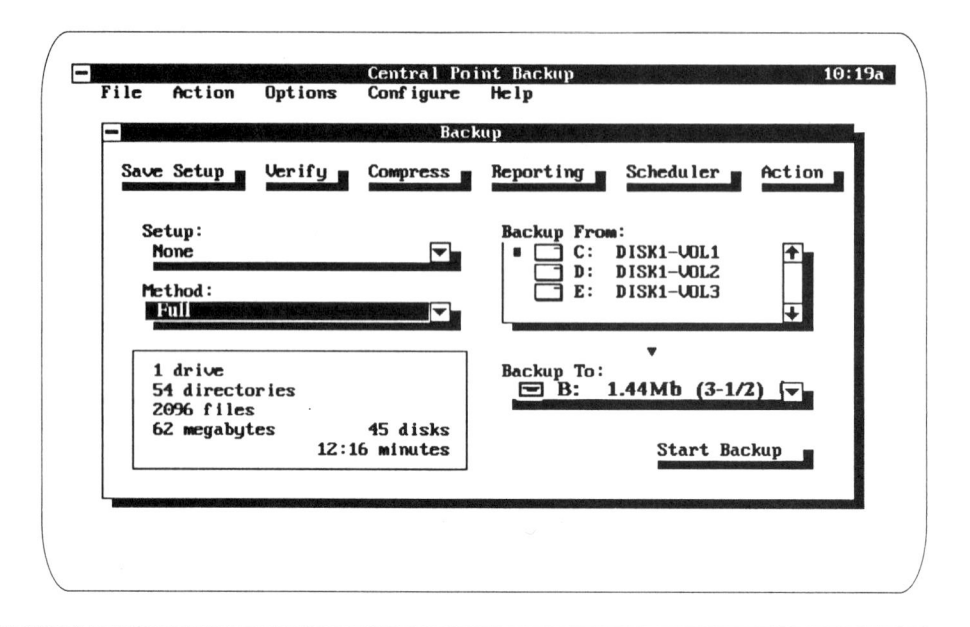

Figure CP-6 *CP Backup* set to do a full backup of drive C

function. Then, you use the arrow keys to move the highlight to the drive you want to back up, and you press the Spacebar to select the drive.

After you select the drive, *CP Backup* scans the disk and confirms the selection by putting a marker next to the hard-drive icon. In figure CP-6, for example, the marker shows that drive C has been selected. The information in the lower left of the screen shows that drive C has 54 directories, 2096 files, and 62MB of data on it. This part of the screen also displays an estimate of the number of diskettes and the amount of time the backup will require.

To execute the backup operation, you select the Start-backup function. Figure CP-7 shows the four screens that are displayed during the backup. Part 1 shows the dialog box that's displayed just after you start the backup. This box lets you assign a description to the backup set. I recommend that you assign a description because it makes it easier to distinguish one backup from another.

However, this doesn't mean that you need a different description each time you back up. Instead, you should use the same description for each

Utility 1: Central Point Backup

Part 1:

The dialog box that asks you to name the backup.

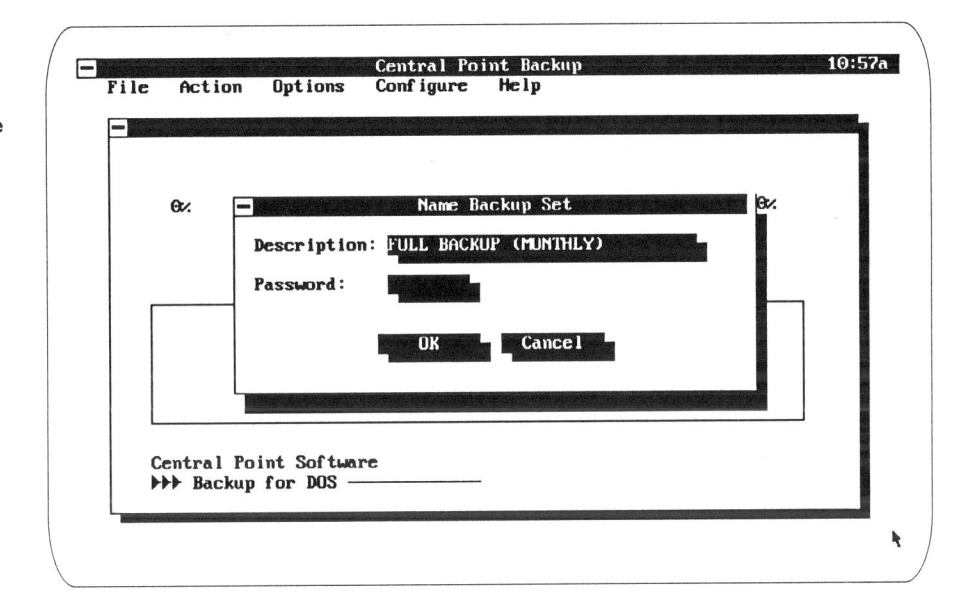

Figure CP-7 The screens *CP Backup* displays during a full backup operation (Part 1 of 4)

backup procedure. For example, if you use the description FULL C (MONTHLY) to describe the full backup of drive C that you do each month, you should use this description each month for the full backup. This way, the old backup is overwritten with the current backup, which is what you want. If you use a different description for the same backup procedure, you'll have a harder time choosing the appropriate backup to restore from.

The second field in figure CP-7 part 1 lets you assign a password. Since you generally don't need a password for a backup, you can omit this entry.

As the backup operation continues, a series of dialog boxes like the one in part 2 of figure CP-7 are displayed. These boxes tell you which diskette to insert. Then, each time the program fills a diskette, it displays a similar dialog box telling you insert the next diskette.

Part 3 of figure CP-7 shows the screen that details the progress of the backup operation. Here, you can see that the backup operation has been running for one minute, and that it is still on the first diskette. You can also see how much time has elapsed, how much time remains, and how much data remains to be backed up.

Part 2:

The dialog box that asks you to insert the appropriate diskette.

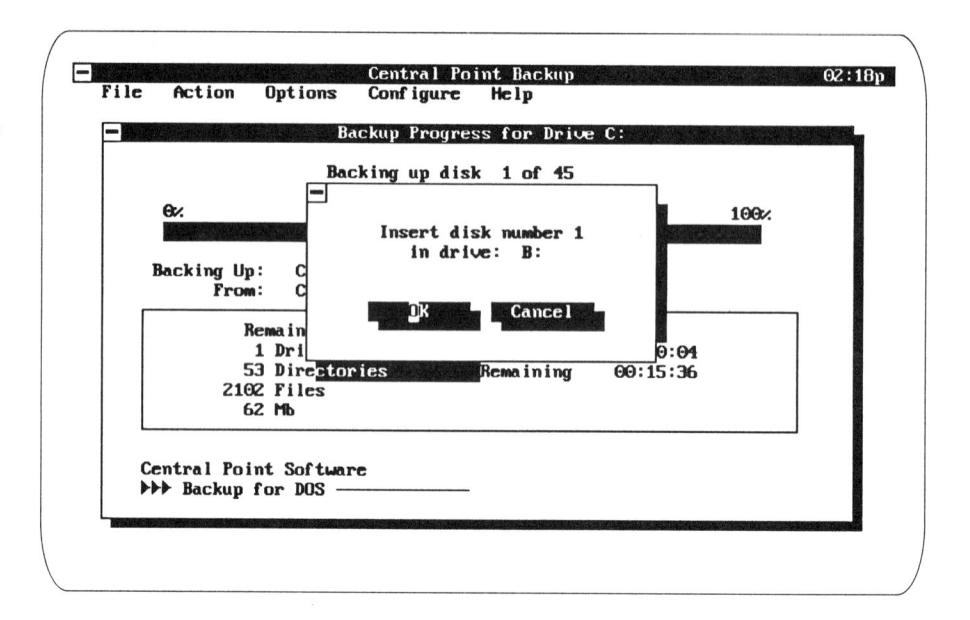

Figure CP-7   The screens *CP Backup* displays during a full backup operation (Part 2 of 4)

Part 3:

The screen that shows the progress of the backup operation.

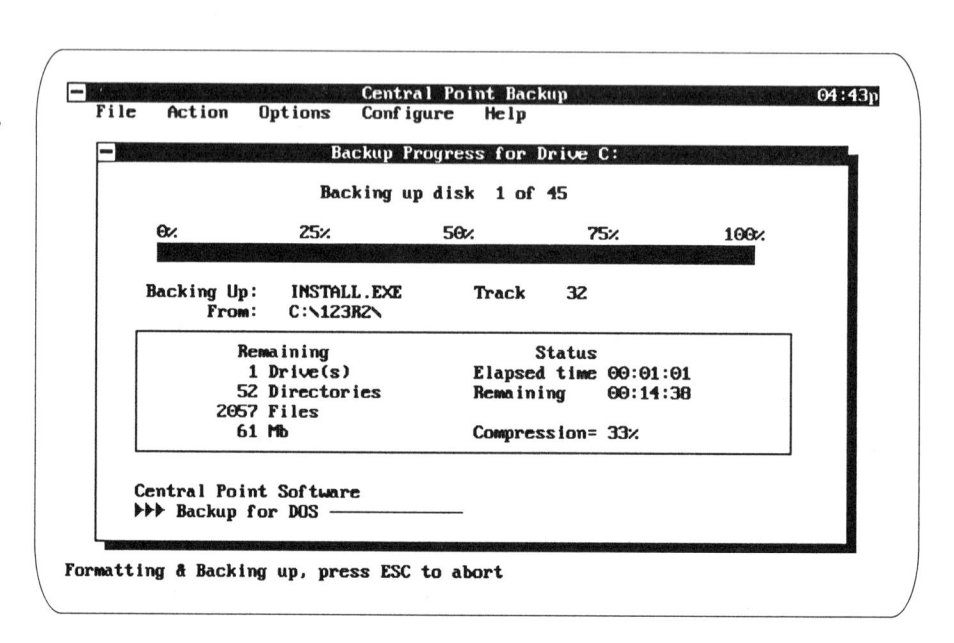

Figure CP-7   The screens *CP Backup* displays during a full backup operation (Part 3 of 4)

Part 4:

The information that's displayed at the end of the backup operation.

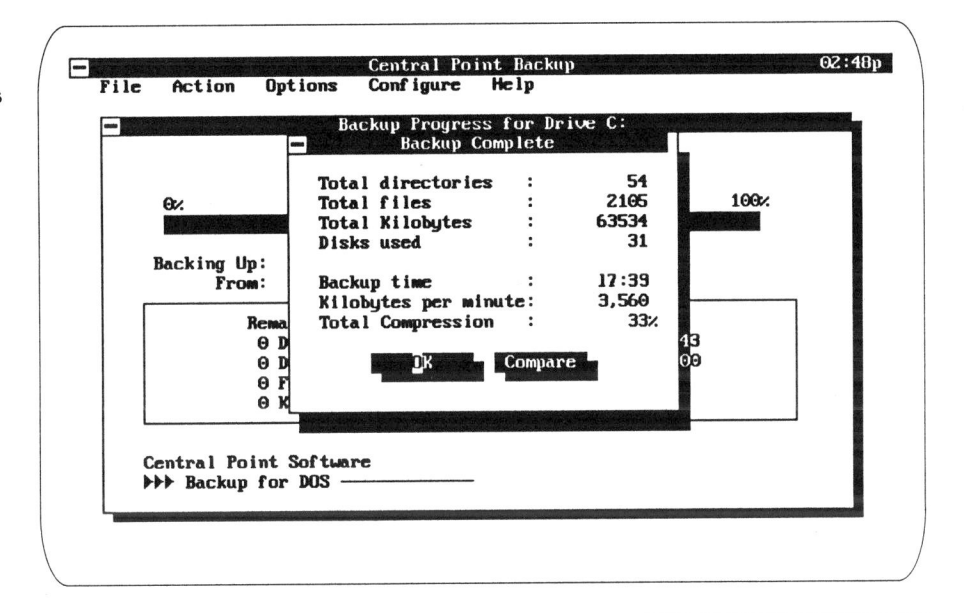

```
┌─────────────────────────────────────────────────────────────────┐
│ ─                     Central Point Backup              02:48p  │
│  File    Action    Options    Configure    Help                 │
│  ┌─────────────────────────────────────────────────────────┐    │
│  │ ─               Backup Progress for Drive C:            │    │
│  │         ┌─────────────── Backup Complete ──────────┐    │    │
│  │    0%   │                                          │    │    │
│  │         │   Total directories     :        54      │    │    │
│  │         │   Total files           :      2105      │ 100%│   │
│  │         │   Total Kilobytes       :     63534      │    │    │
│  │         │   Disks used            :        31      │    │    │
│  │  Backing Up:                                       │    │    │
│  │        From:│ Backup time         :     17:39      │    │    │
│  │         │   Kilobytes per minute: :     3,560      │    │    │
│  │      Rema   │ Total Compression   :       33%      │    │    │
│  │         0 D │                                      │43  │    │
│  │         0 D │       ┌────┐      ┌─────────┐        │00  │    │
│  │         0 F │       │ OK │      │ Compare │        │    │    │
│  │         0 K │       └────┘      └─────────┘        │    │    │
│  │         └──────────────────────────────────────────┘    │    │
│  │                                                         │    │
│  │   Central Point Software                                │    │
│  │  ▶▶▶ Backup for DOS ─────────                           │    │
│  └─────────────────────────────────────────────────────────┘    │
└─────────────────────────────────────────────────────────────────┘
```

Figure CP-7 The screens *CP Backup* displays during a full backup operation (Part 4 of 4)

When the backup operation is complete, a box like the one in part 4 of figure CP-7 is displayed. This box summarizes the backup operation and reports any errors that occurred. If errors are reported, you should run the Compare function immediately. I'll tell you how to do that later in this chapter.

How to do an appended incremental backup   To do an appended incremental backup, first you select the Method function as shown in part 1 of figure CP-8. Then, you select the backup method you want to use. For an appended incremental backup, you select the Incremental function. Then, you select the hard drive you want to back up, and you start the backup by selecting the Start-backup function. After you start the backup, a dialog box like the one in part 2 of figure CP-8 is displayed. This box instructs you to insert the last diskette of your backup set. After you insert the correct diskette, *CP Backup* displays the same series of dialog boxes that it does for a full backup.

If you look again at the Method function in part 1 of figure CP-8, you can see that you can also do separate incremental and differential backups. Because you have to know how to use additional features of *CP Backup* to use these functions, I'm not going to cover them in this chapter. The two other functions you see aren't backup methods. They're here because they are other functions that are associated with backup functions. The Full-copy method is useful when you want to use the backup format to transfer files to another PC, but you don't want to interrupt your backup schedule. The Virus-scan-only function is useful for excluding files from your current backup that have been damaged by a destructive program called a *virus*.

How to do a partial backup To do a partial backup, first you set the backup method to Full. Then, you select the hard drive you want to back up using a slightly different technique than you use for appended backups. If you're using a mouse, you double-click on the hard-drive icon instead of clicking on it once. If you're using the keyboard, you highlight the hard drive and press the Enter key instead of the Spacebar. Either way, *CP Backup* displays a directory and file listing like the one shown in figure CP-9.

Here, you can see that the directories are listed on the left side of the screen, and the files are listed on the right side of the screen. To switch between these two sides, you can click on the listing you want with the mouse, or you can press the Tab key. To select an entire directory for a backup, you select the directory in the directory listing. To select individual files for a backup, you select them from the file listing.

However, before you can select the directories or files you want to include in a partial backup, you must first clear the file selections. To do that, you position the highlight on the root directory and press the Spacebar. All of the directories and files in the listing will change color or intensity to show that they have been cleared. Next, you move to the directory or files you want to back up, and you make your selections by clicking the mouse or pressing the Spacebar. Finally, you press the F10 key to return to the Backup screen. Then, you can start the backup by selecting the Start-backup function.

In figure CP-9, you can see that the \QA\FILES directory has been selected for the backup. And you can see that this directory contains 18 files. When you press the F10 key, the backup screen shown in figure CP-10 is

Utility 1: Central Point Backup **87**

Part 1:

The Incremental function selected from the Method panel.

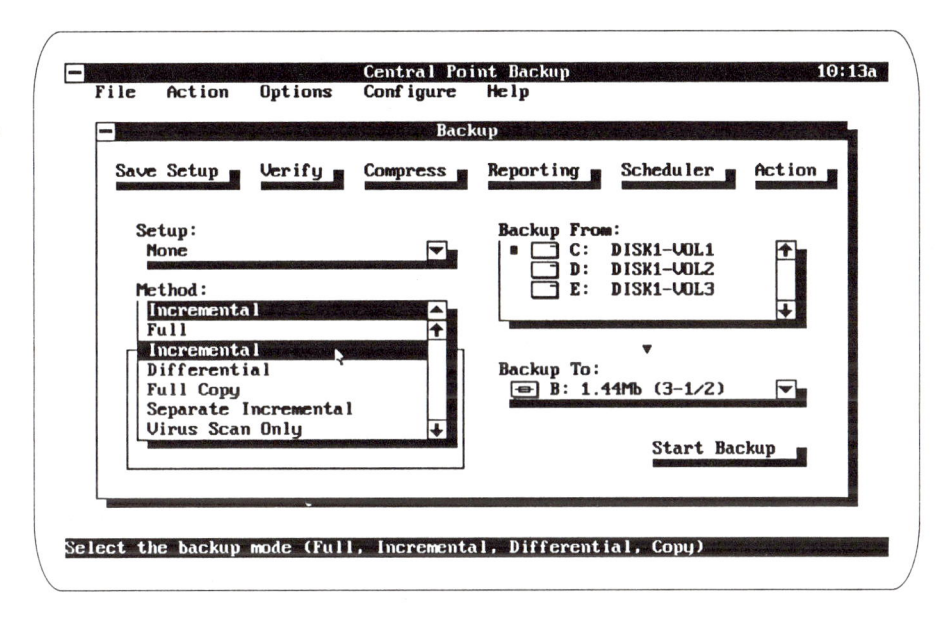

Figure CP-8 How to do an appended incremental backup (Part 1 of 2)

Part 2:

The dialog box that instructs you to insert the last diskette in your backup set.

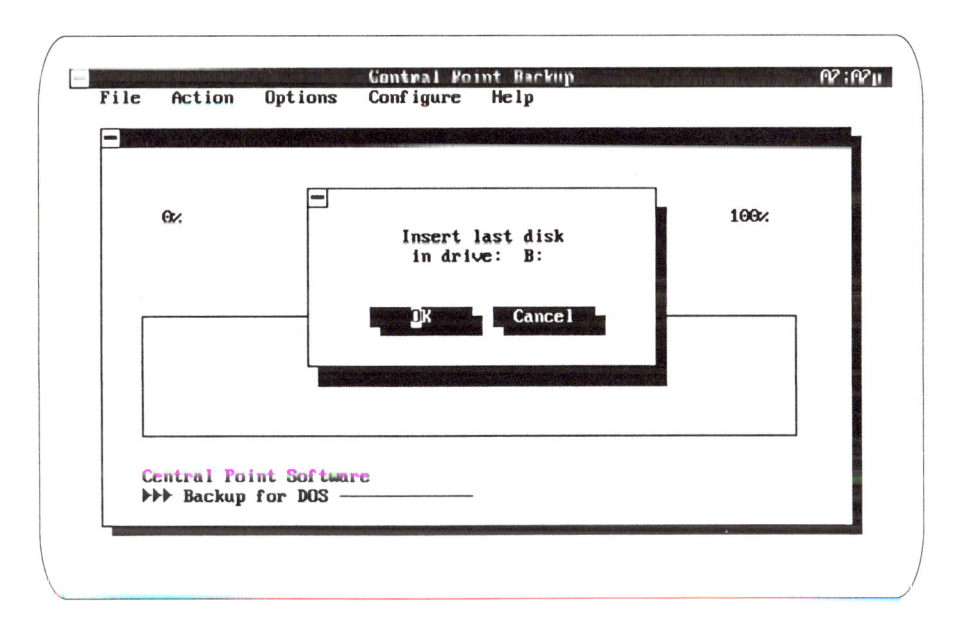

Figure CP-8 How to do an appended incremental backup (Part 2 of 2)

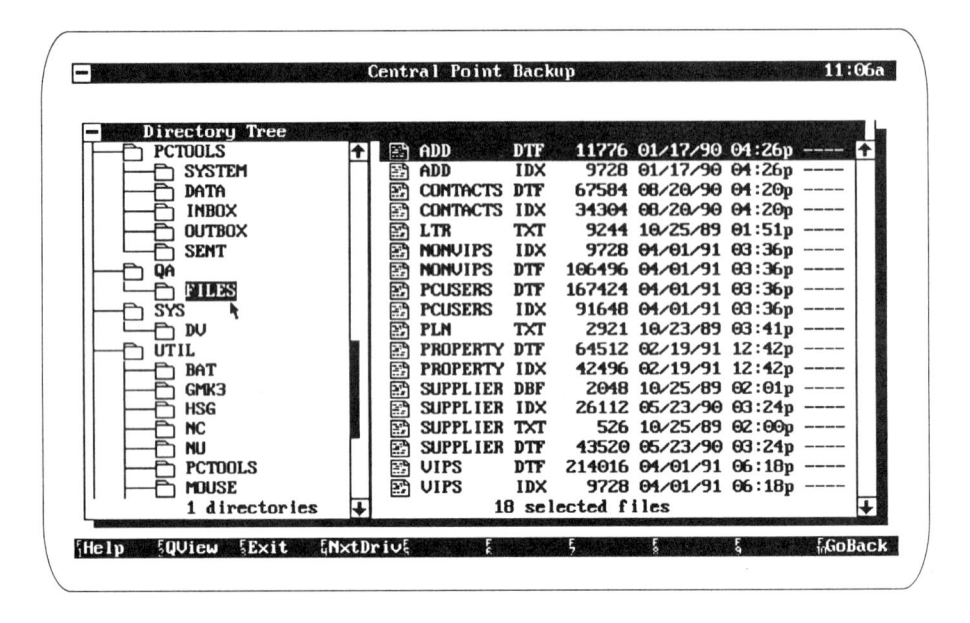

Figure CP-9 One directory that contains 18 files selected for a partial backup

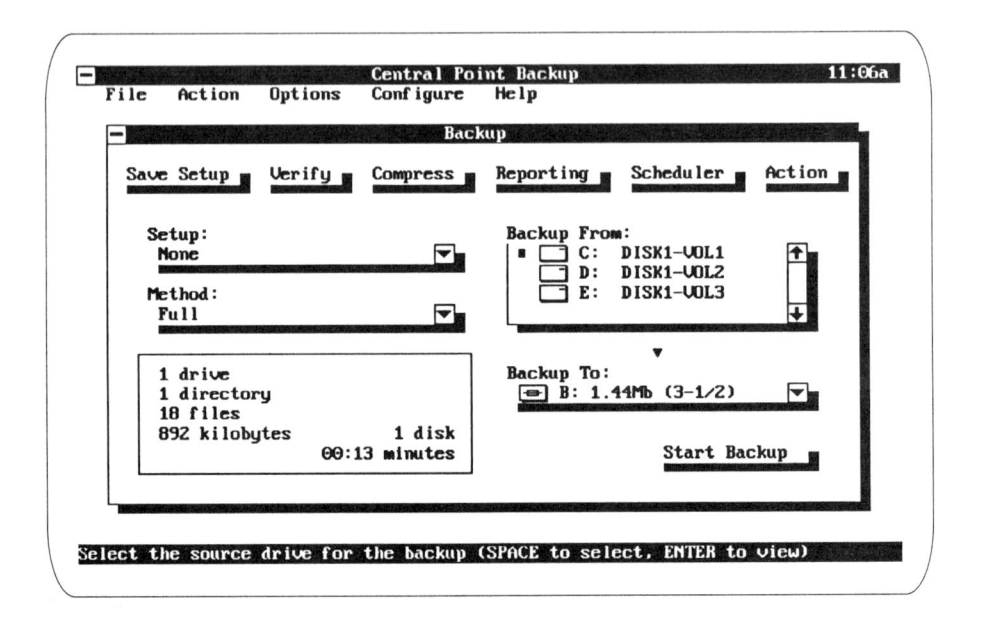

Figure CP-10 *CP Backup* set to do a partial backup

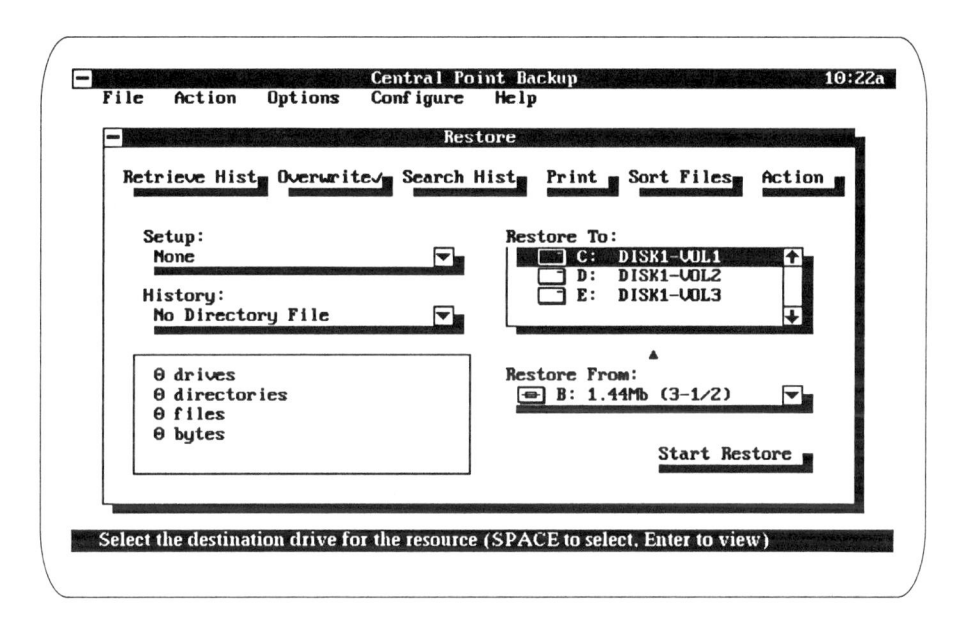

Figure CP-11 The Restore screen

displayed. The information in the lower left of this screen confirms that the backup operation will include one directory with 18 files.

How to restore files

Figure CP-11 shows the Restore screen you use to restore files from your backups to a hard disk. To access this screen, you select the Restore function from the opening screen. Then, you use this screen to select the drive, directories, and other settings required for your restore operation. To start the restore, you select the Start-restore function.

How to use the history files feature   Before you restore data, you should know that *CP Backup* automatically keeps track of the drives, directories, and files that have been backed up. It always keeps this backup-history information on the last diskette of a backup set. But it also keeps this information on the hard disk if the Save-history function on the Options

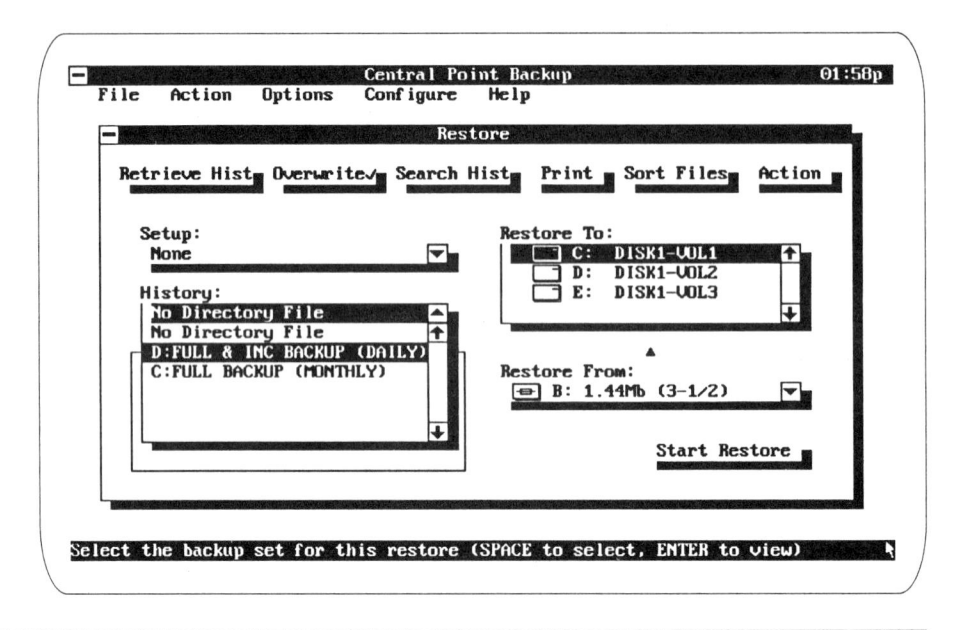

Figure CP-12 A history file named D:FULL & INC BACKUP (DAILY) selected from the History panel

menu is turned on. Then, you can use the *history file* to easily select the directories and files you want for a full or partial restore.

To list the history files, you select the History function from the Restore screen. In figure CP-12, you can see the history files for two different backup sets. The first history file is for full and incremental backups of drive D, and the second file is for a full backup of drive C. If you want to restore data to drive D, you select the first history file. To restore data to drive C, you select the second history file.

How to do a full restore   To do a full restore, first you select the History function as shown in CP-12. Then, to select the history file you want, you click on it with the mouse, or you use the arrow keys to highlight it and press the Spacebar. For example, figure CP-13 shows the settings that are automatically displayed based on the history file that was selected in figure CP-12. Here, the history file for drive D has been loaded. Thus, all of the directories and files for this drive have been selected for the restore. To start the restore operation, just select the Start-restore function. Then, like the Backup func-

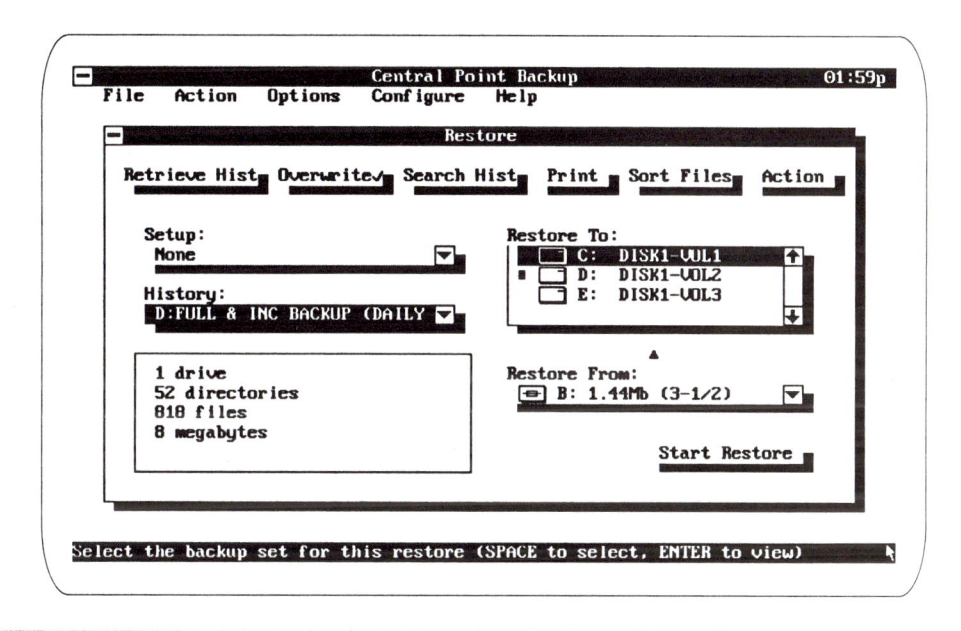

Figure CP-13 *CP Backup* set to do a full restore of the drive D

tion, dialog boxes appear that ask you to insert the backup diskettes in the proper order.

How to do a partial restore To do a partial restore, first you select the history file you want to use from the Restore screen. But you use a slightly different technique than you do for a full restore. If you're using a mouse, you double-click on the history file. Or if you're using the keyboard, you highlight the history file and press the Enter key instead of the Spacebar.

CP Backup then displays a directory and file listing like the one shown in part 1 of figure CP-14. When it displays this listing, all the directories and files are automatically selected. To clear the selection, highlight the root directory and press the Spacebar. Then, you can select the directories or files you want to restore using the same techniques you use for a partial backup. As you can see in part 1, one file named C4.TXT has been selected.

Since a history file can include a combination of full and incremental backups, there can be several different backups listed. If you look again at the directory listing in part 1 of CP-14, for example, you can see history

Part 1:

The C4.TXT file and the most recent backup selected for a partial restore.

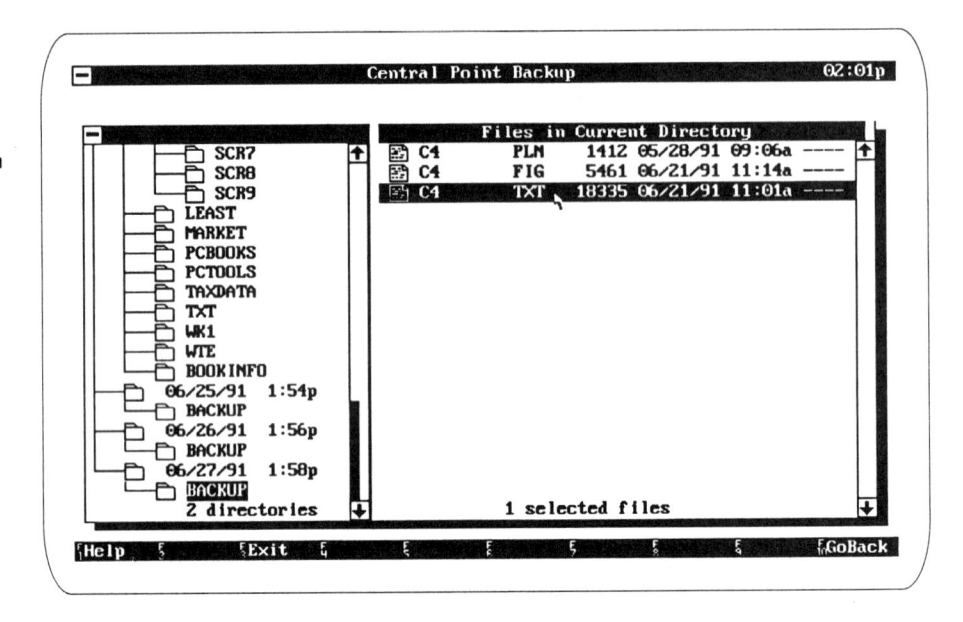

```
┌─────────────────────────────────────────────────────────────────────┐
│ ─                    Central Point Backup                   02:01p  │
│  ┌──────────────────────────┬────────────────────────────────────┐  │
│  │ ─                        │      Files in Current Directory    │  │
│  │       ┌─ SCR7          ↑ │  C4      PLM   1412 05/28/91 09:06a│↑ │
│  │       ├─ SCR8            │  C4      FIG   5461 06/21/91 11:14a│  │
│  │       ├─ SCR9            │  C4      TXT  18335 06/21/91 11:01a│  │
│  │       ├─ LEAST           │                                    │  │
│  │       ├─ MARKET          │                                    │  │
│  │       ├─ PCBOOKS         │                                    │  │
│  │       ├─ PCTOOLS         │                                    │  │
│  │       ├─ TAXDATA         │                                    │  │
│  │       ├─ TXT             │                                    │  │
│  │       ├─ WK1             │                                    │  │
│  │       ├─ WTE             │                                    │  │
│  │       └─ BOOKINFO        │                                    │  │
│  │     ┌─ 06/25/91  1:54p   │                                    │  │
│  │     └─ BACKUP            │                                    │  │
│  │     ┌─ 06/26/91  1:56p   │                                    │  │
│  │     └─ BACKUP            │                                    │  │
│  │     ┌─ 06/27/91  1:58p   │                                    │  │
│  │     └─ BACKUP            │                                    │  │
│  │        2 directories   ↓ │         1 selected files           │↓ │
│  └──────────────────────────┴────────────────────────────────────┘  │
│  Help      Exit                                             GoBack  │
└─────────────────────────────────────────────────────────────────────┘
```

Figure CP-14 How to do a partial restore (Part 1 of 3)

listings for backups on three consecutive days. As a result, you must make sure you select the correct backup for the file you want to restore. Generally, that will be the most recent backup.

After you select the files you want to restore and the backup that you want to restore them from, you press the F10 key to return to the Restore screen as shown in part 2 of figure CP-14. Here, the information at the lower left of the screen shows that one file has been selected to be restored. To begin the restore operation, you select the Start-restore function.

CP Backup then displays a dialog box like the one shown in part 3 of figure CP-14. This box tells you the number of the diskette that has the data you want. As a result, you don't have to insert the first diskette in the backup set and continue through the set until you find the right diskette.

Part 2:

The Restore screen showing that one file will be restored.

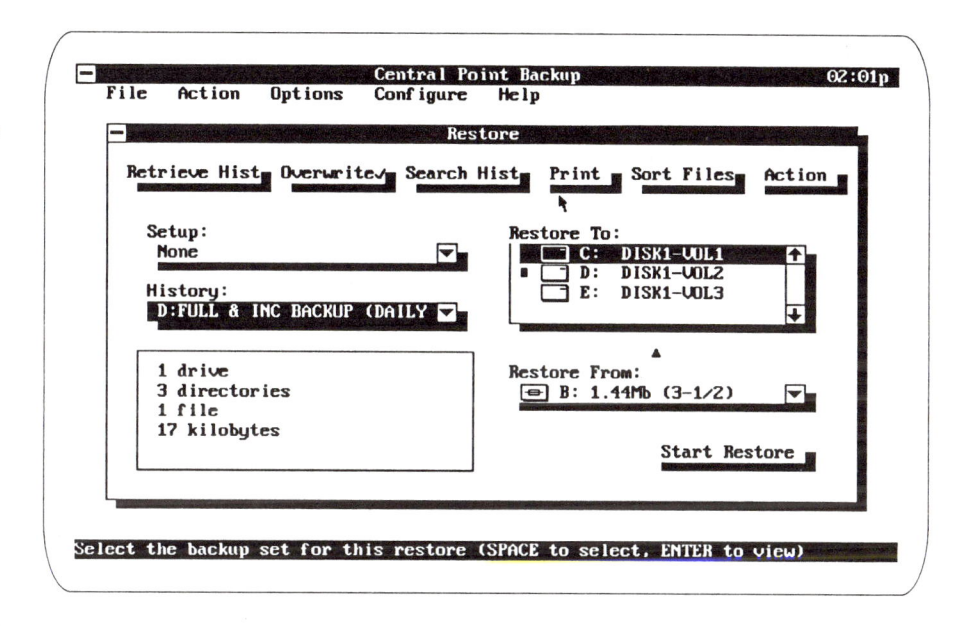

Figure CP-14 How to do a partial restore (Part 2 of 3)

Part 3:

The dialog box that tells you which diskette to insert.

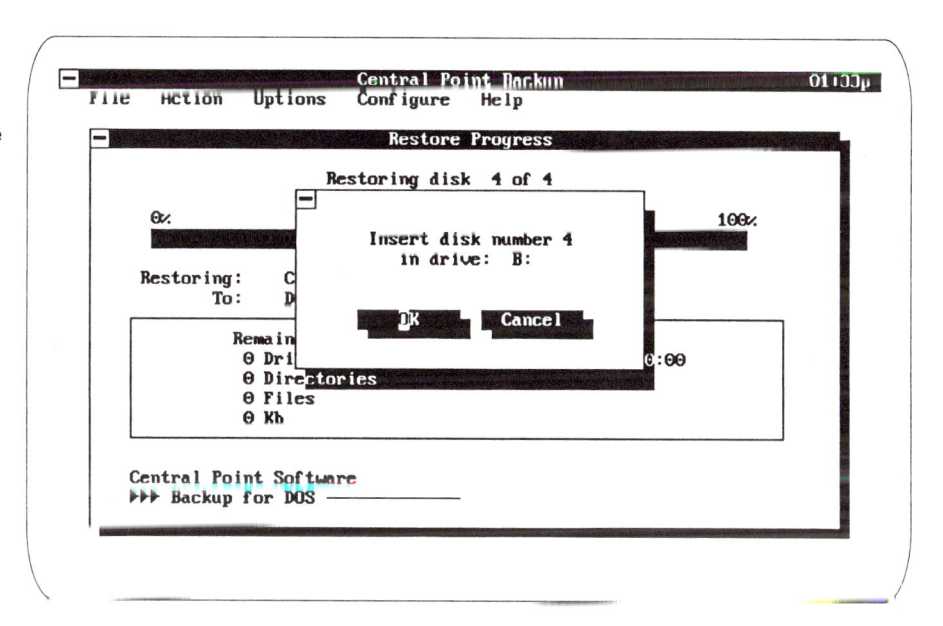

Figure CP-14 How to do a partial restore (Part 3 of 3)

How to compare a backup

As a rule, you can count on *CP Backup* to do reliable backups. So you don't need to compare every backup you do. However, you should occasionally compare a backup to make sure that the utility is working correctly. Then, you can rest assured that your backups will work when you need to restore data.

The best time to compare a backup is right after you do it. This is also the easiest time because you don't have to set up the compare operation. Instead, you just select the Compare function from the dialog box shown in figure CP-15. The program displays a box like this after it completes each backup operation.

When you select the Compare function, you are prompted to insert the first diskette from the backup set. Then, the program reads the data from the diskette and compares it to the data on the hard disk. As it completes each diskette, *CP Backup* prompts you to insert the next diskette until it has compared the data on all the diskettes in the backup set. Finally, the program displays a dialog box that summarizes the compare operation and reports any errors it has found. If it doesn't find any errors, you know that the backup is reliable. If it does find errors, you must determine how to correct them so you can get a reliable backup set.

If you want to compare a backup after you have exited from the screen shown in figure CP-15, you use the same basic procedure that you use to do a full restore. The only difference is that you select the Compare function from the opening screen instead of selecting the Restore function.

How to automate your backups

So far, you've learned how to select functions from various menus to do different types of backups. In some cases, this is the most efficient way to do a backup. However, *CP Backup* provides several features that you can use to automate your backups. In particular, you can create *setup files* that store all of the settings that are required for a backup. You can also use these setup files in batch files to further automate your backups. Since you generally do the same backup operations over and over again, automating them can significantly improve your backup procedures.

Utility 1: Central Point Backup **95**

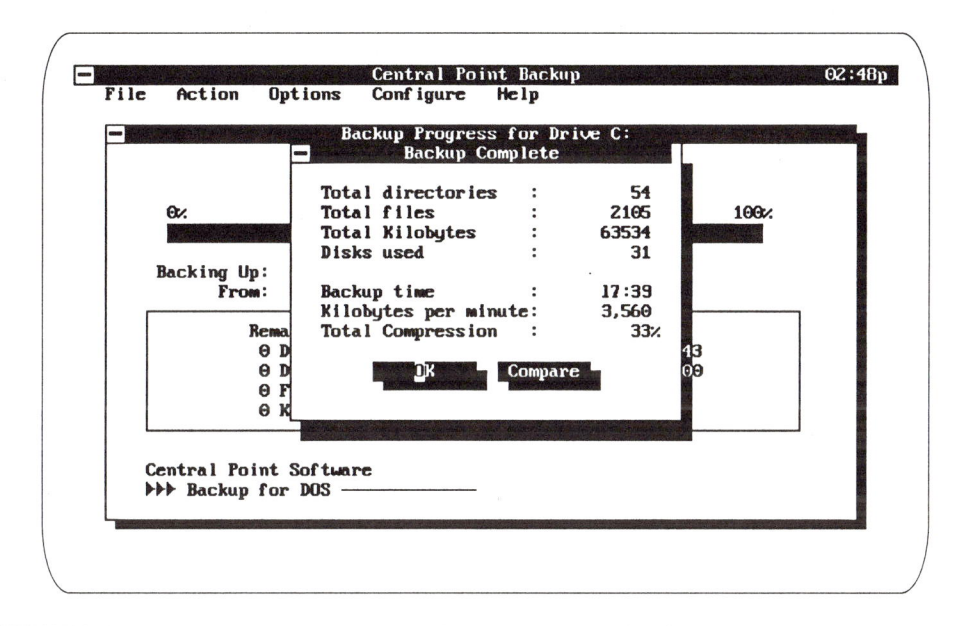

```
┌─────────────────────────────────────────────────────────────┐
│ ─                    Central Point Backup         02:48p    │
│  File   Action   Options   Configure   Help                 │
│     ┌──────────────────────────────────────────────────┐    │
│     │ ─           Backup Progress for Drive C:         │    │
│     │              Backup Complete                     │    │
│     │         Total directories    :        54         │    │
│     │  0%     Total files          :      2105    100% │    │
│     │         Total Kilobytes      :     63534         │    │
│     │         Disks used           :        31         │    │
│     │  Backing Up:                                     │    │
│     │       From:   Backup time    :     17:39         │    │
│     │               Kilobytes per minute:  3,560       │    │
│     │        Rema   Total Compression :     33%        │    │
│     │         0 D                                  43  │    │
│     │         0 D        ┌──┐    ┌───────┐         00  │    │
│     │         0 F        │OK│    │Compare│             │    │
│     │         0 K        └──┘    └───────┘             │    │
│     │                                                  │    │
│     │  Central Point Software                          │    │
│     │  ▶▶▶ Backup for DOS ──────                       │    │
│     └──────────────────────────────────────────────────┘    │
└─────────────────────────────────────────────────────────────┘
```

Figure CP-15   The dialog box *CP Backup* displays at the end of a backup operation

How to create and use a setup file   To create a setup file, you just select the functions that are required for the backup. But instead of starting the backup operation, you select the Save-setup function from the Backup screen. Then, you name the setup file and save it. So the next time you want to run the backup operation, you can do so by using the setup file.

To illustrate, I'll show you how to create a setup file for an appended incremental backup of drive D. First, you make the selections from the Backup screen that are required to run the appended incremental backup. Then, you select the Save-setup function to display the dialog box shown in figure CP-16. Here, you enter a name for the setup file; I used INC-D for the file name. In addition to naming the file, you must save it by selecting the Save-file-selections function. Now, the next time you want to do an appended incremental backup of drive D, you don't have to go through the selection process. Instead, all you have to do is load the INC-D setup file to run the backup.

To load a setup file, you select the Setup function from the Backup screen. *CP Backup* then displays the setup files like the ones shown in figure

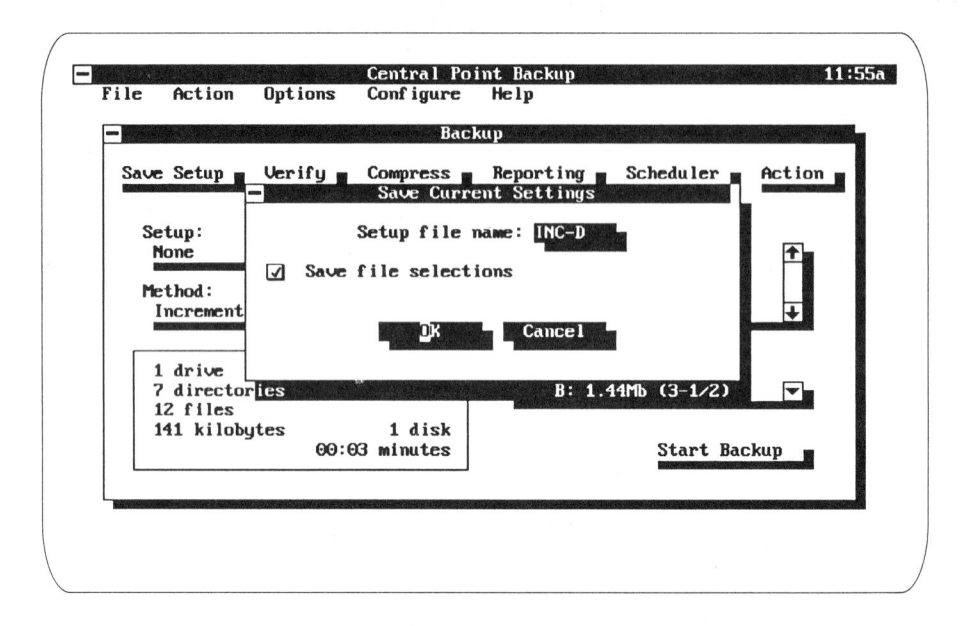

Figure CP-16 The dialog box you use to save the current settings to a setup file

CP-17. In this figure, the FULL-C file does a full backup of the C drive; the FULL-D file does a full backup of the D drive; the INC-C file does an incremental backup of the C drive; and the INC-D file does an incremental backup of the D drive. To load one of these setup files, you either click on it with the mouse, or you move the highlight to it and press the Enter key. Then, as soon as you select the Start-backup function, the backup operation begins.

How to start a setup file from a batch file   Figure CP-18 shows how you can use batch files to run the setup files shown in figure CP-17. Here, the name of each setup file is included with the commands that start *CP Backup*. If you're running *CP Backup* from *PC Tools Deluxe*, you should use the \PC-TOOLS directory in place of the \CPBACKUP directory in the second command line of these batch files. When you execute one of these batch files, it starts *CP Backup* and automatically loads and runs the setup file. Then, when the operation is complete, it returns you to the DOS command prompt. In other words, all you have to do to run your backup operation is

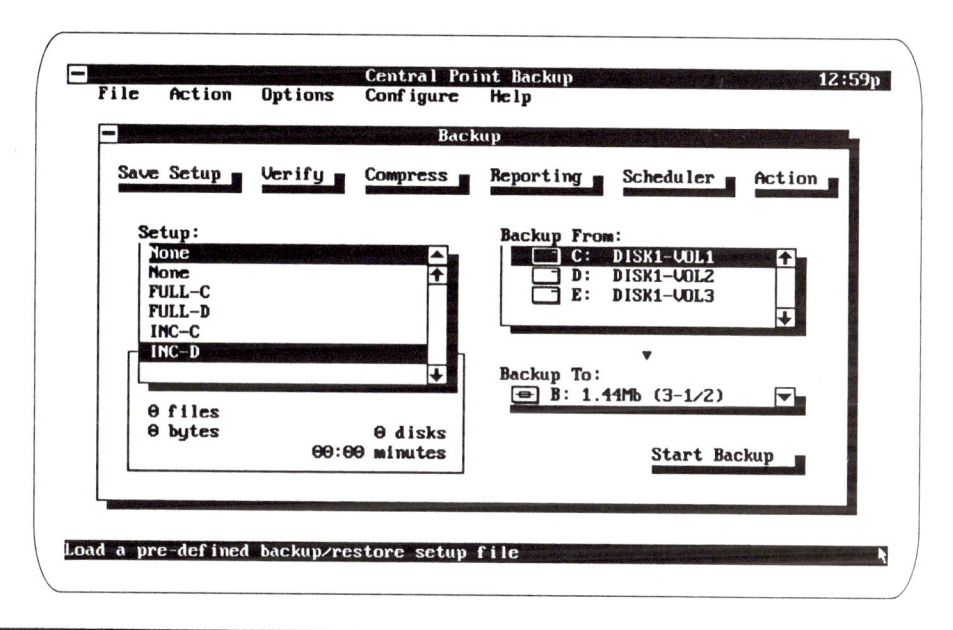

Figure CP-17 The INC-D setup file selected from the Setup panel

enter the name of a batch file at the DOS prompt and press the Enter key. As you can see, this technique greatly simplifies your backups. As a result, you may want to use batch files for your regular backups.

Is *Central Point Backup* the right utility for your backups?

Now that you've seen how to use *Central Point Backup* for the most common backup and restore operations, you should be able to decide if it's the right utility for you. As you've seen, this utility makes it easy to perform these operations. And it's as fast and reliable as any program on the market. Also, if you buy it as part of *PC Tools Deluxe*, it's an excellent value because you also get a DOS shell, advanced disk utilities, and other utilities. Furthermore, *CP Backup* provides better tape support than any of the other utilities. It also provides an excellent backup utility that's compatible with *Windows*. So if you're using *Windows*, you should definitely consider getting *CP Backup*.

```
FULL-C.BAT

    C:
    CD \CPBACKUP
    CPBACKUP FULL-C

INC-C.BAT

    C:
    CD \CPBACKUP
    CPBACKUP INC-C

FULL-D.BAT

    C:
    CD \CPBACKUP
    CPBACKUP FULL-D

INC-D.BAT

    C:
    CD \CPBACKUP
    CPBACKUP INC-D
```

Figure CP-18 Four batch files that load setup files and start the backup operation

Terms

PC Tools Deluxe
dialog box
virus
history file
setup file
Windows

Utility 2: Norton Backup

Norton Backup version 1.1 from *Symantec Corp.* is a good backup utility. It's fast and easy to use, and it offers about as many features as any other backup utility. However, it doesn't provide a feature for doing appended incremental backups. Instead, *Norton Backup* suggests that you do differential backups. So if appended incremental backups are an important part of your backup plan, you'll want to keep this in mind as you read about this utility.

At a price of about $105, *Norton Backup* is a bit more expensive than *Central Point Backup* and *PC-Fullbak+*. However, it offers the best features for automating backups. So if you need to set up a backup utility so it's easy for other people to use, you should consider *Norton Backup*.

To start *Norton Backup* from the DOS command prompt, you change to the appropriate drive and directory. Then, you type the following command and press the Enter key:

    nbackup

If it's the first time you've run the program, *Norton Backup* also runs an operation to set up the utility. You'll learn about this setup operation in a moment. Then, the program displays the opening screen shown in figure NB-1 Here, the Backup option starts the backup function; the Restore option starts the restore function; the Configure option starts the configure function; and the Quit option exits the program.

To select one of these functions using a mouse, you move the mouse cursor to the function you want and click the left mouse button. To select one of those functions using the keyboard, you can use two different techniques. You can press the arrow keys to highlight the function you want and then press the Enter key. Or you can press the letter of the function that appears in a different color or intensity.

99

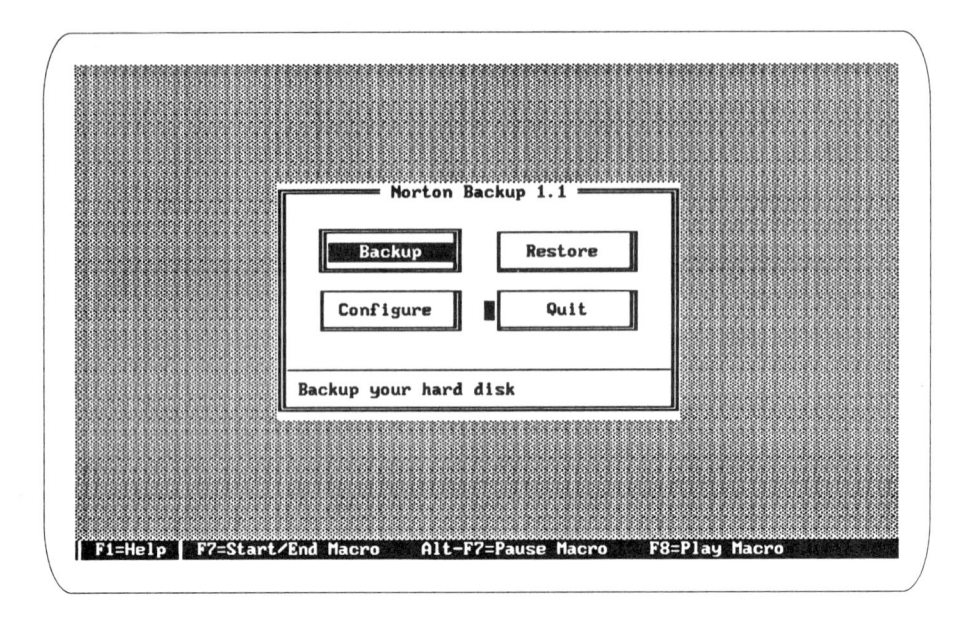

Figure NB-1 The opening screen of *Norton Backup*

If at any point you need help, you can press the F1 key. *Norton Backup* then displays a Help screen with information on the function you're using. To exit the Help screen, you press the Esc key once, or you can select the Cancel function from the screen.

How to set up *Norton Backup*

The first time you start *Norton Backup*, it runs a special setup operation. This operation displays a series of screens that ask you to identify the physical components and the drives on your PC. The program also runs several tests so that it can set itself to run with maximum speed and reliably on your PC. After it completes these operations, *Norton Backup* displays the opening screen shown earlier in figure NB-1.

If you decide you want to change how *Norton Backup* is set up, you use many of the same screens that you use during the setup operation. In addition, you'll probably want to use at least one other menu to set up *Norton*

```
             ┌─── Norton Backup Configuration ───┐
             │  Program Level:    Advanced       │
             │                                   │
             │     Mouse:         Right Handed, Medium Sensitivity │
             │                                   │
             │  Video Display:    25 Lines       │
             │                                   │
             │  Floppy Drives:    Drive A: 5¼" 1.2Mb High Density │
             │                    Drive B: 3½" 1.44Mb High Density│
             │ Configuration Tests: High DMA, Fastest Read │
             │                                   │
             │ Save Configuration    OK    Esc=Cancel │
             └───────────────────────────────────┘
             F1=Help  Select the program functionality level
```

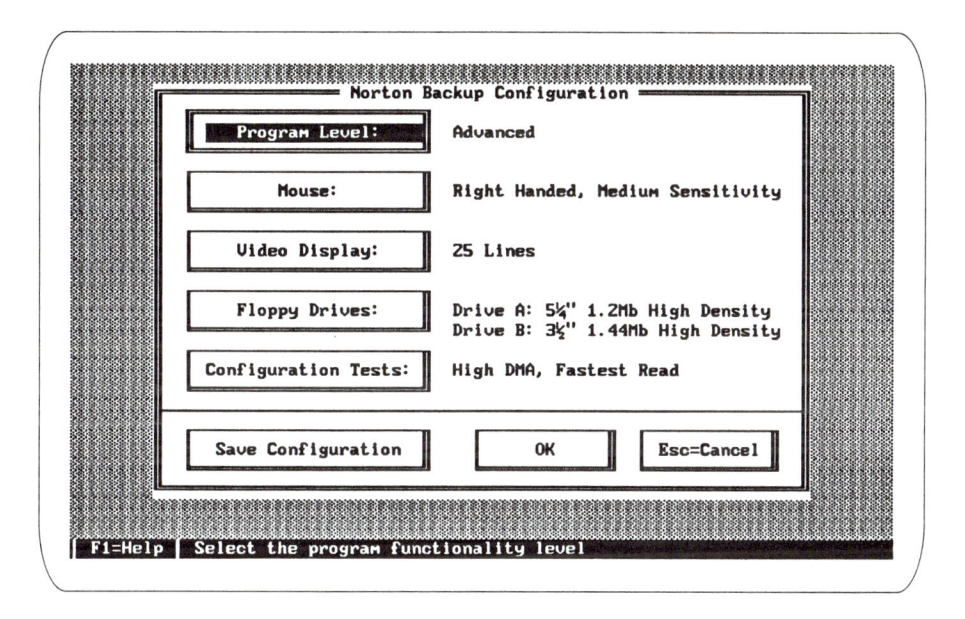

Figure NB-2   The Configure menu

Backup. So I'll show you how to use both the Configure and the Backup-options menus now.

The Configure menu   To get to the Configure menu shown in figure NB-2, select the Configure function from the opening screen. This function displays the same screens and options that *Norton Backup* displays the first time you run it. To illustrate, figure NB-2 shows the main Configuration screen. Here, the functions appear in boxes on the left of the screen, and their current settings appear on the right. When you select one of the functions, a *dialog box* like the one shown in figure NB-3 is displayed.

Figure NB-3 shows the dialog box that's displayed when you select the Program-level function. This dialog box provides three settings: Basic, Advanced, or Preset. The Basic level displays fewer functions on several of the menus. The Advanced level displays all of the functions that are available. And the Preset level displays only those functions that are necessary to do backups using the setup files you create. I'll explain this function in greater detail later. Although the Basic level is the default setting, I recommend you use the Advanced level. The Basic level doesn't make backups any easier. Instead, it just removes some functions that you'll probably want to use.

After the initial setup operation runs, you shouldn't need to use the other four functions on the Configure screen in figure NB-2. The Mouse function, for instance, lets you control the operational characteristics of your mouse. Unless you're using a left-handed mouse or prefer a more sensitive mouse, you'll want to use the default settings. Similarly, you shouldn't need to change the default setting for the Video function because *Norton Backup* automatically detects your video hardware and adjusts the setting accordingly. And you shouldn't need to change the default setting for the Floppy-drives function unless you add or change a drive on your PC.

Because you should be familiar with the tests *Norton Backup* does during the initial setup operation, figure NB-4 presents the Configuration-tests screen. Here, the DMA-tests function tests the capabilities of your PC. In particular, this test determines whether the utility can use the high speed memory access and fastest hard disk access speed. If it can, the utility automatically sets the options as shown in this figure. In addition, the Confidence-test function runs an actual backup operation. Then, it compares the backup to verify that the operation worked correctly. As a result, you know that *Norton Backup* can do reliable backups on your PC.

After you've set the Configuration functions the way you want them, you need to save them as the default settings for the program. To do this, you press the Esc key to return to the Configure Screen in figure NB-3, and you select the Save-configuration function.

The Backup-options menu   In addition to the settings you specify using the Configure menu, *Norton Backup* lets you set several options that control how a backup operation works. You set these options on the Backup-options screen. To access this screen, you must first select the Backup function from the opening screen. Then, the program displays the Backup screen shown in figure NB-5. Next, you select the Options function from this screen. When you do that, the Backup-options screen shown in NB-6 is displayed.

As you can see in figure NB-6, there are ten options you can set. When you select one of the options on the left, *Norton Backup* displays a dialog box that offers you a choice of several settings. In contrast, you can only turn

Utility 2: Norton Backup   **103**

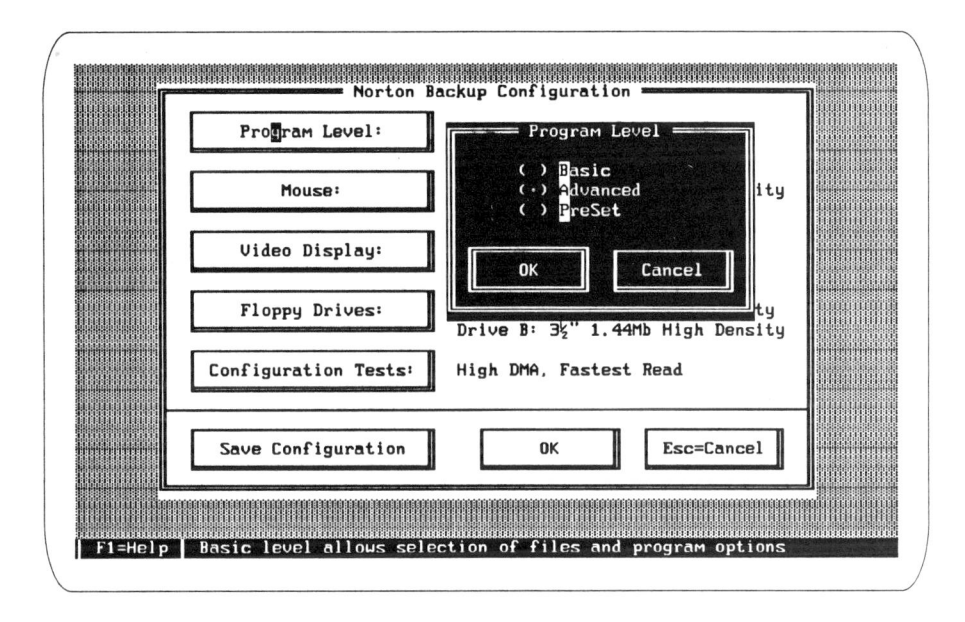

Figure NB-3   The Program-level dialog box you use to set the level of menu choices

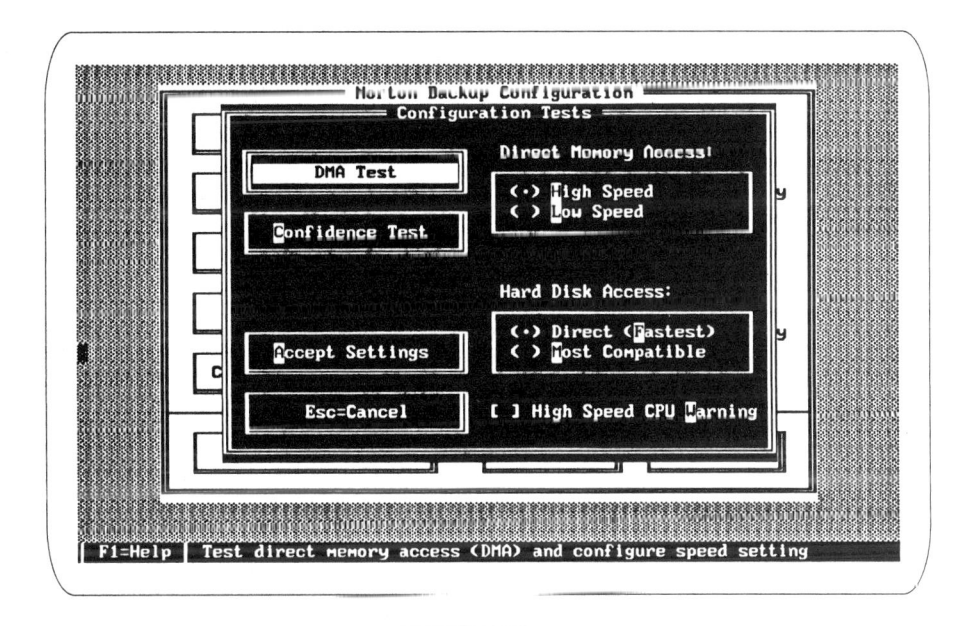

Figure NB-4   The Configuration-tests screen *Norton Backup* displays when it tests your PC hardware

the options on the right on or off. If the option is on, an *X* appears next to it. Otherwise, the option is off.

The Data-verification option lets you specify the level of error checking you want during a backup operation. I recommend that you change the default setting (Off) to the Read-only setting shown here. This setting reads the data as it's written to diskette to insure that the operation is reliable. You'll want to use the Read-only setting because it improves the reliability of your backups without slowing down the backup operation much.

The Data-compression option lets you specify the level of data compression you want *Norton Backup* to do. You can turn off all data compression, set the data compression to save time, or set it to save diskettes. Here, the Data-compression option is set to save time, which is the default setting.

The Overwrite-warning option lets you specify when you want the program to display a warning during a backup operation. Since you use the same backup diskettes over and over again, you don't need to be warned when you use these diskettes. However, it's useful to have *Norton Backup* warn you if a diskette has other data on it. That's why I recommend that you set this option to Regular-DOS-diskettes instead of accepting the default setting of Off.

The Full-backup-cycle option lets you specify the number of days between full backups. When this option is activated, *Norton Backup* automatically configures itself to do a full backup at the specified number of days, and it then reminds you when it's time for a full backup. Although this feature is supposed to make backups simpler, it actually complicates them. Because it only lets you specify a set number of days, it doesn't provide for the irregular number of days required for most backup schedules. If, for example, you want to back up your C drive on the first Monday of each month, this feature can't help you. That's why I think you'll want to leave this feature turned off as shown here.

The Audible-prompts option lets you control the sound that the utility uses to alert you of a condition. When you need to change diskettes during a backup operation, for example, the program can beep to alert you. Since these beeps are useful, you should accept the default setting shown here.

The first two options on the right side of the Backup-options screen control how *Norton Backup* formats backup diskettes. By turning on the

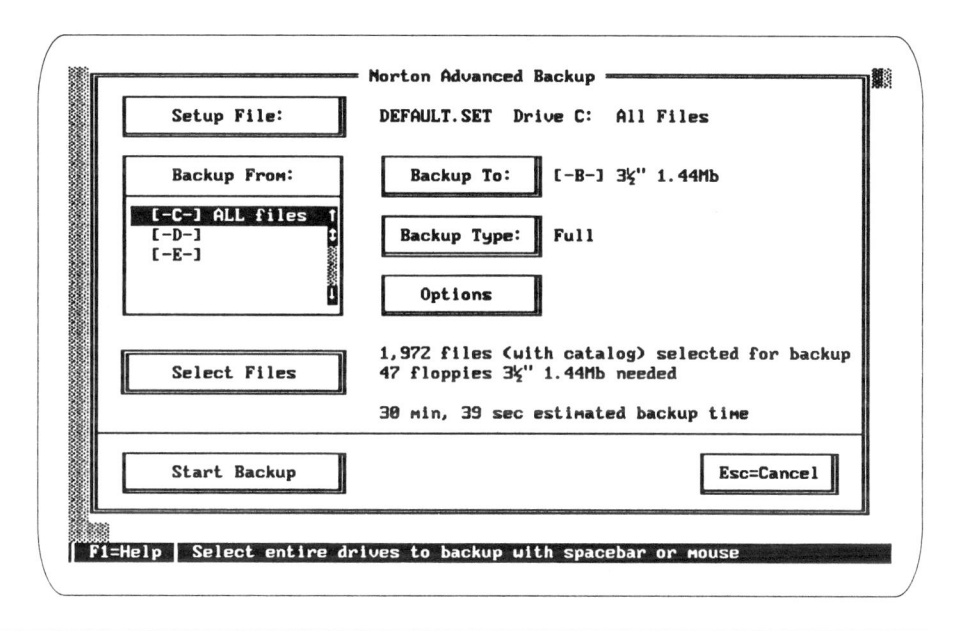

Figure NB-5 The Backup screen

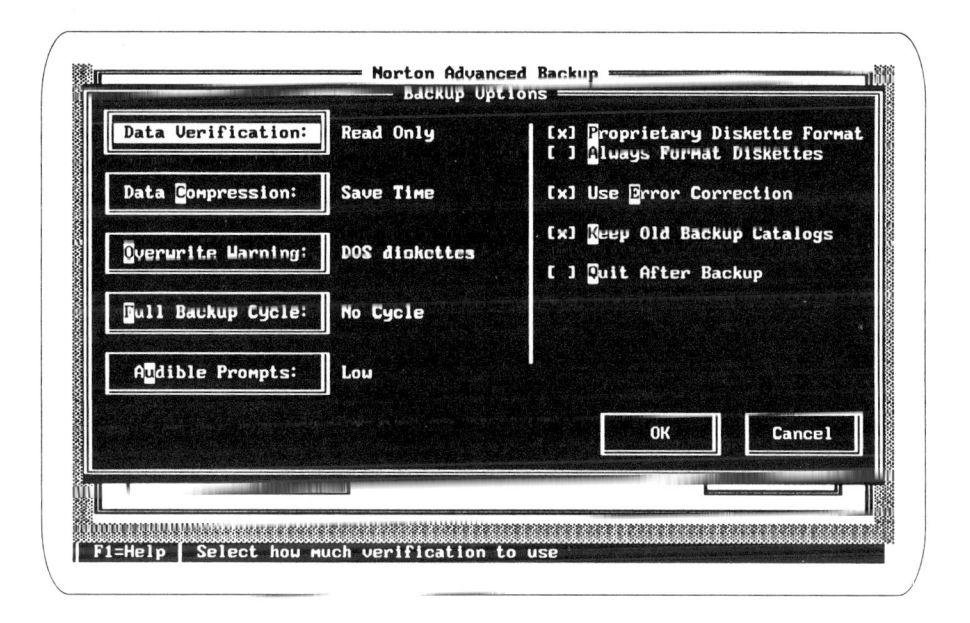

Figure NB-6 The Backup-options menu

Proprietary-diskette-format option as shown here, your backups will run faster. Also, more data can be stored on each diskette. Thus, reducing the number total number of diskettes you need. In contrast, you should leave the Always-format-diskettes option turned off. Otherwise, your backups will take about three times longer to run.

You should accept the default setting for the last three options on the right. Because the Use-error-correction option enables another feature that makes your backups run more reliably without slowing them down, you should leave this option on. Also, you should leave the Keep-old-backup-catalogs option on. This option causes *Norton Backup* to keep the backup catalogs you need for a restore operation. Similarly, you should leave the Quit-after-backup option off because you may want to use the utility to do more than one backup operation during a work session.

After you set the Backup options the way you want them and select the OK function, they remain in effect for the current session. Then, when you exit from the Backup screen, the program displays the dialog box shown in figure NB-7. At this box, you select the Save-changes function to save the backup options. Then, the same options will be in effect the next time you use *Norton Backup*.

In addition to the Backup options, *Norton Backup* lets you set several options for restore operations. To access the Restore-options screen, first you return to the opening screen. Then, you select the Restore function. Next, you select the Options function from the Restore screen. The program then displays the Restore-options screen shown in figure NB-8. I won't explain all of the options on this screen because they're similar to the ones on the Backup-options screen. Furthermore, you probably won't need to change them. If you do, however, you can use the settings displayed here for efficient and reliable restore operations.

How to do a backup

To do a backup, you select the Backup function from the opening screen shown in figure NB-1. *Norton Backup* then displays the Backup screen shown in figure NB-9 part 1. At this screen, you select the type of backup you want to do, the hard drive you want to back up, and the drive you want

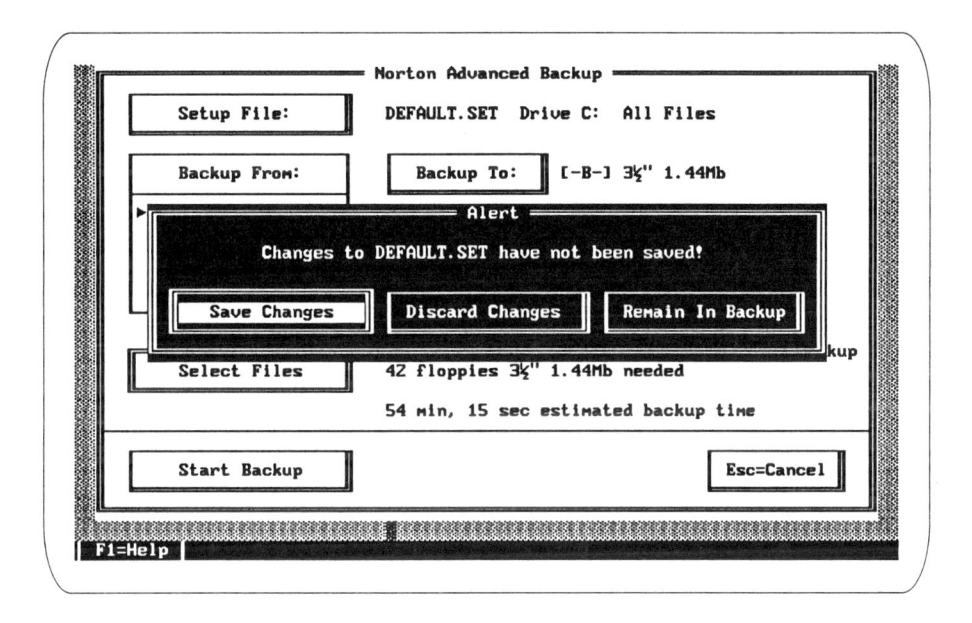

Figure NB-7 The dialog box that lets you save the options you set with the Backup-options menu

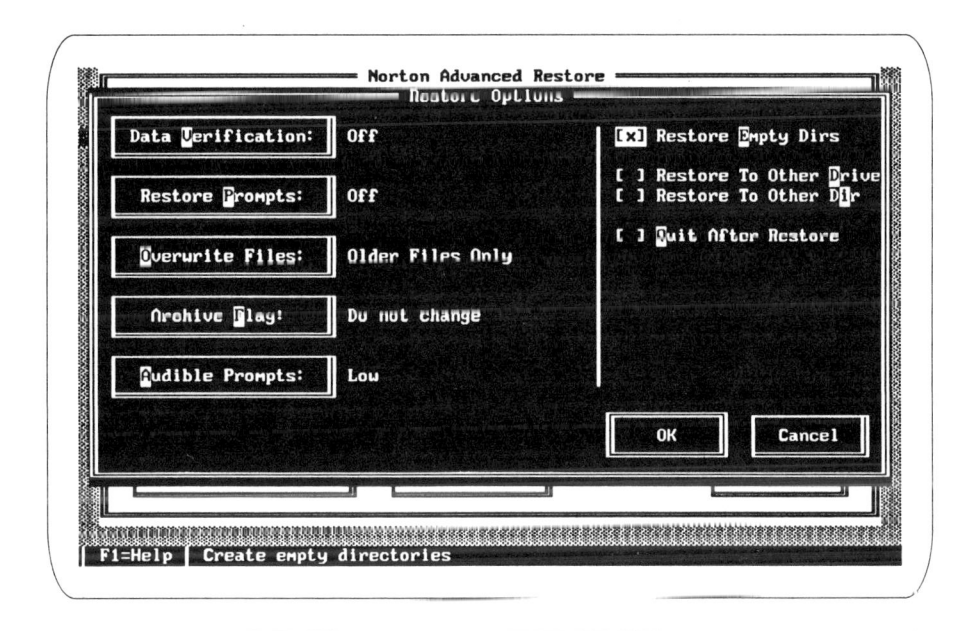

Figure NB-8 The Restore-options screen

to back up to. In other words, you can select the settings that you need for performing the most common backup operations.

How to do a full backup   In part 1 of figure NB-9, the functions have been set to do a full backup of drive C. You shouldn't have to set the Backup-type or Backup-to functions because you already set them to default to the proper settings for a full backup. However, you can change them if you need to by selecting the function you want to change, then selecting the proper setting from the choices offered.

To select the hard drive you want to back up, you move the mouse cursor to the drive you want to back up and click the left mouse button twice in rapid succession. If you don't have a mouse, you press the Tab key to activate the Backup-from function. Then, you use the arrow keys to move the highlight to the hard drive you want, and you press the Spacebar to select the drive.

After you select the appropriate hard drive, *Norton Backup* scans the drive and selects all the directories files to be backed up. In part 1 of figure NB-9, for example, all the directories and files on drive C are selected. The information in the lower right of the screen shows that this drive has 1,972 files on it. The utility also estimates that the backup operation will require 47 diskettes and take over 30 minutes.

To start the backup operation, you select the Start-backup function. *Norton Backup* then displays the Backup-in-progress screen shown in part 2 of figure NB-9. Here, the top of the screen displays the directories and files as they are backed up. The bottom left of the screen displays information on diskette use. And the bottom right displays other information on the progress of the backup operation. In this figure, for example, you can see that the backup operation has just started and that the program is prompting you to insert the first diskette.

As the backup operation continues, its progress is displayed as shown in part 3 of figure NB-9. Here, the Diskette-progress portion of the screen shows that the current diskette in the B drive is almost full. And the Backup-set-information portion of the screen shows that the current diskette is the second one in the backup set. When the second diskette is full, the program prompts you to insert the third diskette in the set, and so on.

Part 1:

In the Backup-from panel, select the drive you want to back up.

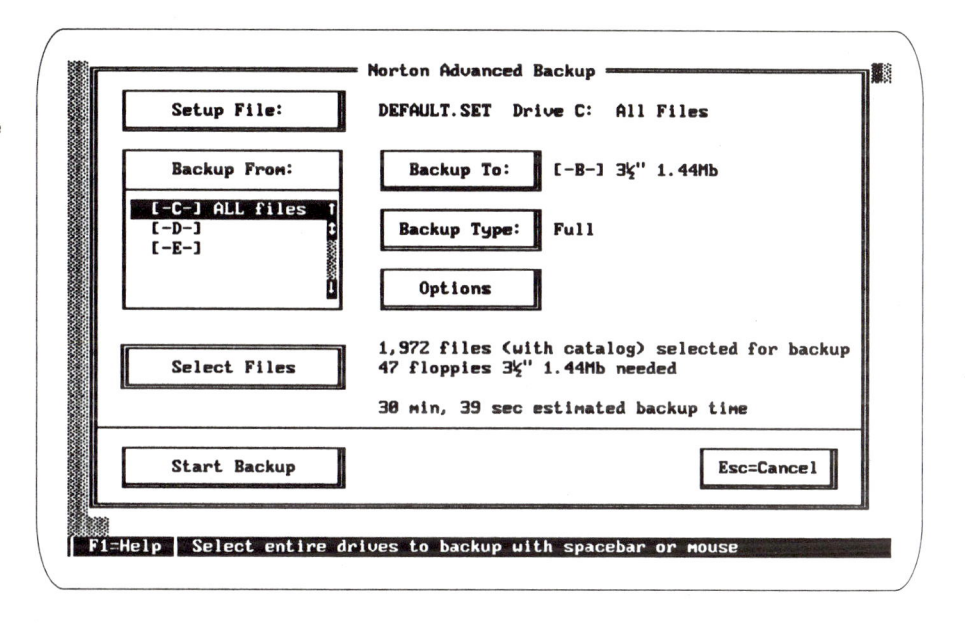

```
┌─────────────────── Norton Advanced Backup ───────────────────┐
│                                                              │
│   ┌─────────────────┐   DEFAULT.SET  Drive C:  All Files     │
│   │   Setup File:   │                                        │
│   └─────────────────┘                                        │
│                         ┌─────────────┐                      │
│   ┌─────────────────┐   │ Backup To:  │  [-B-] 3½" 1.44Mb    │
│   │  Backup From:   │   └─────────────┘                      │
│   ├─────────────────┤                                        │
│   │ [-C-] ALL files │   ┌─────────────┐                      │
│   │ [-D-]           │   │Backup Type: │  Full                │
│   │ [-E-]           │   └─────────────┘                      │
│   │                 │                                        │
│   │                 │   ┌─────────────┐                      │
│   │                 │   │   Options   │                      │
│   └─────────────────┘   └─────────────┘                      │
│                                                              │
│   ┌─────────────────┐   1,972 files (with catalog) selected  │
│   │  Select Files   │   for backup                           │
│   └─────────────────┘   47 floppies 3½" 1.44Mb needed        │
│                                                              │
│                         30 min, 39 sec estimated backup time │
│                                                              │
│   ┌─────────────────┐                     ┌───────────────┐  │
│   │  Start Backup   │                     │  Esc=Cancel   │  │
│   └─────────────────┘                     └───────────────┘  │
│                                                              │
│ F1=Help │ Select entire drives to backup with spacebar or mouse│
└──────────────────────────────────────────────────────────────┘
```

Figure NB-9   How you do a full backup (Part 1 of 4)

Part 2:

Insert the appropriate diskette as prompted by *Norton Backup*.

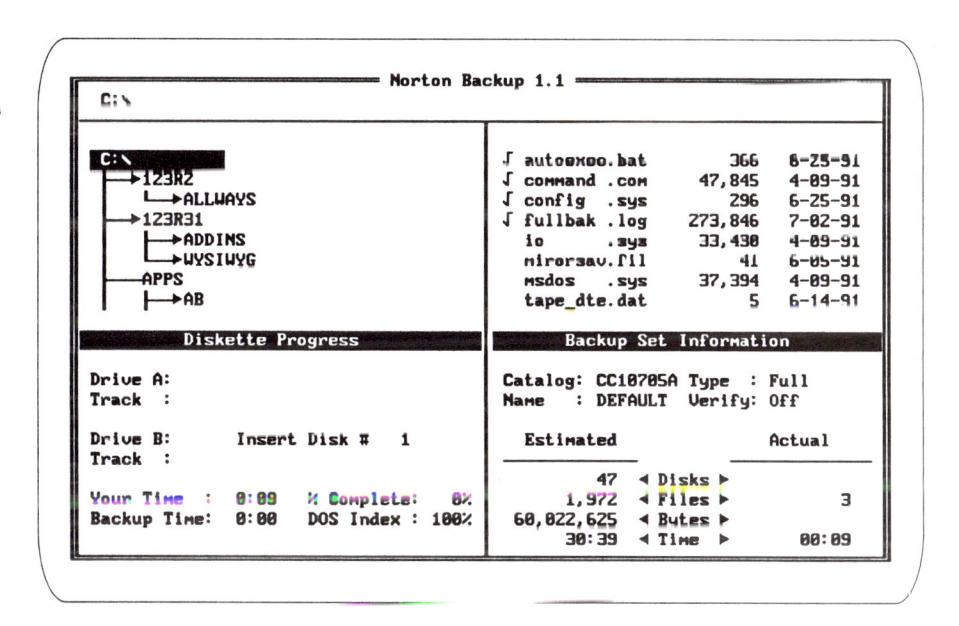

```
┌─────────────────────── Norton Backup 1.1 ────────────────────┐
│ C:\                                                          │
│                                                              │
│ C:\                              √ autoexec.bat   366 6-25-91│
│   →123R2                         √ command .com 47,845 4-09-91│
│      └→ALLWAYS                   √ config  .sys   296 6-25-91│
│   →123R31                        √ fullbak .log 273,846 7-02-91│
│      └→ADDINS                      io      .sys 33,430 4-09-91│
│      └→WYSIWYG                     mirorsav.fil      41 6-05-91│
│   →APPS                            msdos   .sys 37,394 4-09-91│
│      └→AB                          tape_dte.dat       5 6-14-91│
│                                                              │
├────── Diskette Progress ──────┬───── Backup Set Information ─┤
│                               │                              │
│ Drive A:                      │ Catalog: CC10705A Type : Full│
│ Track  :                      │ Name   : DEFAULT  Verify: Off│
│                               │                              │
│ Drive B:    Insert Disk # 1   │    Estimated          Actual │
│ Track  :                      │                              │
│                               │         47 ◄ Disks ►         │
│ Your Time :  0:09  % Complete:│      1,972 ◄ Files ►       3 │
│ Backup Time: 0:00  DOS Index : 100% │ 60,022,625 ◄ Bytes ►   │
│                               │      30:39 ◄ Time  ►   00:09 │
└──────────────────────────────────────────────────────────────┘
```

Figure NB-9   How you do a full backup (Part 2 of 4)

When the backup operation is complete, *Norton Backup* displays a screen like the one in part 4 of figure NB-9. In the Backup-set-information portion of the screen, you get a summary of how much data was backed up, how many diskettes were required, and how long the backup took.

How to do a separate incremental backup As I mentioned earlier, you can't do appended incremental backups with *Norton Backup*. But you can do separate incremental backups, which means you must use a separate backup set for each incremental backup. If, for example, you do a full backup on Monday and incremental backups Tuesday through Friday, you must use a separate backup set for each incremental backup. As a result, you'll have four sets of incremental backups. Fortunately, you should need only one diskette for each incremental set, so it shouldn't be too hard to keep track of the diskettes.

Figure NB-10 shows you how to do a separate incremental backup. First, you select the Backup-type function from the Backup screen to get the dialog box shown in part 1. At this box, you select the Incremental option by clicking the mouse on it or by highlighting the option and pressing the Enter key. *Norton Backup* then returns you to the Backup screen.

At the Backup screen, you select the hard drive you want to back up. Then, the program displays the screen shown in part 2 of figure NB-10. Here, the information near the bottom of the screen shows that 31 files on drive D will be backed up. This screen also shows that the incremental backup requires only one diskette and that the operation will take about 22 seconds.

When you select the Start-backup function, *Norton Backup* displays the same screens that you use for a full backup. It shows you the progress of the backup operation and prompts you to insert the appropriate diskette. And when the operation is complete, a screen that summarizes the backup operation is displayed.

How to do a differential backup *Norton Backup* recommends that you use differential backups instead of incremental backups. That way, you only have to keep two backup sets: one for your full backup, and one for your differential backup. As you learned earlier in this chapter, differential backups are particularly effective if you generally work on the same files. If that

Utility 2: Norton Backup **111**

Part 3:

The screen that shows the progress of the backup operation.

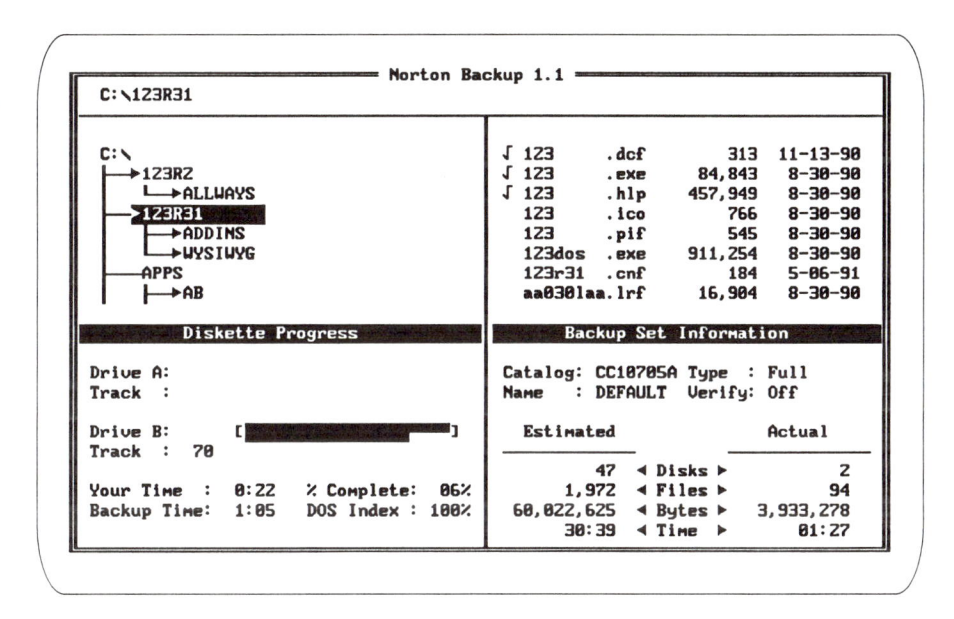

```
┌─────────────────────── Norton Backup 1.1 ───────────────────────┐
│ C:\123R31                                                        │
│                                                                  │
│  C:\                          │ √ 123      .dcf      313  11-13-90│
│    ├─►123R2                   │ √ 123      .exe   84,843   8-30-90│
│    │    └─►ALLWAYS            │ √ 123      .hlp  457,949   8-30-90│
│    ├─►123R31                  │   123      .ico      766   8-30-90│
│    │    ├─►ADDINS             │   123      .pif      545   8-30-90│
│    │    └─►WYSIWYG            │   123dos   .exe  911,254   8-30-90│
│    ├─APPS                     │   123r31   .cnf      184   5-06-91│
│    │    └─►AB                 │   aa0301aa.lrf    16,904   8-30-90│
│ ┌──────── Diskette Progress ────────┐ ┌──── Backup Set Information ────┐
│ │ Drive A:                          │ │ Catalog: CC10705A Type  : Full │
│ │ Track  :                          │ │ Name   : DEFAULT  Verify: Off  │
│ │                                   │ │                                │
│ │ Drive B:    [██████████████████]  │ │ Estimated            Actual    │
│ │ Track  :  70                      │ │                                │
│ │                                   │ │       47  ◄ Disks ►         2  │
│ │ Your Time  :  0:22  % Complete: 06%│ │    1,972  ◄ Files ►        94  │
│ │ Backup Time:  1:05  DOS Index : 100%│ │60,022,625 ◄ Bytes ► 3,933,278 │
│ │                                   │ │    30:39  ◄ Time  ►     01:27  │
│ └───────────────────────────────────┘ └────────────────────────────────┘
```

Figure NB-9 How you do a full backup (Part 3 of 4)

Part 4:

The summary information *Norton Backup* displays at the end of the backup operation.

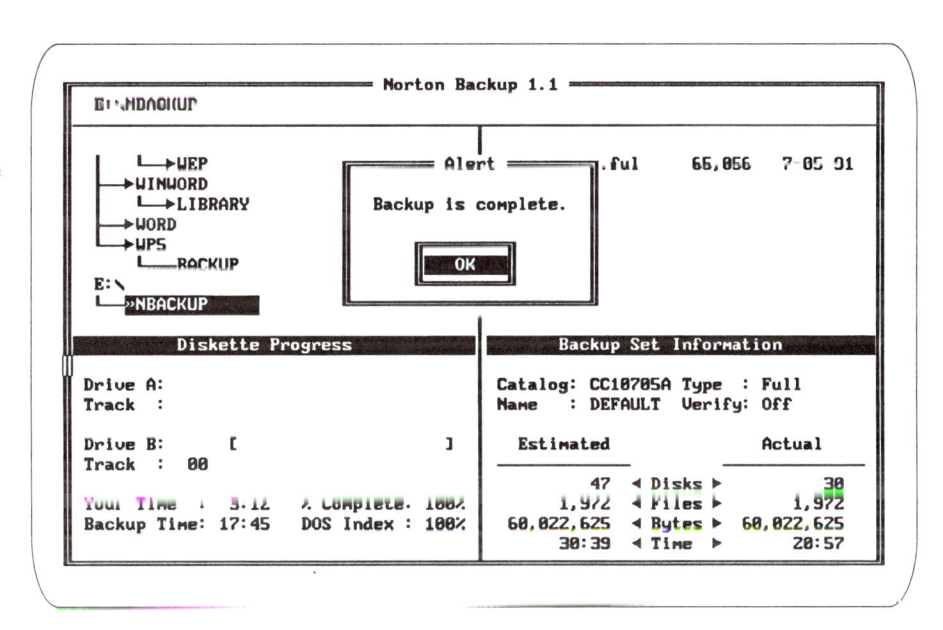

```
┌─────────────────────── Norton Backup 1.1 ───────────────────────┐
│ B:\NBACKUP                                                       │
│                                                                  │
│       └─►WEP              ┌──── Alert ────┐ .ful  66,056  7-05-91│
│    ├─►WINWORD             │                │                     │
│    │    └─►LIBRARY        │Backup is complete.│                  │
│    ├─WORD                 │                │                     │
│    ├─►WP5                 │     [  OK  ]   │                     │
│    │    └─►BACKUP         └────────────────┘                     │
│  E:\                                                             │
│    └─►»NBACKUP                                                   │
│ ┌──────── Diskette Progress ────────┐ ┌──── Backup Set Information ────┐
│ │ Drive A:                          │ │ Catalog: CC10705A Type  : Full │
│ │ Track  :                          │ │ Name   : DEFAULT  Verify: Off  │
│ │                                   │ │                                │
│ │ Drive B:    [                  ]  │ │ Estimated            Actual    │
│ │ Track  :  00                      │ │                                │
│ │                                   │ │       47  ◄ Disks ►        30  │
│ │ Your Time  :  3:12  % Complete:100%│ │    1,972  ◄ Files ►     1,972  │
│ │ Backup Time: 17:45  DOS Index : 100%│ │60,022,625 ◄ Bytes ► 60,022,625│
│ │                                   │ │    30:39  ◄ Time  ►     20:57  │
│ └───────────────────────────────────┘ └────────────────────────────────┘
```

Figure NB-9 How you do a full backup (Part 4 of 4)

describes you and if you decide to do differential backups, you won't be bothered by the fact that you can't do appended incremental backups.

To do a differential backup, you use the same procedure you use for a separate incremental backup. The only difference is that you select the Differential option from the Backup-type dialog box instead of the Incremental option. Then, when you select the Start-backup function, the program displays the Backup-in-progress screen followed by the summary screen that indicates that the backup is complete.

If you look again at the Backup-type dialog box shown in figure NB-10 part 1, you can see two other backup options. The Full-copy and Incremental-copy options do a full or incremental backup, but they don't reset the archive bits. These methods are useful when you want to use a backup to transfer files to another PC, but you don't want to interrupt your backup schedule.

How to do a partial backup   Figure NB-11 shows you how to do a partial backup. First, you set the Backup type to Full or Full-Copy as shown in part 1. Then, you highlight the hard drive you want to back up and select the Select-files function. *Norton Backup* then displays a directory and file listing like the one shown in part 2 of figure NB-11.

At this screen, you can see that the directories for the drive you selected are listed on the left and the files are listed on the right. To switch between these two listings, you can click the mouse on the listing you want, or you can press the Tab key. To select all the files in a directory for a backup, you use the directory listing. To select individual files for a backup, you use the file listing. Either way, you can select files or directories by double-clicking on them with a mouse or by pressing the Spacebar after you highlight your selection.

To illustrate, part 2 of figure NB-11 shows that all the files in the \QA\FILES directory have been selected. To indicate which files have been selected, the program puts a check mark next to the file. As you can see here, all the files in the \QA\FILES directory have been checked.

After you select the files you want to back up, you select the OK function. *Norton Backup* then displays a screen like the one shown in part 3 of figure NB-11. Here, the Backup-from function shows that *SOME files* have been selected from drive C. The information near the bottom of the screen confirms that 19 files have been selected and that the backup operation will

Utility 2: Norton Backup   113

Part 1:

Select the Incremental option from the Backup-type dialog box.

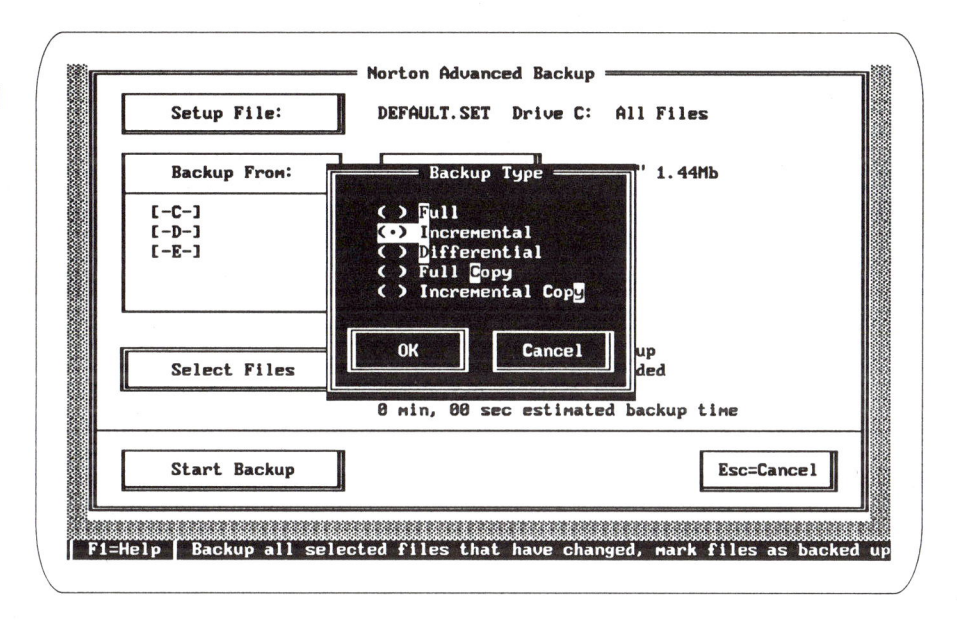

Figure NB-10 How you do an incremental backup (Part 1 of 2)

Part 2:

Select the drive you want to back up and select the Start-backup function to start the backup operation.

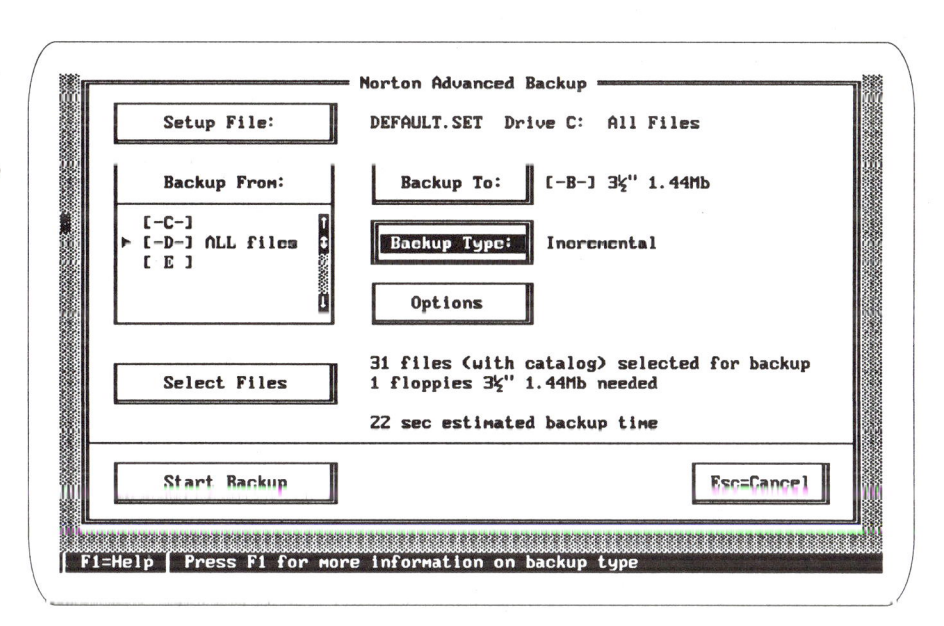

Figure NB-10 How you do an incremental backup (Part 2 of 2)

require only one diskette. To start the backup, you select the Start-Backup function.

How to restore files

To restore files, you select the Restore function from the opening screen. *Norton Backup* then displays the Restore screen shown in figure NB-12. Here, you can select the drive, directories, and other settings required for your restore operation. Then, to start the restore, you select the Start-restore function.

How to select a catalog file for a restore operation   Before you learn how to restore data, you should know that *Norton Backup* automatically keeps track of the directories and files of each backup you do. It keeps this backup information in special files called *catalog files*, and it stores these files in the *Norton Backup* program directory. From the directory and file listings that catalog files display, you select the data you want to restore. As you'll see in just a moment, you can select all the directories and files to do a full restore. Or you can select just the file or files you want for a partial restore.

Before you do a restore, though, you have to select the catalog file for the backup set that you want to restore from. To do this, first you select the Catalog function from the Restore screen. Then, a Select-catalog dialog box like the one shown in figure NB-13 is displayed. At this box, you select the catalog file you want by double-clicking on it with the mouse or by highlighting it and pressing the Spacebar. Next, you select the Load function. However, to select the right catalog for a restore, you must understand how the catalog files are named. Since the naming scheme isn't completely obvious, I'll take a moment to explain it.

The first two letters of a catalog file indicate the drive that was backed up. The first catalog file shown in figure NB-13, for example, is for a backup of drive C because the file name begins with CC. Similarly, the second catalog file that's shown is for a backup of drive D. The numbers that follow the drive indicate the date of the backup. For instance, CC10708A.FUL means that the catalog file is for a backup of drive C that was done on the first year of the decade (91), in the seventh month (07), on the eighth day (08). In other

Utility 2: Norton Backup **115**

Part 1:

Highlight the drive you want to back up and select the Select-files function.

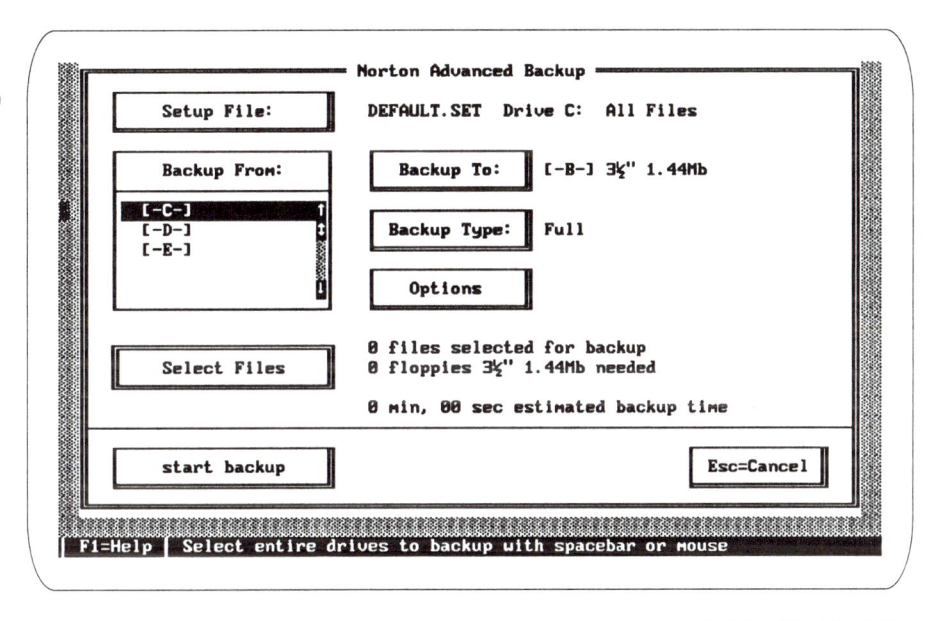

Figure NB-11 How you do a partial backup (Part 1 of 3)

Part 2:

Select the files you want to back up and select the OK function.

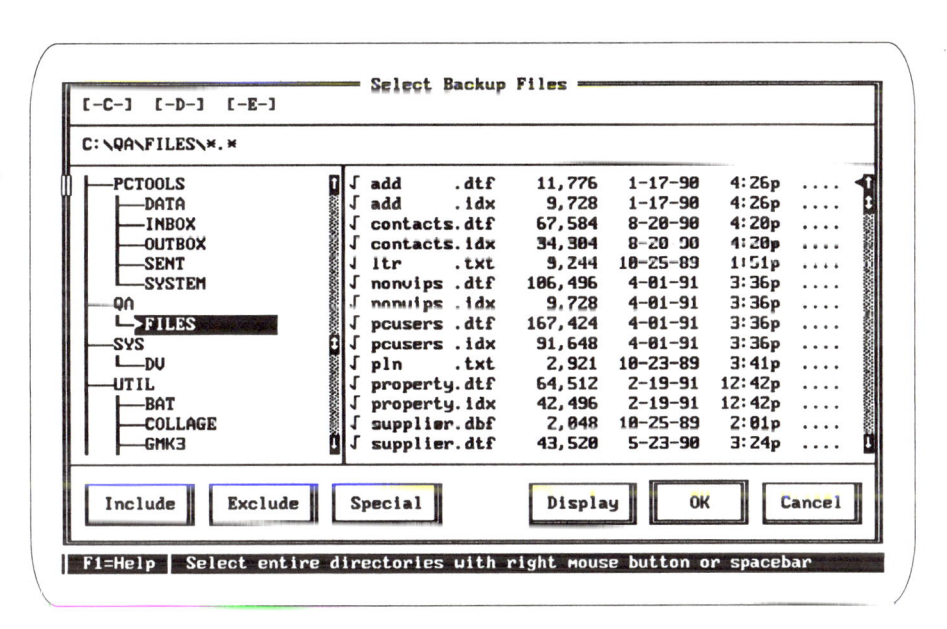

Figure NB-11 How you do a partial backup (Part 2 of 3)

Part 3:

Select the Start-backup function to start the backup operation.

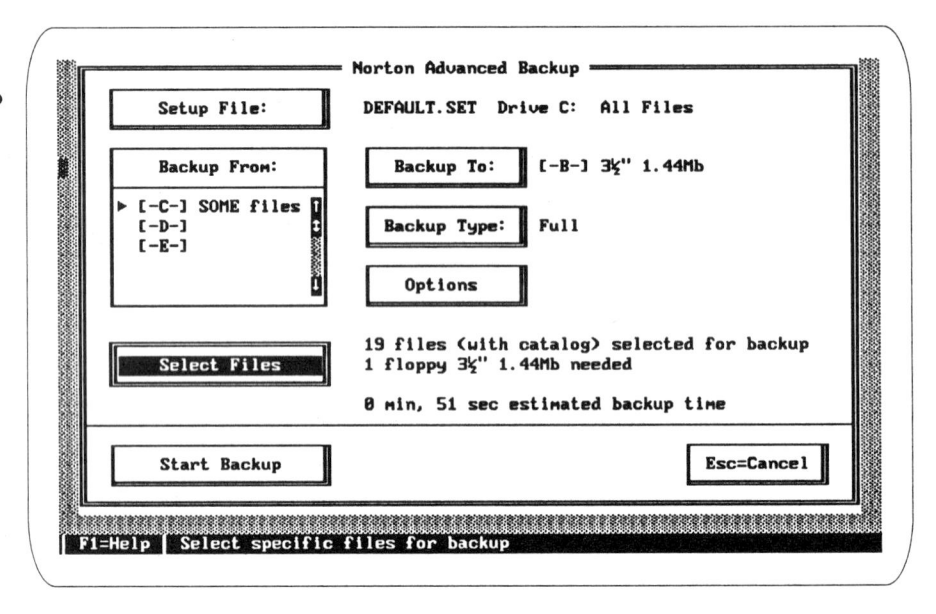

```
┌─────────────── Norton Advanced Backup ───────────────┐
│                                                      │
│  ┌ Setup File: ┐   DEFAULT.SET  Drive C:  All Files  │
│                                                      │
│  ┌ Backup From: ┐  ┌ Backup To: ┐  [-B-] 3½" 1.44Mb  │
│  ► [-C-] SOME files                                  │
│    [-D-]           ┌ Backup Type: ┐  Full            │
│    [-E-]                                             │
│                    ┌  Options  ┐                     │
│                                                      │
│                    19 files (with catalog) selected for backup │
│  ┌ Select Files ┐  1 floppy 3½" 1.44Mb needed        │
│                    0 min, 51 sec estimated backup time │
│                                                      │
│  ┌ Start Backup ┐                        ┌ Esc=Cancel ┐ │
│                                                      │
│ F1=Help │ Select specific files for backup           │
└──────────────────────────────────────────────────────┘
```

Figure NB-11 How you do a partial backup (Part 3 of 3)

words, this catalog is for a backup done on July 8, 1991. The letter *A* indicates that this was the first backup done on that day. And the .FUL extension indicates that the catalog is for a full backup. Other extensions you might see are .INC for incremental or .DIF for differential backups.

If you lose all the files on your hard disk, you'll also lose the catalog files that you need for the restore operation. That's why *Norton Backup* also keeps a copy of the catalog file on the last diskette in the backup set. To use the catalog file off the diskette, you insert the last diskette of your backup set, and you use the Retrieve function from the Select-catalog dialog box shown in figure NB-13.

Over time, *Norton Backup* will store many catalog files on your hard disk. However, many of these catalog files will be for outdated backups. If, for example, you do a full backup of your data files on drive D each week, this week's backup makes last week's backup obsolete. To make it easier to select catalog files, you should occasionally delete the outdated ones. You can use DOS commands to delete outdated files, or you can delete them

Utility 2: Norton Backup   **117**

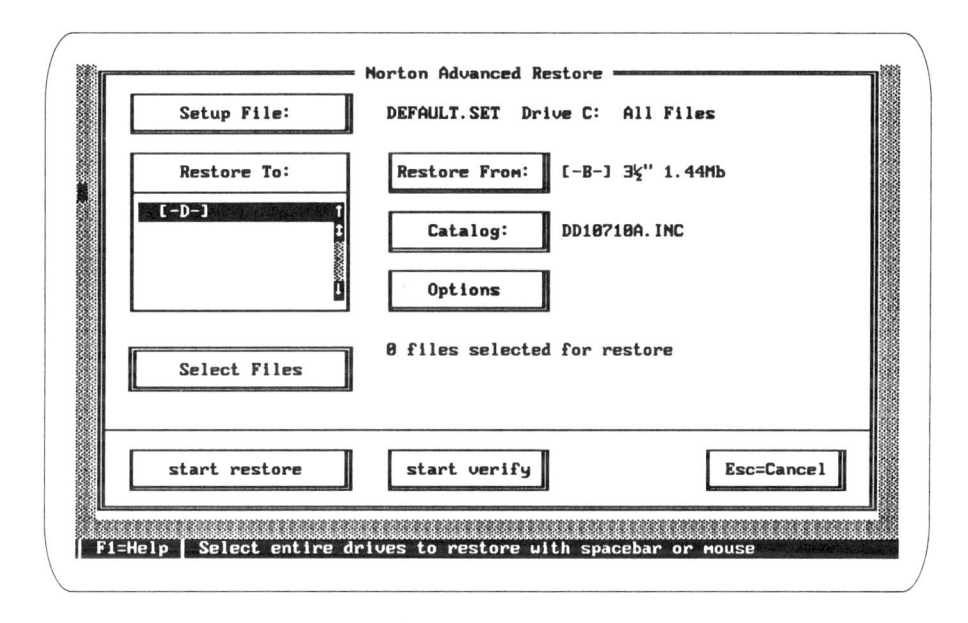

Figure NB-12 The Restore screen

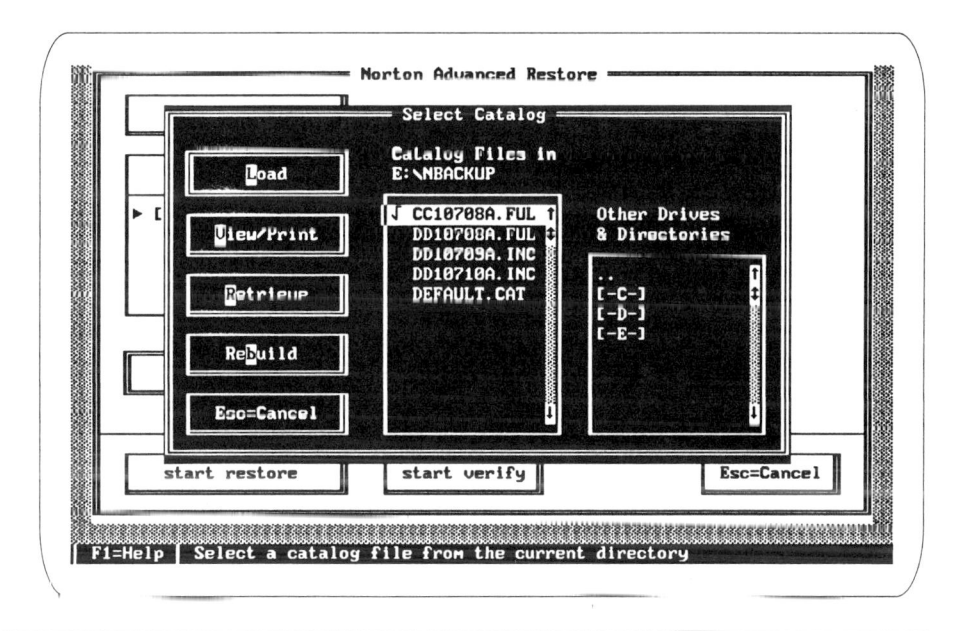

Figure NB-13 The Select-catalog dialog box

using a shell program. Once again, you'll find these catalog files in the *Norton Backup* program directory, which is usually called \NBACKUP.

How to do a full restore   Figure NB-14 shows you how to do a full restore. In part 1, a catalog file named CC10708A.FUL has already been selected. This catalog is for a full backup of drive C that was performed on July 8th, 1991.

After you select the catalog file, you have to select the drive that you are restoring to. To select the drive in the Restore-to function, you can either double-click on the drive with the mouse, or you can move the highlight to it and press the Spacebar. In part 2 of figure NB-14, you can see that the program then displays information on how many files will be restored. In this case, all 1,965 files from a backup set of drive C will be restored.

To start the restore, you select the Start-restore function. When you do, a screen like the one in part 3 of figure NB-14 is displayed. This screen tells you to insert the first diskette in the backup set. As each diskette is restored, you are prompted to insert the next diskette in the set. As you can see, this screen also shows you the progress of the restore operation.

How to do a partial restore   When you do a partial restore, you use the same basic procedure that you use for a full restore. But instead of selecting the drive from the Restore-to function, you just highlight the drive. Then, you select the Select-files function to display a directory and file listing. At this screen, you use the same procedure to select files for a partial restore that you use to select files for a partial backup.

To illustrate, figure NB-15 shows you how to select files and start a partial restore. In part 1, all the files in the \QA\FILES directory have been selected for the restore operation. After you select the directories and files you want to restore, you select the OK function. Then, a screen like the one shown in part 2 of figure NB-15 is displayed. Here, the Restore-to function shows that some of the files from the backup set have been selected for the restore operation, and the information at the bottom of the screen shows that 18 files will be restored.

When you select the Start-restore function, a screen like the one in part 3 of figure NB-15 is displayed. At this screen, the prompt tells you which backup diskette to insert. Here, for example, the prompt tells you to insert the

Utility 2: Norton Backup **119**

Part 1:

Use the Catalog function to select the catalog file you want to use for the restore.

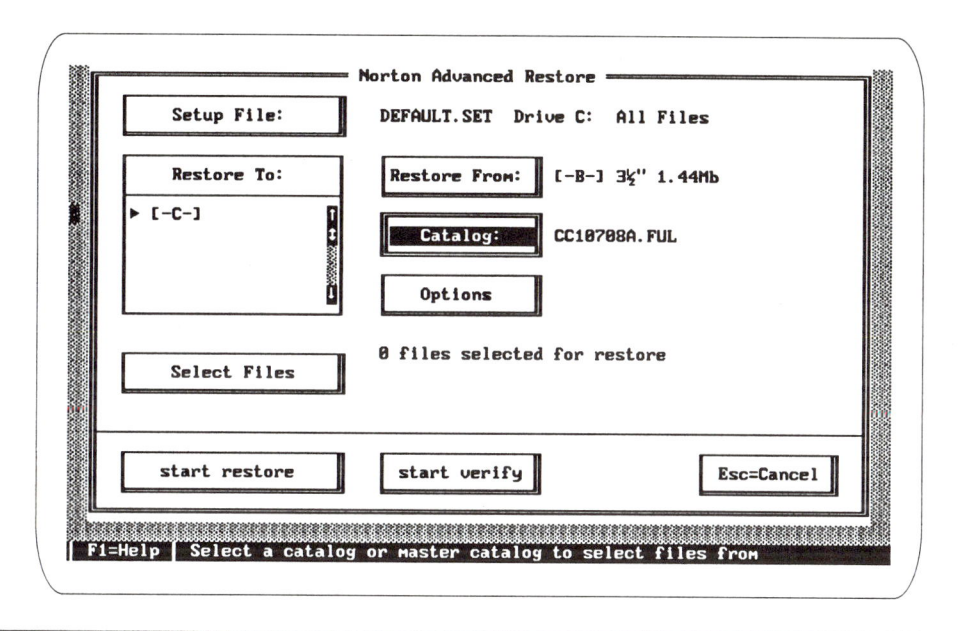

Figure NB-14 How you do a full restore (Part 1 of 3)

Part 2:

Select the drive you want to restore to from the Restore-to panel.

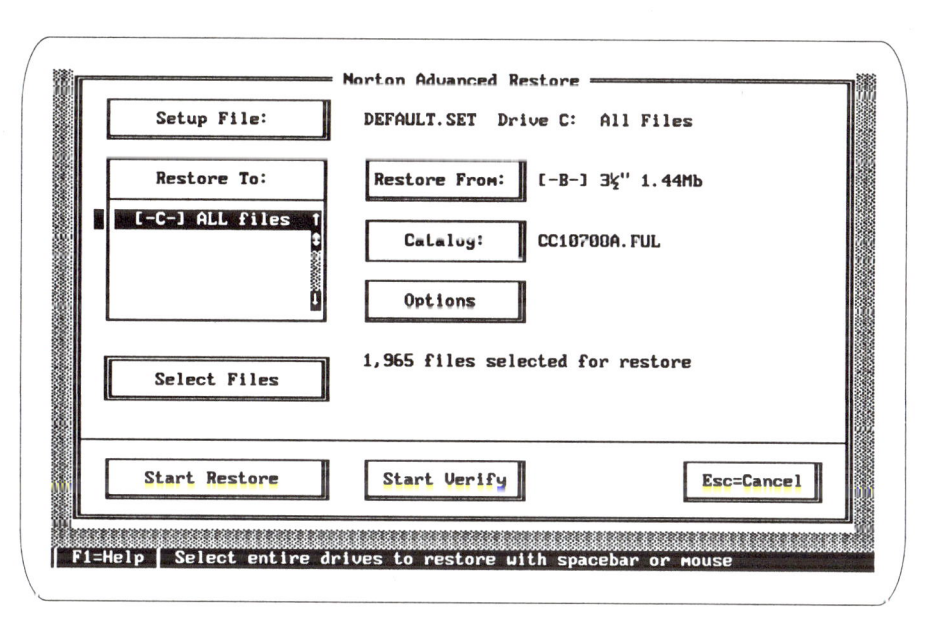

Figure NB-14 How you do a full restore (Part 2 of 3)

Part 3:

Start the restore operation and insert the appropriate diskette as prompted by *Norton Backup*.

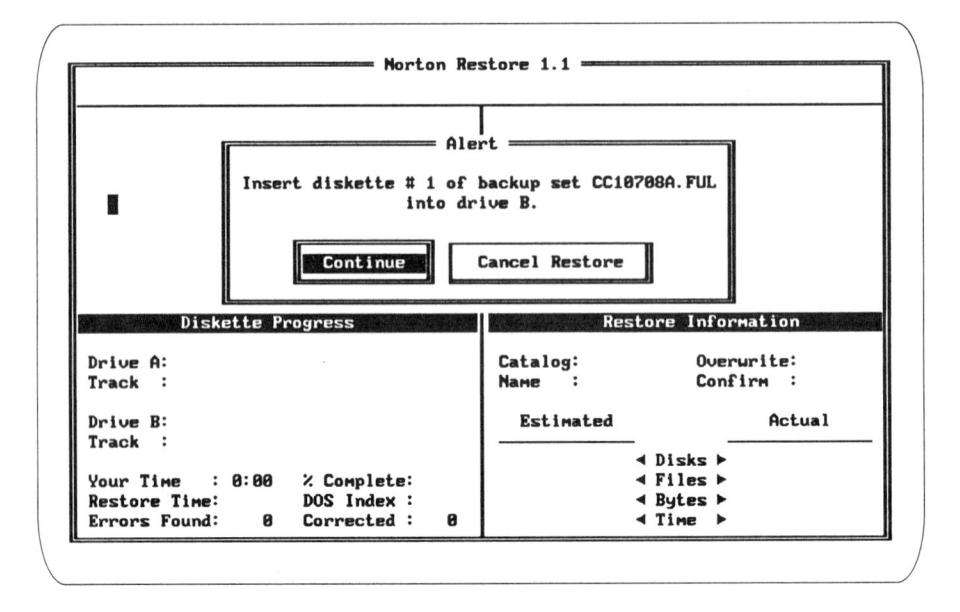

```
╔══════════════════ Norton Restore 1.1 ══════════════════╗
║                                                         ║
║              ┌──────────── Alert ────────────┐          ║
║              │ Insert diskette # 1 of backup │          ║
║              │ set CC10708A.FUL into drive B.│          ║
║              │                               │          ║
║              │   [Continue]  Cancel Restore  │          ║
║              └───────────────────────────────┘          ║
║ ┌─── Diskette Progress ───┐ ┌── Restore Information ──┐ ║
║ │ Drive A:                │ │ Catalog:    Overwrite:  │ ║
║ │ Track  :                │ │ Name    :   Confirm  :  │ ║
║ │ Drive B:                │ │ Estimated       Actual  │ ║
║ │ Track  :                │ │                         │ ║
║ │ Your Time   : 0:00      │ │           ◄ Disks ►     │ ║
║ │ Restore Time:  % Complete│ │          ◄ Files ►     │ ║
║ │ Errors Found: 0  DOS Index:│◄ Bytes ►               │ ║
║ │              Corrected: 0 │ │         ◄ Time  ►     │ ║
║ └─────────────────────────┘ └─────────────────────────┘ ║
╚═════════════════════════════════════════════════════════╝
```

Figure NB-14 How you do a full restore (Part 3 of 3)

18th diskette because it's the one that contains the selected files. This prompt speeds up the restore operation because you don't have to insert the first diskette in the backup set and continue through the set until you find the right diskette.

How to compare a backup

As a rule, you can count on *Norton Backup* to do reliable backups. So you don't need to compare every backup you do. However, you should occasionally compare a backup to make sure that the utility is working correctly. Then, you can rest assured that your backups will work when you need to restore data. The best time to compare a backup is right after you back up, before any changes occur.

To compare a backup, you use the same basic procedure you use for a full restore. You just select the Start-verify function from the Restore screen instead of the Start-restore function. *Norton Backup* then prompts you to

Utility 2: Norton Backup **121**

Part 1:

Highlight the drive you want to restore and use the Select-files function to select the files you want to restore.

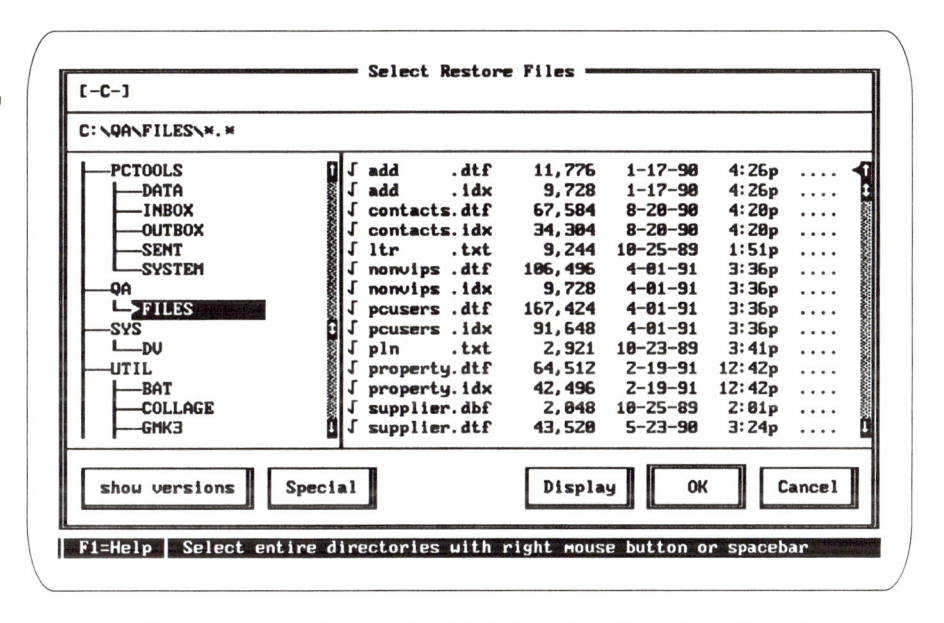

```
┌─────────────────── Select Restore Files ───────────────────┐
│ [-C-]                                                       │
│ C:\QA\FILES\*.*                                             │
│                                                             │
│   ┌─PCTOOLS        │ ♪ add      .dtf   11,776  1-17-90  4:26p  ....│
│   │  ├─DATA        │ ♪ add      .idx    9,728  1-17-90  4:26p  ....│
│   │  ├─INBOX       │ ♪ contacts.dtf   67,584  8-20-90  4:20p  ....│
│   │  ├─OUTBOX      │ ♪ contacts.idx   34,304  8-20-90  4:20p  ....│
│   │  ├─SENT        │ ♪ ltr      .txt    9,244 10-25-89  1:51p  ....│
│   │  └─SYSTEM      │ ♪ nonvips  .dtf  106,496  4-01-91  3:36p  ....│
│   ├─QA             │ ♪ nonvips  .idx    9,728  4-01-91  3:36p  ....│
│   │  └▶FILES       │ ♪ pcusers  .dtf  167,424  4-01-91  3:36p  ....│
│   ├─SYS            │ ♪ pcusers  .idx   91,648  4-01-91  3:36p  ....│
│   │  └─DV          │ ♪ pln      .txt    2,921 10-23-89  3:41p  ....│
│   ├─UTIL           │ ♪ property.dtf   64,512  2-19-91 12:42p  ....│
│   │  ├─BAT         │ ♪ property.idx   42,496  2-19-91 12:42p  ....│
│   │  ├─COLLAGE     │ ♪ supplier.dbf    2,048 10-25-89  2:01p  ....│
│   │  └─GMK3        │ ♪ supplier.dtf   43,520  5-23-90  3:24p  ....│
│                                                             │
│  [ show versions ] [ Special ]    [ Display ] [ OK ] [ Cancel ]│
│                                                             │
│ F1=Help │ Select entire directories with right mouse button or spacebar │
└─────────────────────────────────────────────────────────────┘
```

Figure NB-15   How you do a partial restore (Part 1 of 3)

Part 2:

Use the Start-restore function to start the restore operation.

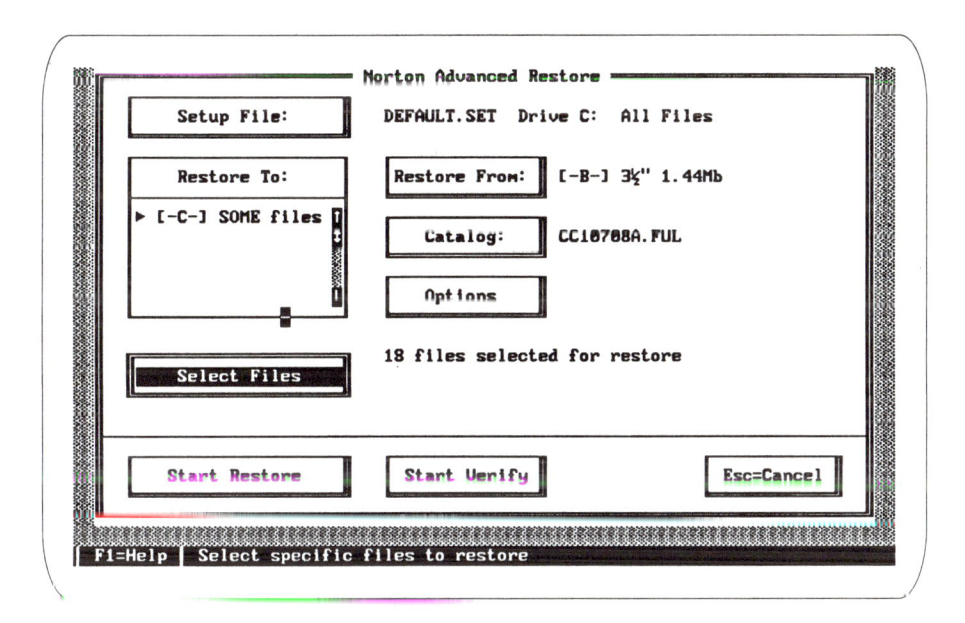

```
┌─────────────── Norton Advanced Restore ───────────────┐
│                                                        │
│  [ Setup File: ]      DEFAULT.SET  Drive C:  All Files │
│                                                        │
│  [ Restore To: ]     [ Restore From: ]  [-B-] 3½" 1.44Mb│
│  ▶ [-C-] SOME files                                    │
│                       [ Catalog: ]       CC10708A.FUL  │
│                                                        │
│                       [ Options ]                      │
│                                                        │
│                       18 files selected for restore    │
│    [ Select Files ]                                    │
│                                                        │
│                                                        │
│  [ Start Restore ]    [ Start Verify ]    [ Esc=Cancel ]│
│                                                        │
│ F1=Help │ Select specific files to restore             │
└────────────────────────────────────────────────────────┘
```

Figure NB-15   How you do a partial restore (Part 2 of 3)

Part 3:

Insert the appropriate diskette as prompted by *Norton Backup*.

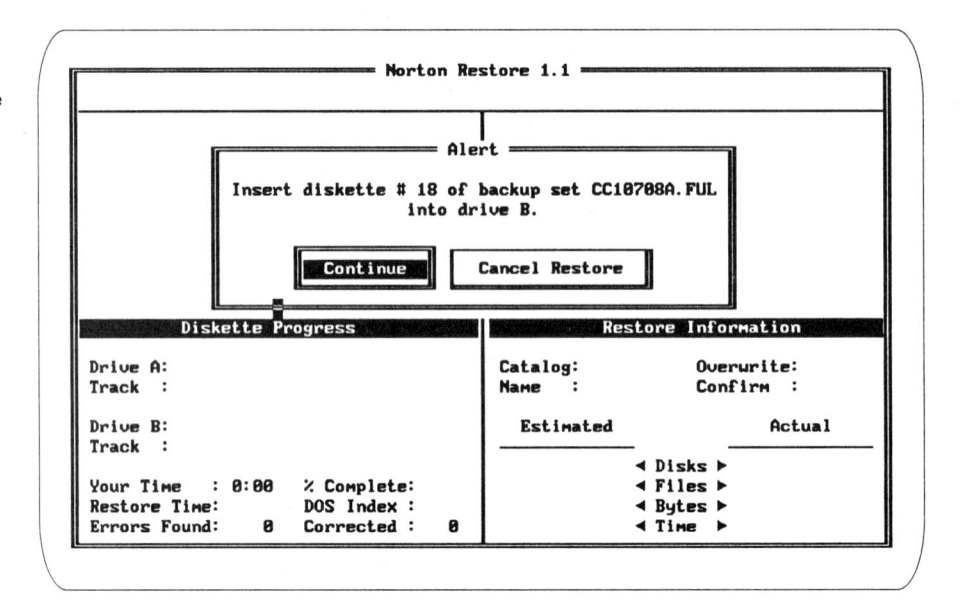

```
┌──────────────────────── Norton Restore 1.1 ────────────────────────┐
│                                                                     │
│                          ┌──── Alert ────┐                          │
│                  Insert diskette # 18 of backup set CC10708A.FUL    │
│                                 into drive B.                       │
│                                                                     │
│                          [ Continue ]   [ Cancel Restore ]          │
│                                                                     │
│   ──── Diskette Progress ────        ──── Restore Information ────  │
│   Drive A:                           Catalog:        Overwrite:     │
│   Track  :                           Name    :       Confirm  :     │
│                                                                     │
│   Drive B:                           Estimated             Actual   │
│   Track  :                                                          │
│                                                  ◄ Disks ►          │
│   Your Time    : 0:00   % Complete:              ◄ Files ►          │
│   Restore Time:         DOS Index :              ◄ Bytes ►          │
│   Errors Found:     0   Corrected :    0         ◄ Time  ►          │
└─────────────────────────────────────────────────────────────────────┘
```

Figure NB-15 How you do a partial restore (part 3 of 3)

insert the first diskette from the backup set. The program reads the data from the diskette and compares it to the data on the hard disk. As the program completes this process for each diskette, it prompts you to insert the next diskette until it has compared the data on all the diskettes in the backup set. If the program doesn't find any errors, you know that the backup is reliable. On the other hand, if the compare operation does find errors, it alerts you of the condition. Then, you must determine how to correct the errors so you have a reliable backup.

How to automate your backups

So far, you've learned how to select functions from various screens to set up and do different types of backups. In some cases, this is the most efficient way to do a backup. However, *Norton Backup* provides several features that you can use to automate your backups. In particular, you can create *setup files* that store all of the settings that are required for a backup. You can also

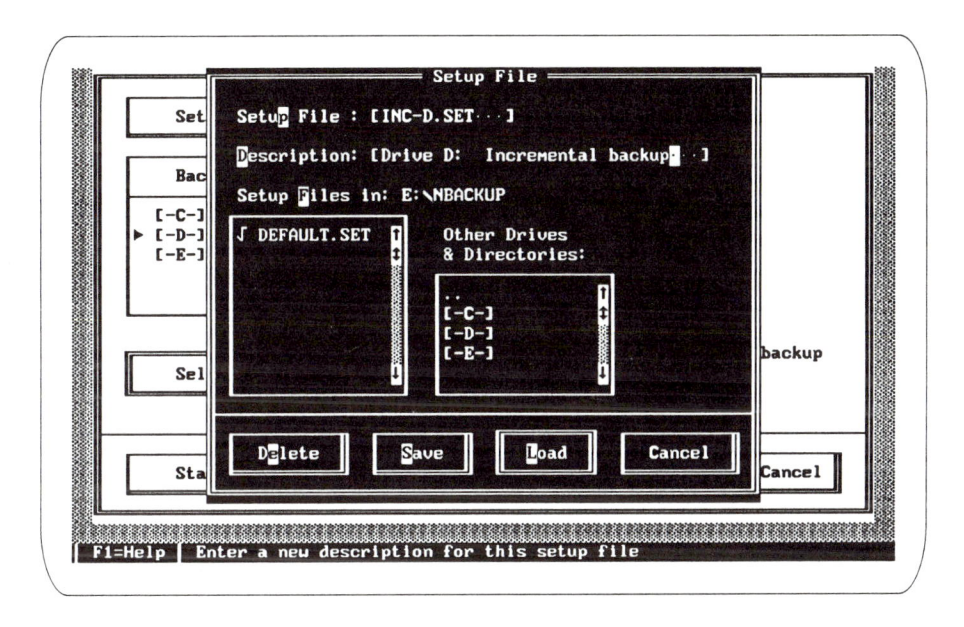

Figure NB-16 The Setup-file dialog box you use to create and save a setup file

use these setup files in batch files. In addition, you can use a simple routine called a *macro* with setup files to fully automate your backups. And you can take maximum advantage of setup files by using a special menu that *Norton Backup* provides. Since you generally do the same backup operations over and over again, automating your backups can significantly improve your backup procedures.

How to create and use a setup file   To create a setup file, you set the functions for the backup operation as if you were going to run the backup. But you don't start the backup. Instead, you select the Setup-file function from the Backup screen. *Norton Backup* then displays a dialog box like the one in figure NB-16. In the Setup-file field, you enter a name for the setup file that includes an extension of *.SET*. In the next field, you enter a description of the setup file. Here, for example, I typed *INC-D.SET* as the name, and *Drive D: Incremental backup* as the description. To save the setup file, you select the Save function at the bottom of the box.

Figure NB-17 shows you how to load and use a setup file for a backup. First, you select the Setup-file function from the Backup screen. Then, when *Norton Backup* displays a dialog box like the one shown in part 1, you select the setup file by double-clicking on it with the mouse or by highlighting it and pressing the Spacebar. To confirm your selection, the program places a check mark beside the setup file.

Next, you select the Load function from the bottom of the dialog box. Then, the program loads the setup file and returns you to the Backup screen. In part 2 of figure NB-17, for example, you can see that the FULL-D.SET that I selected in part 1 has been loaded. Since the setup file contains all the settings that are required for the backup operation, you can run the backup by simply selecting the Start-backup function.

How to start a setup file from a batch file   Figure NB-18 shows you how to use batch files to run setup files. Here, the setup file is included with the commands that start *Norton Backup*. When you execute one of these batch files, it automatically starts *Norton Backup*, loads the setup file, and displays the Backup screen. Then, you can just select the Start-backup function to run the backup operation.

How to create and use macros   *Norton Backup* doesn't automatically start a backup operation when you start a setup file from a batch file. You can, however, create and use a simple routine called a macro that causes a backup operation to run automatically. Since these macros are stored with setup files, you can use them in combination with setup files started from batch files to run your backups.

Figure NB-19 lists the steps for creating a macro. To create a macro, first you load the appropriate setup file. Then, you return to the opening screen shown in figure NB-20, and you press the F7 key to start *recording the macro*. To show that the program is ready to record, the word *Recording* is displayed at the bottom left of the screen as you can see in figure NB-20.

Next, you use keystrokes to select the functions that are required to start the backup operation. But you don't start the backup. Instead, you highlight the Start-backup function and you hold down the Ctrl key as you press the Enter key. This simulates starting the backup operation and returns you to the opening screen.

Utility 2: Norton Backup **125**

Part 1:

Select the Setup-file function and select the setup file you want. Then, select the Load function from the Setup-file dialog box.

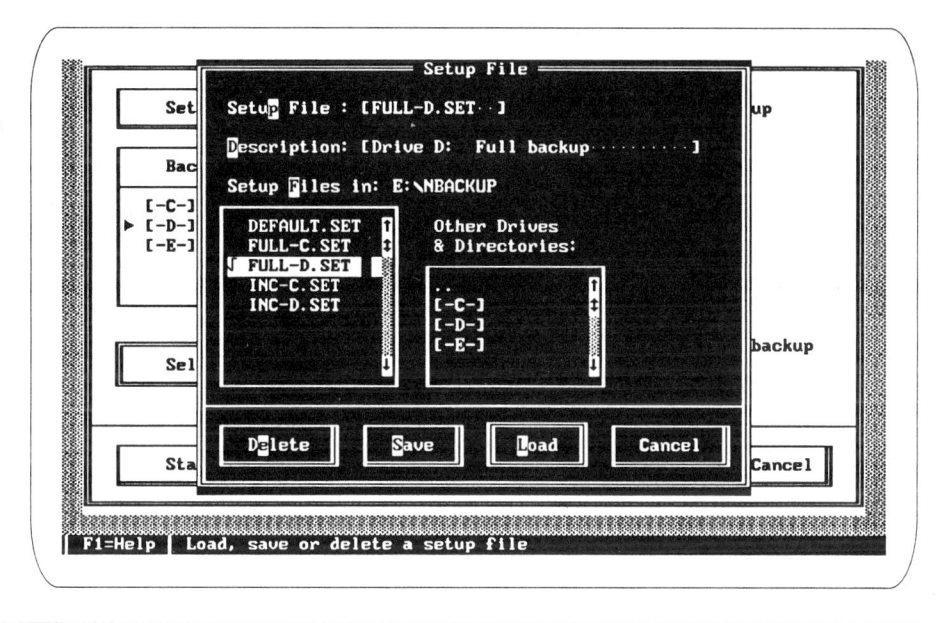

Figure NB-17 How you load a setup file (Part 1 of 2)

Part 2:

The Backup screen that shows that the FULL-D.SET setup file has been loaded.

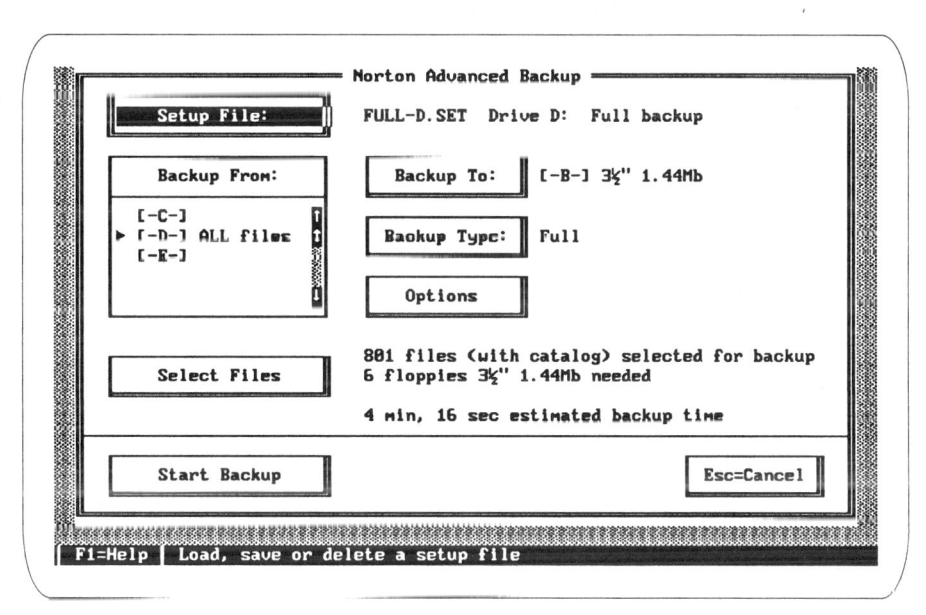

Figure NB-17 How you load a setup file (Part 2 of 2)

```
FULL-C.SET

    C:
    CD \NBACKUP
    NBACKUP FULL-C.SET

INC-C.SET

    C:
    CD \NBACKUP
    NBACKUP INC-C.SET

FULL-D.SET

    C:
    CD \NBACKUP
    NBACKUP FULL-D.SET

INC-D.SET

    C:
    CD \NBACKUP
    NBACKUP INC-D.SET
```

Figure NB-18 Four batch files that start *Norton Backup* and load setup files

At the opening screen, you press the F7 key again to stop recording the macro. And you select the Quit function. A dialog box like the one in figure NB-21 is then displayed. Finally, you select the Save-changes function. This saves the macro you just recorded with the setup file.

To use the macro, you just type the @ character in front of the setup file name. For example, the following command line starts *Norton Backup*, loads a setup file, and executes the macro that starts the backup operation:

```
C:\NBACKUP>nbackup @inc-d.set
```

1. At the Backup screen, use the Setup-file function to load the appropriate setup file.

2. Press the Esc key to return to the opening screen. Then, press the F7 key to start recording the macro.

3. Using keystrokes, select the Backup function. Then, complete the selections as if you were going to run the backup operation but don't start the backup.

4. Highlight the Start-backup function. Then, press the Ctrl+Enter key combination to simulate starting the backup operation.

5. At the opening screen, press the F7 key to end the process of recording the macro.

6. Select the Quit function. Then, from the dialog box that appears, select the Save-changes function to complete the procedure.

Figure NB-19 The steps for creating a macro that loads a setup file and automatically runs a backup operation

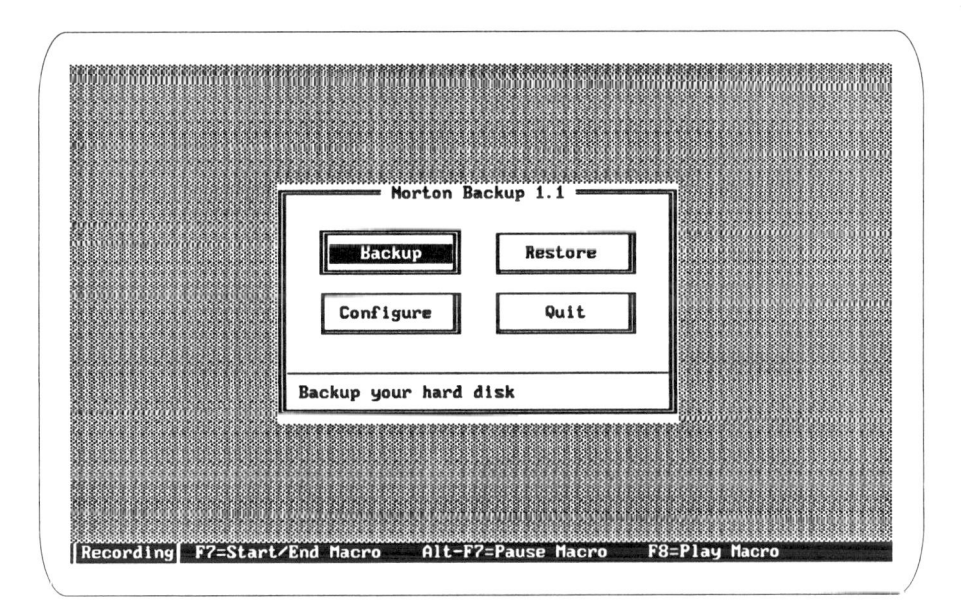

Figure NB-20 The Start-macro function (F7 key) selected from the opening screen

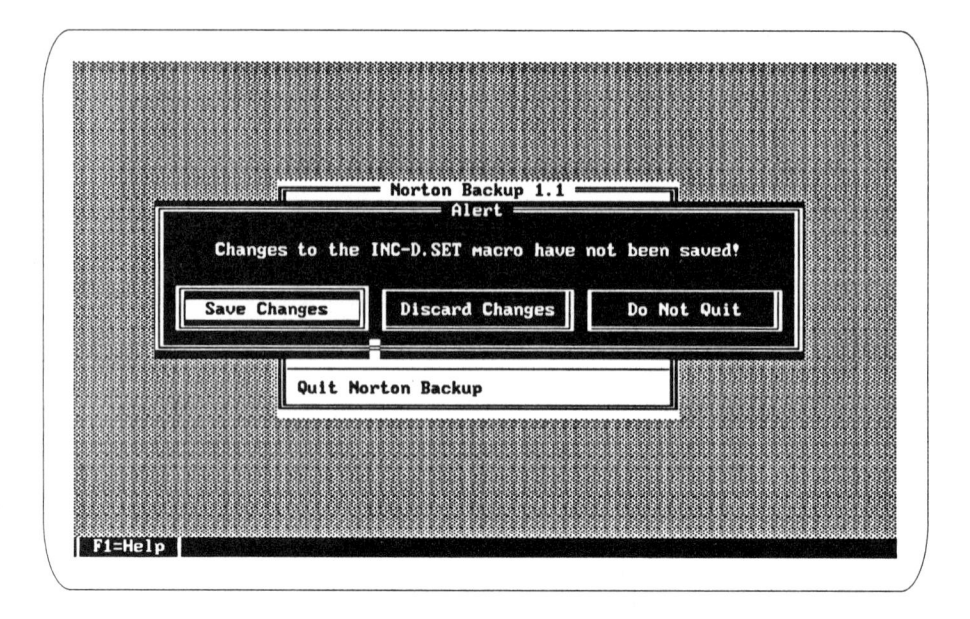

Figure NB-21 The dialog box you use to save a macro with a setup file

Of course, you can also the @ character with setup files that are in batch files. Since combining macros and setup files streamlines your backup as much as possible, you may want to use this technique for all your regular backup procedures.

How to use the Preset menu   Figure NB-22 shows the Preset menu screen. When you use the Preset menu instead of the standard menus, you can take maximum advantage of setup files. That's because the Preset menu lists only the functions required to do backups using setup files. This simplified menu is ideal if you're setting up *Norton Backup* for another person to use, especially, if that person is a novice PC user.

To activate the Preset menu, you select the Configure function at the opening screen. Next, select the Program-level function and set it to Preset. Then, when you select the Backup function, *Norton Backup* uses the Preset menu with the setup files you've already created in place of the Backup screen you've seen throughout this chapter.

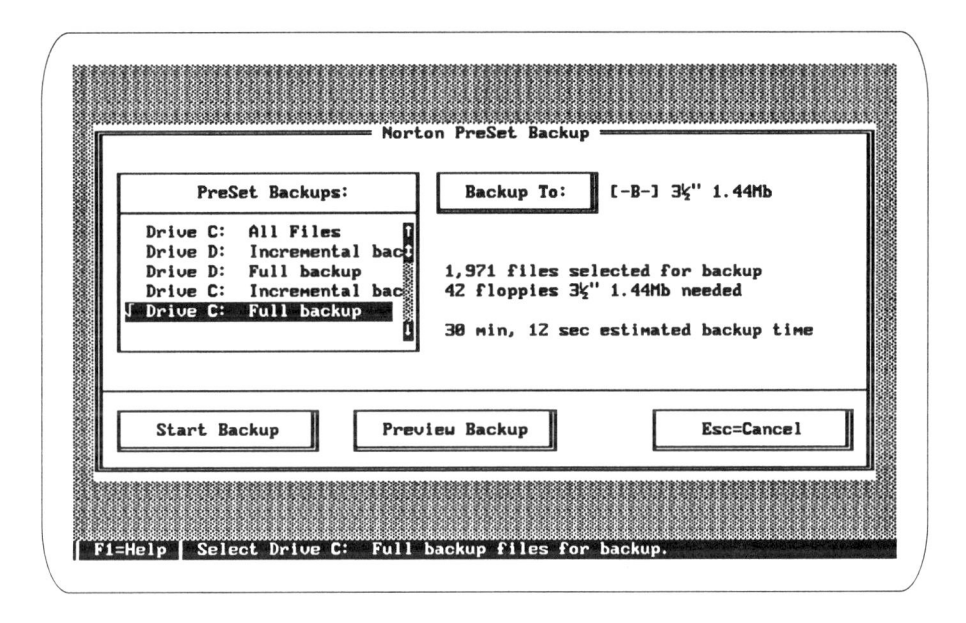

Figure NB-22 The Preset menu screen

You can see the Preset menu in use in figure NB-22. Here, the setup files I created earlier are displayed in the Preset-backups panel. To do a backup, you just select one of these setup files and start the backup.

Is *Norton Backup* the right utility for your backups?

Now that you've seen how to use *Norton Backup* for the most common backup and restore operations, you should be able to decide if it's the right utility for you. This utility is as fast as any on the market. In addition, it has more features that insure its reliability than the three other utilities presented in this chapter.

But if you compare it with *Central Point Backup*, I think you'll agree that it's a bit harder to use. In part, that's because you can't do appended incremental backups. This makes it harder to manage your backups because each incremental backup requires a separate backup set. Also, the catalog files that you need for restore operations make it a bit harder to use than *Central Point Backup*.

If, however, you want to set up a backup utility for other people to use, you should consider *Norton Backup*. As you've seen, with setup files, macros, and its Preset menu, this utility has several features that make it better suited to this purpose than any of the other utilities in this chapter.

Terms

dialog box
catalog file
setup file
macro
recording a macro

Utility 3: PC-Fullbak+

PC-Fullbak+ version 2.02 from *Westlake Data Products* doesn't have some of the advanced features that the other utilities have. In particular, it doesn't provide for setup files or macros that you can use to automate your backups. In addition, the standard menu system that *PC-Fullbak+* provides isn't as easy to use as the menu system that *Central Point Backup* provides.

On the other hand, *PC-Fullbak+* is the least expensive backup utility presented in this book at a price of around $50. Also, it's about as fast as any of the other utilities. And it provides a simplified menu for the most common backup options. If this menu will work with your backup plan, *PC-Fullbak+* may be the easiest utility for you to use. So if you're looking for a backup utility, don't overlook this one.

To start *PC-Fullbak+* from the DOS command prompt, you change to the appropriate drive and directory. Then, you type the following command and press the Enter key:

```
fullbak
```

The utility then displays the main screen shown in figure PC-1. As you can see, there's a menu line at the top of the screen, and the highlight identifies the selected function. In this menu line, the Backup option starts the backup function, the Compare option starts the compare function, and so on.

To select one of these functions, you use the arrow keys to highlight the function you want, and you press the Enter key. Or you can press the first letter of the function you want. In other words, you press the B key to start the backup function, the C key to start the compare function, and so on. Since most of the *PC-Fullbak+* menus work like this, I'll assume that you now know how to select functions from the menus. If a menu works a little differently, though, I'll show you how to use it.

132 Chapter 5

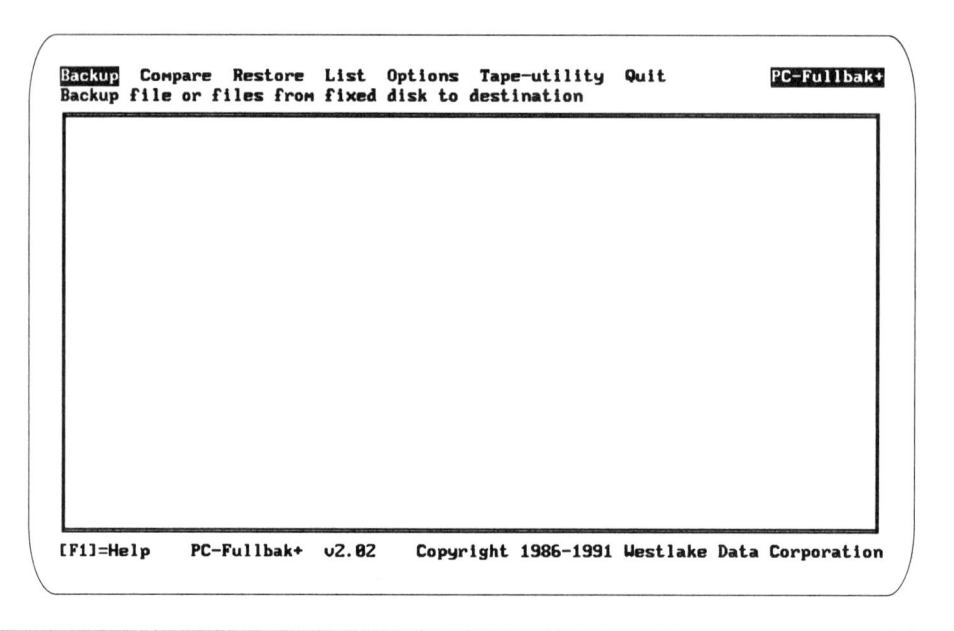

```
┌─────────────────────────────────────────────────────────────┐
│ Backup  Compare  Restore  List  Options  Tape-utility  Quit     PC-Fullbak+ │
│ Backup file or files from fixed disk to destination         │
│ ┌─────────────────────────────────────────────────────────┐ │
│ │                                                         │ │
│ │                                                         │ │
│ │                                                         │ │
│ │                                                         │ │
│ │                                                         │ │
│ │                                                         │ │
│ │                                                         │ │
│ │                                                         │ │
│ │                                                         │ │
│ │                                                         │ │
│ └─────────────────────────────────────────────────────────┘ │
│  [F1]=Help    PC-Fullbak+  v2.02    Copyright 1986-1991 Westlake Data Corporation │
└─────────────────────────────────────────────────────────────┘
```

Figure PC-1   The main screen of *PC-Fullbak+*

If at any point you need help, you can press the F1 key to display a Help screen. This screen displays information about the function you're using. To exit the Help screen, you press the Esc key.

If you already have *PC-Fullbak+* version 1, you should know that it uses the same type of menu system and provides the same basic features as version 2.02. So you can apply what you learn in this chapter even if you are using version 1. However, you may want to consider upgrading to the new version because it provides several features that make the program more reliable and easier to use.

How to set up *PC-Fullbak+*

To set up *PC-Fullbak+*, you use the Options function from the main screen shown in figure PC-1. When you select this function, the Options screen shown in figure PC-2 is displayed. On the left side of the screen, you can see that there are six categories of options. The Backup-options category sets the

Utility 3: PC-Fullbak+   **133**

```
┌─────────────────────────────────────────────────────────────────────────┐
│  [F1]=Help     PC-Fullbak+  v2.02    Copyright 1986-1991 Westlake Data Corporation │
│                                                                         │
│  ┌──────────────────┬──────────────────────BACKUP───────────────────┐   │
│  │ Backup Options   │ Drive to backup ........................... C │   │
│  │                  │ Device to which backup will be written ... Diskette_drive │
│  │ Compare Options  │ Write a log file .......................... Yes │   │
│  │                  │ Data Compression method ............... SaveTime │   │
│  │                  │ Include error correction code ............ Yes │   │
│  │ Restore Options  │ Verify data during backup ................. No │   │
│  │                  │ Set archived attribute on each file ...... Yes │   │
│  │                  │ Backup new/updated files only ............. No │   │
│  │ List Options     │ Append files to previous backup ........... No │   │
│  │                  │ Warn before overwriting existing data .... Any not backup │
│  │                  │ Backup using script file .................. No │   │
│  │ Device Options   │      Script file to use .................. N/A │   │
│  │                  │      Script file name .................... N/A │   │
│  │                  │ DMA setting .............................. Fast │   │
│  │ Video Options    │ Backup by date ............................ No │   │
│  │                  │      Start date .......................... N/A │   │
│  │                  │      End date ............................ N/A │   │
│  │ Quit             │                                                 │   │
│  │                  │                                                 │   │
│  ├──────────────────┴─────────────────────────────────────────────┤    │
│  │  [TAB] Selects         [↑] & [↓] Select Options, [←] & [→] Select Settings │
│  └─────────────────────────────────────────────────────────────────────┘   │
└─────────────────────────────────────────────────────────────────────────┘
```

Figure PC-2   The Options screen with the Backup-options category displayed

options relating to the backup function, the Compare-options category sets the options relating to the compare function, and so on.

To understand how *PC-Fullbak+* works, you need to know that you use the Options screen in figure PC-2 for two purposes. First, you use this screen to set and save the options that you want *PC-Fullbak+* to use as defaults. Second, you use the Options screen to set the options that are required for different types of backups. For example, you use the Options screen to specify which hard drive you want to back up. And you use this screen to specify whether you want to do a full or incremental backup. When you use the Options screen for settings like these, you don't save them as defaults.

Because you have to use the Options screen to specify both temporary and default settings, it's essential that you know how to make selections from it. That's why I'll show you how to set the most important options in each category now. Then, when you need to change some of the settings to perform different types of backups, you can refer back to this material.

To use the Options screen, you press the Tab key to highlight the category of options you want. *PC-Fullbak+* then displays the options relating to that category on the right side the screen. In figure PC-2, for example, the Backup-options category is highlighted. As a result, the right side of the screen displays all of the options relating to the Backup function. To select the option you want to set, you press the Up or Down arrow key to highlight the option. To change the option, you press the Left or Right arrow key to toggle through the settings that are available for that option.

The Backup-options category   As I just mentioned, figure PC-2 shows the 17 options available for the Backup function. You'll probably need to use this category often because you must change several of its options for some of the most common backup procedures. However, don't be overwhelmed by the number of options on this screen for two reasons. First, you have to change only four of these options regularly. Second, the screens for the Restore-options and Compare-options categories don't have nearly as many options to deal with.

The first backup option in figure PC-2 is the Drive-to-backup option. You use it to specify which hard drive you want to back up. If you have more than one hard drive on your PC, you'll change this option regularly.

The next option, Device-to-which-backup-will-be-written, lets you specify the type of drive you're going to use for your backups. Here, this option is set to use a diskette drive. Since this is the most common type of hardware that's used for backups, this is the setting you'll probably use. And you won't need to change it unless you change hardware. In addition to a diskette drive, you can also set this option to back up to a tape drive or to logical devices like a removable hard disk, a bernoulli box, or an optical disk drive.

The Write-a-log-file option lets you activate the log-file feature. When you use this feature, you can restore selected files from a file list instead of having to enter a file specification. Since this feature makes restoring data much easier, you should activate the log-file feature as shown here.

The Data-compression-method option lets you specify the type of data compression you want the utility to use. Generally, you should set this option to save time as shown here. But you can also turn off all data compression, or you can have *PC-Fullbak+* compress the files so the backup takes a little longer but uses fewer diskettes.

The next two options in figure PC-2, Include-error-correction-codes and Verify-data-during-backup, let you specify the level of error checking you want *PC-Fullbak+* to do during a backup. Since the Include-error-correction-codes has little affect on the speed of backups, you should activate it as shown here. On the other hand, you shouldn't activate the Verify-data-during-backup option. When it's on, it doubles your backup time. Furthermore, running a compare operation is a more reliable way to verify your data. That's why you should leave this option set to No as shown here.

The Set-archived-attribute-on-each-file option lets you specify whether or not *PC-Fullbak+* turns off the archive bit for each file when it's backed up. In order to do incremental backups, you accept the default setting of Yes as shown here. If, however, you want to do differential backups, you need to reset this option to No after you do a full backup. Then, you can set up *PC-Fullbak+* to do an incremental backup that doesn't turn off the archive bits. Similarly, if you want to use a backup to transfer files to another PC, you should specify No for this option so you don't interrupt your regular schedule of backups.

The next two options, Backup-new/updated-files-only and Append-files-to-previous-backup, are used for incremental backups. As you can guess, if you set both of these options to Yes, you can do an appended incremental backup.

The Warn-before-overwriting-existing-data option lets you select the type of warnings you want the program to display. The Any-not-backup setting shown here warns you if a backup diskette contains data on it other than data from an earlier backup. This is the most useful setting because it can save you from accidentally losing regular files by overwriting them with backups.

I recommend that you don't use the Backup-using-script-file option because script files are not a useful feature. I'll explain why later. So for now, just set this option to No. Then, the following two script file options are disabled as shown here. Similarly, backing up by date is of little use, so I recommend that you set the Backup-by-date option to No.

You probably won't ever need to change the DMA-setting option. When it's set to Fast as shown here, *PC-Fullbak+* uses the fastest memory access possible. If, however, you find that this setting causes your computer to lock-up when you run a backup operation, you should select the Slower setting for this option.

The Compare-options category   Figure PC-3 shows the five options you can set for the Compare function. The first option lets you specify which hard drive you want to use for the compare. The second option lets you specify the type of drive you want to use for your backups. The type of drive you specify with this option must be the same type as the one you specified for the backup operation.

The third option, Compare-using-point-and-shoot-feature, lets you activate the file-list feature that *PC-Fullbak+* calls the *point-and-shoot feature*. This feature lets you select the files you want to compare using a file list instead of having to enter a file specification. Since a file list is easier to use, you probably want to set this option to Yes as shown here. If, however, you decide to use a file specification, you set this feature to No. Then, you set the Path-to-compare option like this:

```
\*.*
```

And you set the Compare-subdirectories-also option to Yes.

The Restore-options category   Figure PC-4 shows you the six options you can set for the Restore function. Once again, the first option lets you specify the hard drive you want to use for the restore. The second option lets you specify the type of drive you're going to restore from. The Warn-before-overwriting-existing-files option lets you specify whether the program will warn you before it replaces a file on the hard disk with a file from a backup, so I recommend that you set it to Yes. The Restore-using-point-and-shoot-feature option lets you activate the file-list feature that I just described. Generally, you activate this feature and use it for restore operations. Otherwise, you have to use the next two options to enter file specifications.

The List-options category   The List function lets you print or display a listing of the files that are on a backup set. But if you use the point-and-shoot feature that *PC-Fullbak+* provides, you shouldn't need to use this feature. Since I recommend that you use the point-and-shoot feature, I won't show you how to set the options for the List function.

Utility 3: PC-Fullbak+ **137**

Figure PC-3 The Options screen with the Compare-options category displayed

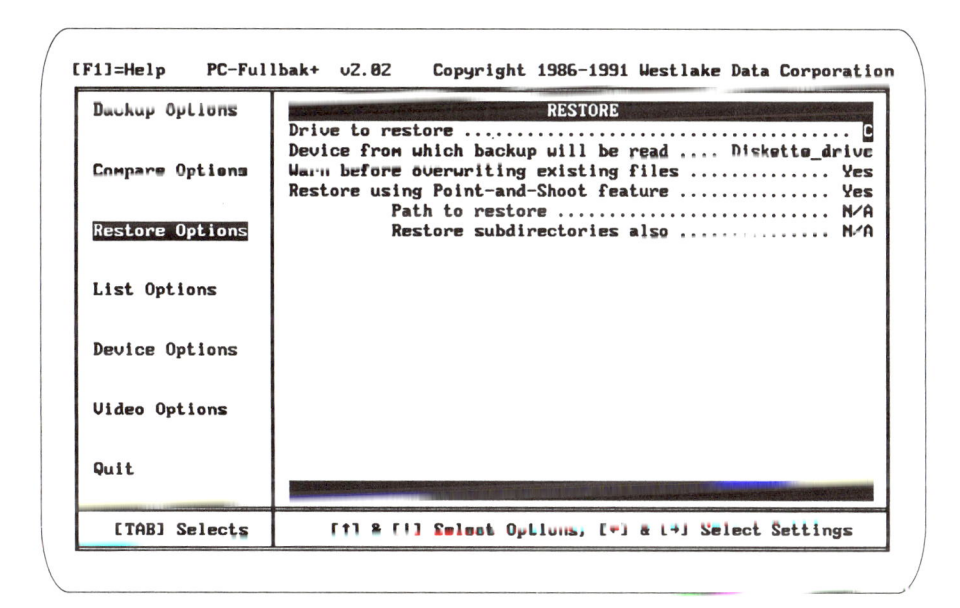

Figure PC-4 The Options screen with the Restore-options category displayed

The Device-options category Figure PC-5 shows you the three groups of options in this category. You use these options to define the device that you're backing up to. Since you'll probably use only one type of device for your backups, you shouldn't need to set all of these options. And since this chapter focuses on how to use a backup utility with diskettes, I'll present only the diskette drive options.

The first option in figure PC-5 lets you specify which diskette drive you want to use for your backups. Here, the A drive is selected. The next option lets you specify the capacity of diskettes you want to use in the drive. If the drive you selected is a 5-1/4 inch drive, you can select the 360 setting for standard-capacity diskettes or the 1.2 setting shown here for high-capacity diskettes. Similarly, if the drive you selected is a 3-1/2 inch drive, you can select the 720 setting for standard-capacity diskettes or the 1.44 setting for high-capacity diskettes.

The Format-to-use option lets you indicate whether you want to format backup diskettes using the DOS format or the *PC-Fullbak+* proprietary format. Since the proprietary format is faster and stores more data on each diskette, you should use it.

You should set the Reformat-during-every-backup option to No as shown here. This way, *PC-Fullbak+* will format backup diskettes only if they weren't previously formatted. Otherwise, the utility will format each diskette every time you back up. This is unnecessary, and it wastes time.

The Estimate-#-of-diskettes-required option controls whether you get an estimate of the number of diskettes required for a backup operation. Since it's useful to know whether you have enough diskettes available for a backup, I recommend that you set this option to Yes as shown here.

The Change-of-diskette-detection option controls how *PC-Fullbak+* detects diskettes. The setting shown here causes the program to automatically detect when a diskette is inserted during an operation. Then, the program continues without requiring further keystrokes from the user. Since this setting works best with most PCs, you'll probably want to use it.

The Video-options category Since you shouldn't need to change the two Video options that *PC-Fullbak+* provides, I'm not going to show them here. If, however, you have an older CGA monitor, you may need to activate the Eliminate-video-snow option to get a clearer display on your monitor.

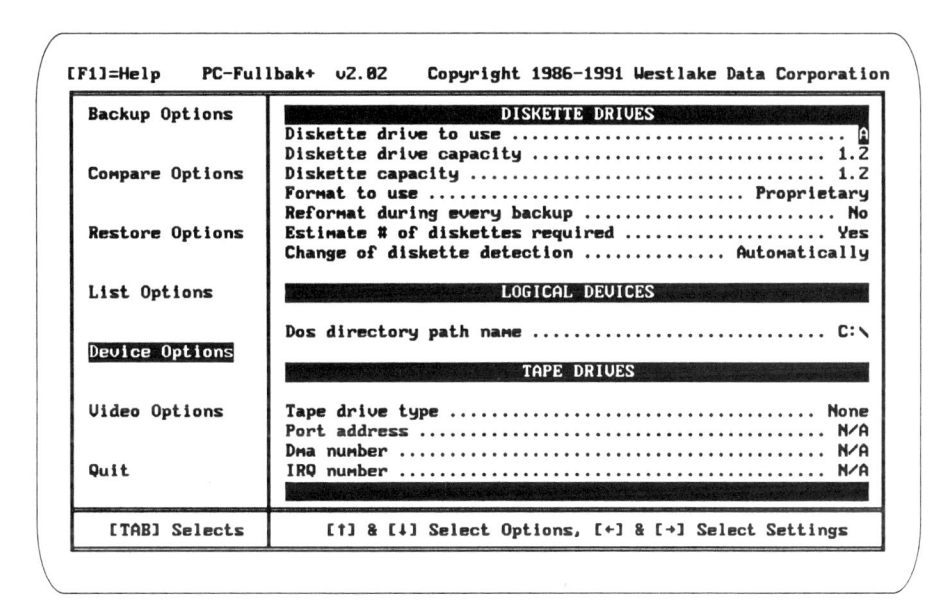

```
[F1]=Help    PC-Fullbak+  v2.02    Copyright 1986-1991 Westlake Data Corporation

Backup Options                          DISKETTE DRIVES
                   Diskette drive to use ..................................... A
                   Diskette drive capacity ................................. 1.2
Compare Options    Diskette capacity ....................................... 1.2
                   Format to use ................................... Proprietary
                   Reformat during every backup ............................. No
Restore Options    Estimate # of diskettes required ........................ Yes
                   Change of diskette detection ................... Automatically

List Options                            LOGICAL DEVICES

                   Dos directory path name ................................. C:\
Device Options
                                          TAPE DRIVES

Video Options      Tape drive type ........................................ None
                   Port address ............................................ N/A
                   Dma number .............................................. N/A
Quit               IRQ number .............................................. N/A

   [TAB] Selects        [↑] & [↓] Select Options, [←] & [→] Select Settings
```

Figure PC-5   The Options screen with the Device-options category displayed

The Quit function   To exit the Options screen, you select the Quit function. The program then displays the screen shown in figure PC-6. If you want the settings you just made to be the default settings, you select Yes as shown here. Then, *PC-Fullbak+* will use these settings the next time you start the utility. On the other hand, if you want to use the current settings for a backup or restore operation, but you don't want to affect the default settings, you select No.

How to do a backup

To start a backup operation, you select the Backup function from the main screen previously shown in figure PC-1. *PC-Fullbak+* then displays a screen like the one shown in figure PC-7 part 1. Here, you can see that the program displays several of the backup options that are in effect for the current backup operation. If these options aren't the ones you want, you must select the Quit function from the menu line to return to the main screen. Then, you

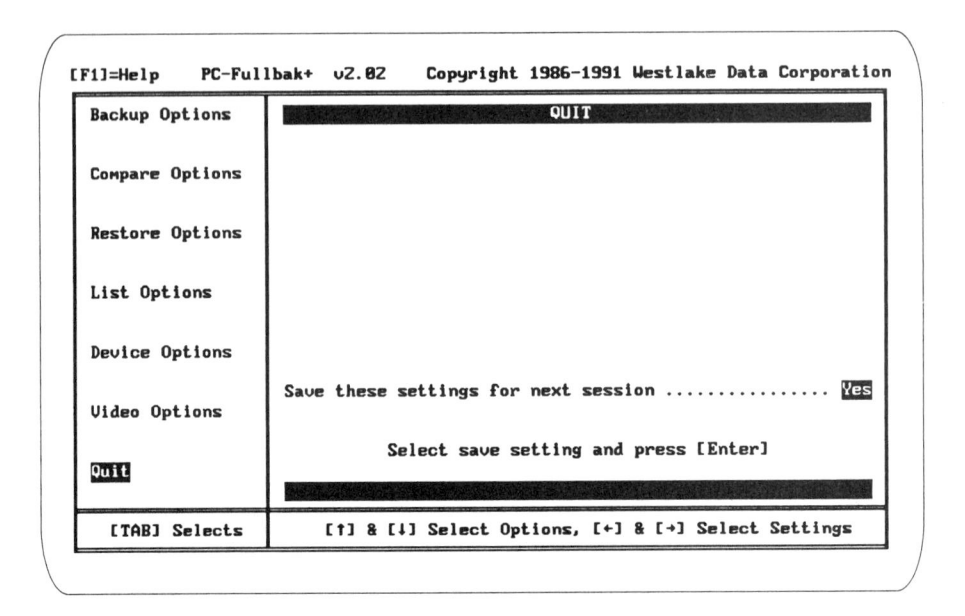

```
[F1]=Help    PC-Fullbak+  v2.02    Copyright 1986-1991 Westlake Data Corporation

Backup Options                        QUIT

Compare Options

Restore Options

List Options

Device Options
                        Save these settings for next session .............. Yes
Video Options
                               Select save setting and press [Enter]
Quit

[TAB] Selects        [↑] & [↓] Select Options, [←] & [→] Select Settings
```

Figure PC-6   The Options screen with the Quit function displayed

can use the Options function to change them. If, for example, *PC-Fullbak+* is set to back up the C drive, but you want to back up the D drive, you must go to the Options screen to change this option.

In other words, once you select the Backup function and *PC-Fullbak+* displays this screen, you can only select the files you want to back up. Consequently, if you don't want to use the default settings for a backup, you must set the backup options from the Options screen before you select the Backup function.

How to do a full backup   Figure PC-7 shows you how to do a full backup of drive C. Part 1 shows the screen that's displayed when you select the Backup function. If the backup options are set correctly, you select the Run function from this screen to start the backup. Then, the program displays a file listing on the left of the screen as shown in part 2 of figure PC-7.

You use the file listing to select the files you want to back up. To select all the files for a full backup, you highlight the root directory and press the Spacebar. Then, *PC-Fullbak+* puts a marker next to every directory and file

Utility 3: PC-Fullbak+   **141**

Part 1:

First, you select the Backup function to display this screen; then, you select the Run function.

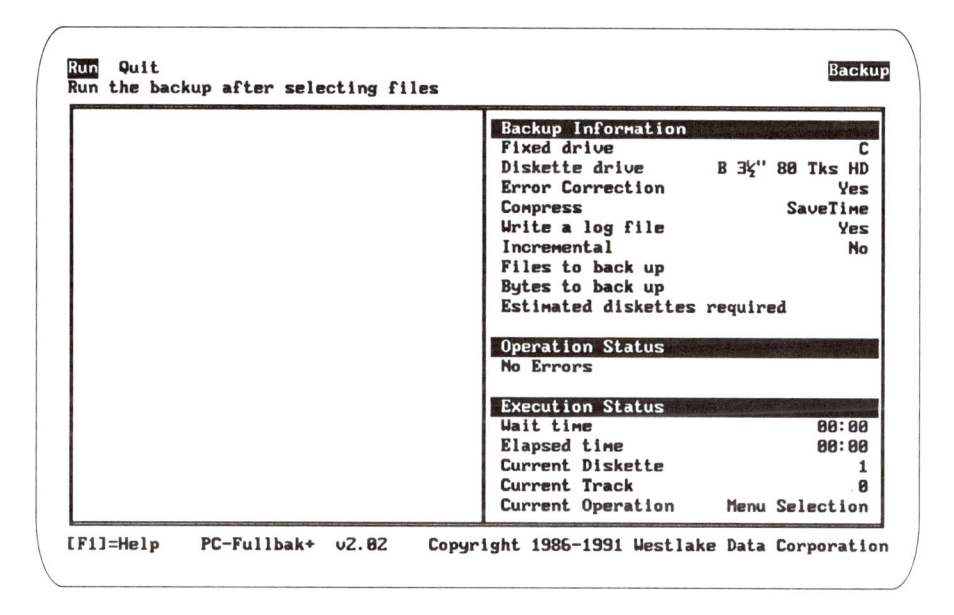

```
┌──────────────────────────────────────────────────────────────────────┐
│ Run  Quit                                                    Backup  │
│ Run the backup after selecting files                                 │
│                          ┌────────────────────────────────────────┐  │
│                          │ Backup Information                     │  │
│                          │ Fixed drive                         C  │  │
│                          │ Diskette drive          B 3½" 80 Tks HD│  │
│                          │ Error Correction                   Yes │  │
│                          │ Compress                      SaveTime │  │
│                          │ Write a log file                   Yes │  │
│                          │ Incremental                         No │  │
│                          │ Files to back up                       │  │
│                          │ Bytes to back up                       │  │
│                          │ Estimated diskettes required           │  │
│                          ├────────────────────────────────────────┤  │
│                          │ Operation Status                       │  │
│                          │ No Errors                              │  │
│                          ├────────────────────────────────────────┤  │
│                          │ Execution Status                       │  │
│                          │ Wait time                        00:00 │  │
│                          │ Elapsed time                     00:00 │  │
│                          │ Current Diskette                     1 │  │
│                          │ Current Track                        0 │  │
│                          │ Current Operation       Menu Selection │  │
│                          └────────────────────────────────────────┘  │
│ [F1]=Help    PC-Fullbak+ v2.02   Copyright 1986-1991 Westlake Data Corporation │
└──────────────────────────────────────────────────────────────────────┘
```

Figure PC-7   How you do a full backup (Part 1 of 4)

Part 2:

First, you highlight the root directory; then, you press the Spacebar to select all the files for a backup.

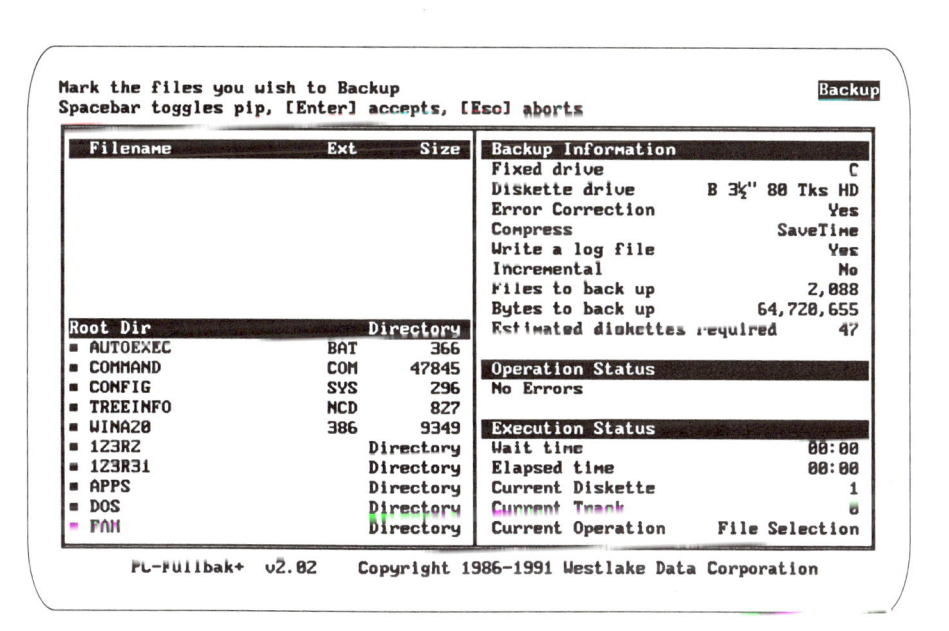

```
┌──────────────────────────────────────────────────────────────────────┐
│ Mark the files you wish to Backup                            Backup  │
│ Spacebar toggles pip, [Enter] accepts, [Esc] aborts                  │
│ ┌───────────────────────────────┐ ┌────────────────────────────────┐ │
│ │ Filename      Ext       Size  │ │ Backup Information             │ │
│ │                               │ │ Fixed drive                 C  │ │
│ │                               │ │ Diskette drive  B 3½" 80 Tks HD│ │
│ │                               │ │ Error Correction           Yes │ │
│ │                               │ │ Compress              SaveTime │ │
│ │                               │ │ Write a log file           Yes │ │
│ │                               │ │ Incremental                 No │ │
│ │                               │ │ Files to back up         2,088 │ │
│ │                               │ │ Bytes to back up    64,720,655 │ │
│ │ Root Dir         Directory    │ │ Estimated diskettes required 47│ │
│ │ ■ AUTOEXEC    BAT       366   │ ├────────────────────────────────┤ │
│ │ ■ COMMAND     COM     47845   │ │ Operation Status               │ │
│ │ ■ CONFIG      SYS       296   │ │ No Errors                      │ │
│ │ ■ TREEINFO    NCD       827   │ ├────────────────────────────────┤ │
│ │ ■ WINA20      386      9349   │ │ Execution Status               │ │
│ │ ■ 123R2            Directory  │ │ Wait time                00:00 │ │
│ │ ■ 123R31           Directory  │ │ Elapsed time             00:00 │ │
│ │ ■ APPS             Directory  │ │ Current Diskette             1 │ │
│ │ ■ DOS              Directory  │ │ Current Track                0 │ │
│ │ ■ FAN              Directory  │ │ Current Operation File Selection│ │
│ └───────────────────────────────┘ └────────────────────────────────┘ │
│         PC-Fullbak+ v2.02   Copyright 1986-1991 Westlake Data Corporation │
└──────────────────────────────────────────────────────────────────────┘
```

Figure PC-7   How you do a full backup (Part 2 of 4)

as shown in part 2 of figure PC-7. The markers indicate that all the directories and files have been selected for the backup. Notice also that on the right of the screen, *PC-Fullbak+* shows you the number of files and bytes of storage that are required for the files you selected. Here, you can see that 2,088 files and 64,720,655 bytes will be backed up. In addition, the program estimates that the operation will require 47 diskettes.

When you press the Enter key to start the backup operation, a screen like the one in part 3 of figure PC-7 is displayed. At the top of this screen, you're prompted to insert the appropriate diskette. This screen also shows you the progress of the backup operation.

Part 4 of figure PC-7 shows you the screen that's displayed when the backup operation is complete. This screen summarizes information on the backup operation. By reviewing this information, you can verify that the backup worked as you expected.

Earlier, you learned how to set a backup option that causes *PC-Fullbak+* to write a log file for a backup. This log file is named FULLBAK.LOG, and it's stored in the root directory of the hard drive that you backed up. The program uses the log file to keep track of the directories and files that are backed up. This log file makes restoring files easier because it displays a file listing that you can use to select files.

Each time you back up a hard disk with the log-file option active, *PC-Fullbak+* adds the new backup information to the file. This is what you want to happen if you're doing an appended incremental backup because these files are appended to the same set of backup diskettes. But *PC-Fullbak+* also adds the new backup information to the log file when you do another full backup. As a result, the log file will soon contain information for many full backup operations. This makes the log file much harder to use when you need to restore data from your backups. That's why I recommend that you delete the FULLBAK.LOG file each time before you do a full backup.

How to do an appended incremental backup Since you probably won't set up *PC-Fullbak+* to do an appended incremental backup by default, you must first set at least two backup options to do this type of backup. As a review, figure PC-8 shows the Backup-options screen that you access by selecting the Options function from the main screen. At the Backup-options screen, you set the Backup-new/updated-file-only option and the

Utility 3: PC-Fullbak+   **143**

Part 3:

The screen that prompts you for the appropriate diskette and that displays the progress of the backup operation.

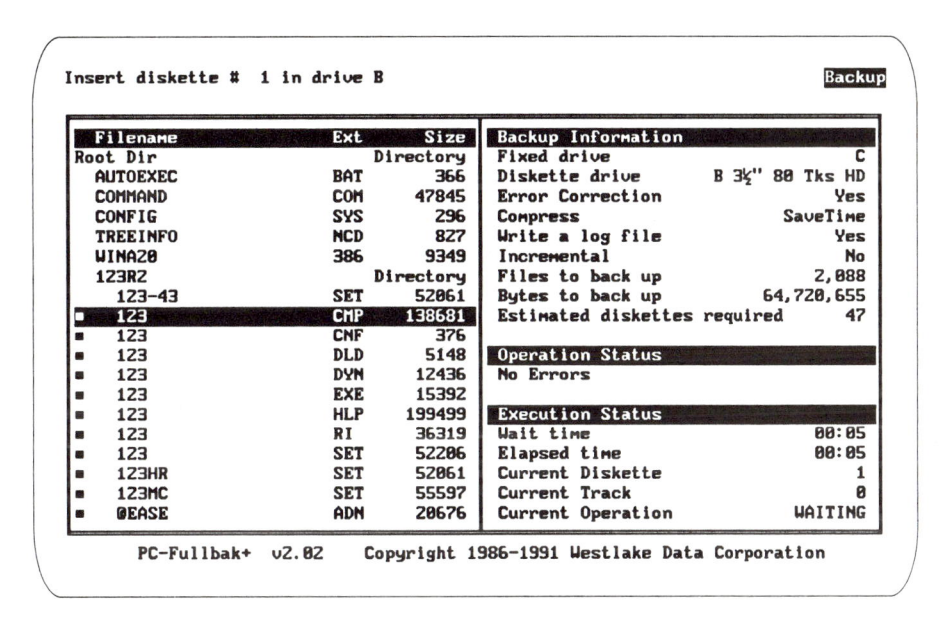

```
Insert diskette # 1 in drive B                                    Backup

 Filename         Ext      Size   Backup Information
Root Dir                Directory  Fixed drive                         C
  AUTOEXEC        BAT       366   Diskette drive          B 3½" 80 Tks HD
  COMMAND         COM     47845   Error Correction                   Yes
  CONFIG          SYS       296   Compress                      SaveTime
  TREEINFO        NCD       827   Write a log file                   Yes
  WINA20          386      9349   Incremental                         No
  123R2                Directory  Files to back up                 2,088
    123-43        SET     52061   Bytes to back up            64,720,655
 ▫  123           CMP    138681   Estimated diskettes required        47
 ▪  123           CNF       376
 ▪  123           DLD      5148   Operation Status
 ▪  123           DYN     12436   No Errors
 ▪  123           EXE     15392
 ▪  123           HLP    199499   Execution Status
 ▪  123           RI      36319   Wait time                        00:05
 ▪  123           SET     52206   Elapsed time                     00:05
 ▪  123HR         SET     52061   Current Diskette                     1
 ▪  123MC         SET     55597   Current Track                        0
 ▪  @EASE         ADN     20676   Current Operation              WAITING

         PC-Fullbak+  v2.02   Copyright 1986-1991 Westlake Data Corporation
```

Figure PC-7   How you do a full backup (Part 3 of 4)

Part 4:

The screen that's displayed at the end of the backup that summarizes the backup operation.

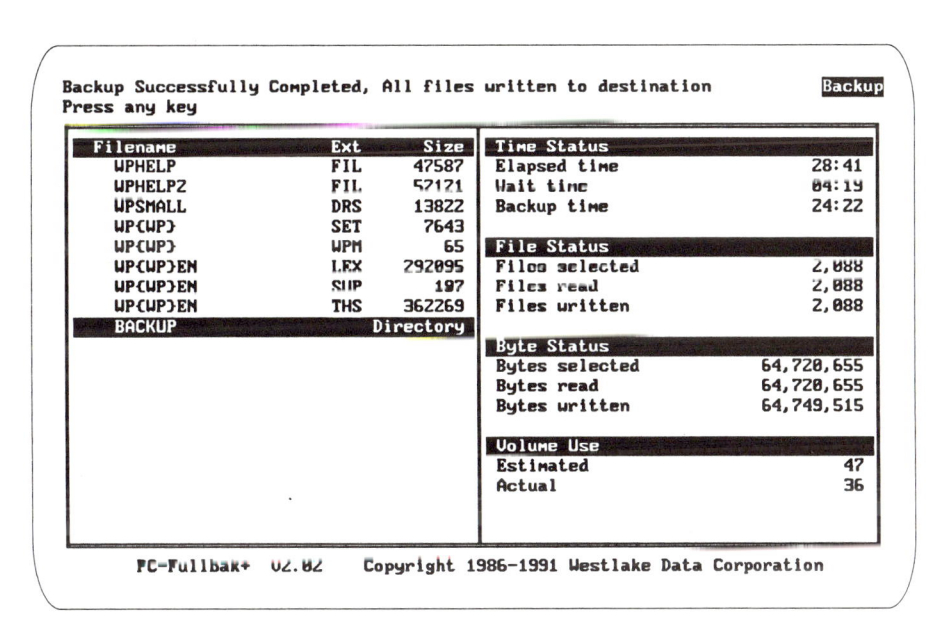

```
Backup Successfully Completed, All files written to destination   Backup
Press any key

 Filename         Ext      Size   Time Status
  WPHELP          FIL     47587   Elapsed time                     28:41
  WPHELP2         FIL     52121   Wait time                        04:19
  WPSMALL         DRS     13822   Backup time                      24:22
  WP{WP}          SET      7643
  WP{WP}          WPM       65    File Status
  WP{WP}EN        LEX    292095   Files selected                   2,088
  WP{WP}EN        SUP       197   Files read                       2,088
  WP{WP}EN        THS    362269   Files written                    2,088
  BACKUP               Directory
                                  Byte Status
                                  Bytes selected              64,720,655
                                  Bytes read                  64,720,655
                                  Bytes written               64,749,515

                                  Volume Use
                                  Estimated                           47
                                  Actual                              36

         PC-Fullbak+  v2.02   Copyright 1986-1991 Westlake Data Corporation
```

Figure PC-7   How you do a full backup (Part 4 of 4)

```
[F1]=Help    PC-Fullbak+  v2.02    Copyright 1986-1991 Westlake Data Corporation

Backup Options                            BACKUP
                    Drive to backup ..................................... D
                    Device to which backup will be written ... Diskette_drive
Compare Options     Write a log file .................................. Yes
                    Data Compression method ...................... SaveTime
                    Include error correction code ..................... Yes
Restore Options     Verify data during backup .......................... No
                    Set archived attribute on each file ............... Yes
                    Backup new/updated files only ..................... Yes
List Options        Append files to previous backup ................... Yes
                    Warn before overwriting existing data .... Any not backup
                    Backup using script file ........................... No
Device Options              Script file to use ....................... N/A
                            Script file name ......................... N/A
                    DMA setting ...................................... Fast
Video Options       Backup by date ..................................... No
                            Start date ............................... N/A
                            End date ................................. N/A
Quit


[TAB] Selects       [↑] & [↓] Select Options, [←] & [→] Select Settings
```

Figure PC-8   The Backup options set to do an appended incremental backup

Append-files-to-previous-backup option to Yes. Then, you return to the main screen by selecting the Quit function without saving the settings you just changed.

Figure PC-9 shows you how to run the backup operation. Part 1 shows the screen that's displayed after you select the Backup function from the main menu. The information that's displayed on the right of the screen reflects the settings from figure PC-8. To start this backup, you select the Run function.

Then, the program displays a file listing on the left of the screen. At this screen, you highlight the root directory. Then, you press the Spacebar to select all of the directories below the root directory. *PC-Fullbak+* displays markers next to all of the selected directories as shown in part 2 of figure PC-9. It also displays the number of files that it found in these directories that require backing up. In part 2, for example, you can see that there are 23 files that need to be backed up. And you can see that the backup requires one diskette.

Utility 3: PC-Fullbak+ **145**

Part 1:

PC-Fullbak+ set to do an appended incremental backup.

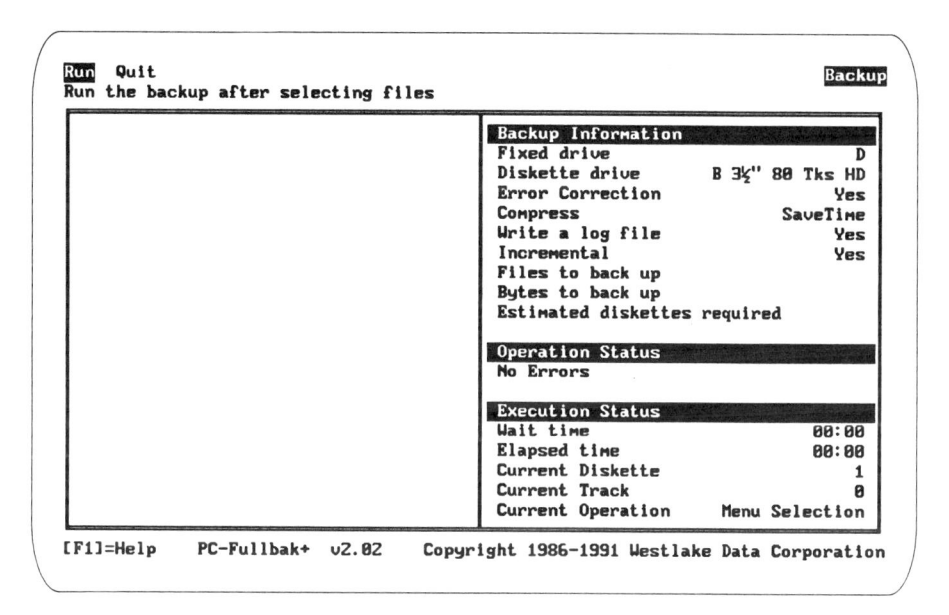

```
Run  Quit                                                    Backup
Run the backup after selecting files

                              ┌─Backup Information─────────────────┐
                              │ Fixed drive                     D  │
                              │ Diskette drive       B 3½" 80 Tks HD│
                              │ Error Correction              Yes  │
                              │ Compress                  SaveTime │
                              │ Write a log file              Yes  │
                              │ Incremental                   Yes  │
                              │ Files to back up                   │
                              │ Bytes to back up                   │
                              │ Estimated diskettes required       │
                              ├─Operation Status───────────────────┤
                              │ No Errors                          │
                              ├─Execution Status───────────────────┤
                              │ Wait time                   00:00  │
                              │ Elapsed time                00:00  │
                              │ Current Diskette                1  │
                              │ Current Track                   0  │
                              │ Current Operation    Menu Selection│
                              └────────────────────────────────────┘
 [F1]=Help    PC-Fullbak+  v2.02    Copyright 1986-1991 Westlake Data Corporation
```

Figure PC-9   How you do an appended incremental backup (Part 1 of 2)

Part 2:

The screen that's displayed at the start of an appended incremental backup.

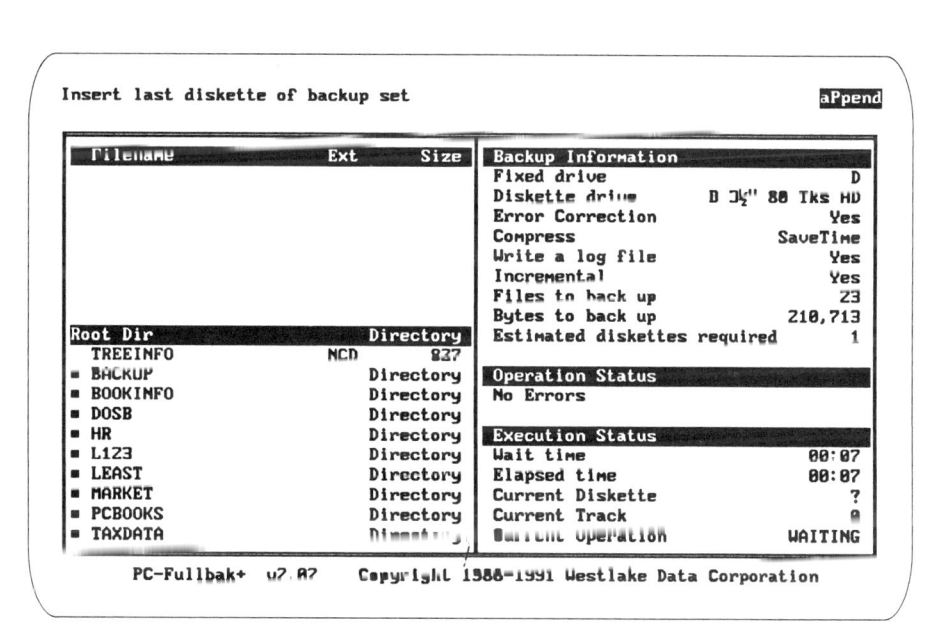

```
Insert last diskette of backup set                          aPpend

┌─Filename──────────Ext─────Size─┐┌─Backup Information─────────────┐
│                                ││ Fixed drive                 D  │
│                                ││ Diskette drive   B 3½" 80 Tks HD│
│                                ││ Error Correction          Yes  │
│                                ││ Compress              SaveTime │
│                                ││ Write a log file          Yes  │
│                                ││ Incremental               Yes  │
│                                ││ Files to back up           23  │
│                                ││ Bytes to back up      210,713  │
├─Root Dir──────────────Directory┤│ Estimated diskettes required  1│
│  TREEINFO         NCD      837 │├─Operation Status───────────────┤
│ ■ BACKUP              Directory││ No Errors                      │
│ ■ BOOKINFO            Directory│├─Execution Status───────────────┤
│ ■ DOSB                Directory││                                │
│ ■ HR                  Directory││                                │
│ ■ L123                Directory││ Wait time              00:07   │
│ ■ LEAST               Directory││ Elapsed time           00:07   │
│ ■ MARKET              Directory││ Current Diskette           ?   │
│ ■ PCBOOKS             Directory││ Current Track              0   │
│ ■ TAXDATA             Directory││ Current Operation    WAITING   │
└────────────────────────────────┘└────────────────────────────────┘
          PC-Fullbak+  v2.02    Copyright 1986-1991 Westlake Data Corporation
```

Figure PC-9   How you do an appended incremental backup (Part 2 of 2)

When you press the Enter key, *PC-Fullbak+* starts the backup operation and displays a message at the top of the screen telling you to insert the last diskette of the backup set. When you insert this diskette, the program displays the progress of the operation as it appends the files to the diskette. If the backup fills the diskette, the program prompts you for another diskette. When the backup is completed, the program displays a summary screen like the one it displays for a full backup.

How to do a partial backup   To do a partial backup, first you set the appropriate backup options from the Options screen. Then, you select the Backup function from the main screen. Next, you select the Run option from the Backup screen. *PC-Fullbak+* then displays file listing like the one shown in figure PC-10 part 1. To back up all the files in a directory, you use the Up and Down arrow keys to highlight the directory; then, you press the Spacebar. To back up individual files, first you use the arrow keys to move the highlight to the appropriate directory. Then, you use the Insert key to expand the directory and list its files. Next, you move the highlight to the file you want, and you press the Spacebar to select it.

If, for example, you want to back up all the files in the \QA\FILES directory, you must first move to the \QA directory as shown in part 1 of figure PC-10. Then, you press the Insert key to expand this directory. Next, you move to the \FILES subdirectory as shown in part 2 of figure PC-10. When you press the Spacebar with this subdirectory highlighted, *PC-Fullbak+* selects all the files in the subdirectory as shown here. Finally, you press the Enter key to start the backup operation.

How to restore files

Before you start a restore operation, you must set the Restore options using the Options screen. Then, you select the Restore function from the main screen. Next, a screen like the one shown in PC-11 part 1 is displayed. This is the screen you use whether you're doing a full or a partial restore.

As I mentioned earlier, the program uses a log file to automatically keep track of the directories and files that have been backed up. The name of this file is FULLBAK.LOG, and it's stored in the root directory of the drive you backed up. When you start a restore operation, the program uses this log file

Utility 3: PC-Fullbak+   **147**

Part 1:

The screen you use to select files for a partial backup.

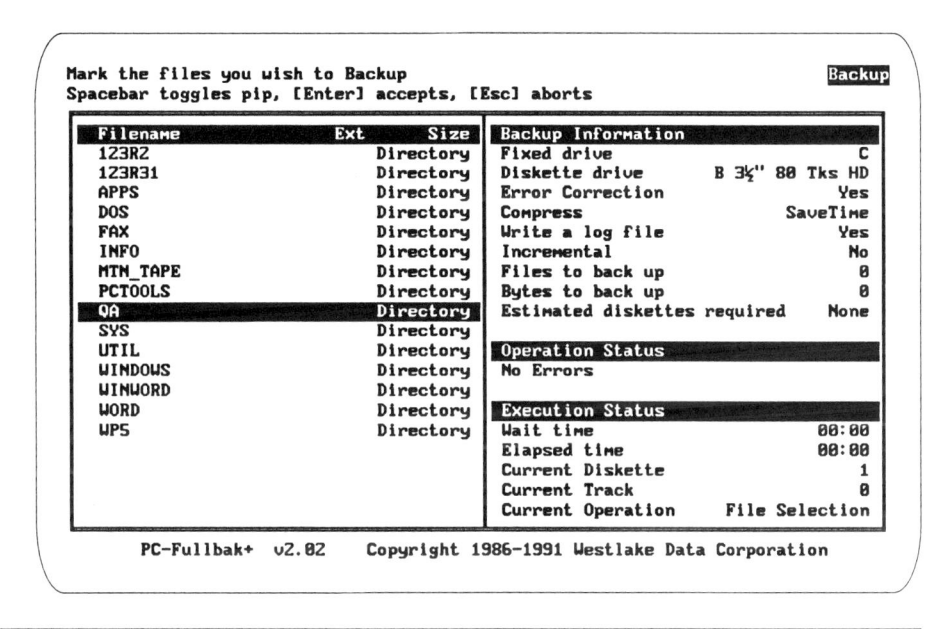

```
Mark the files you wish to Backup                                    Backup
Spacebar toggles pip, [Enter] accepts, [Esc] aborts

 Filename        Ext      Size    Backup Information
 123R2                    Directory  Fixed drive                          C
 123R31                   Directory  Diskette drive        B 3½" 80 Tks HD
 APPS                     Directory  Error Correction                   Yes
 DOS                      Directory  Compress                      SaveTime
 FAX                      Directory  Write a log file                   Yes
 INFO                     Directory  Incremental                         No
 MTM_TAPE                 Directory  Files to back up                     0
 PCTOOLS                  Directory  Bytes to back up                     0
 QA                       Directory  Estimated diskettes required      None
 SYS                      Directory
 UTIL                     Directory  Operation Status
 WINDOWS                  Directory  No Errors
 WINWORD                  Directory
 WORD                     Directory  Execution Status
 WPS                      Directory  Wait time                        00:00
                                     Elapsed time                     00:00
                                     Current Diskette                     1
                                     Current Track                        0
                                     Current Operation       File Selection

         PC-Fullbak+  v2.02   Copyright 1986-1991 Westlake Data Corporation
```

Figure PC-10 How you select files for a partial backup (Part 1 of 2)

Part 2:

All the files in the \QA\FILES directory are selected for the backup.

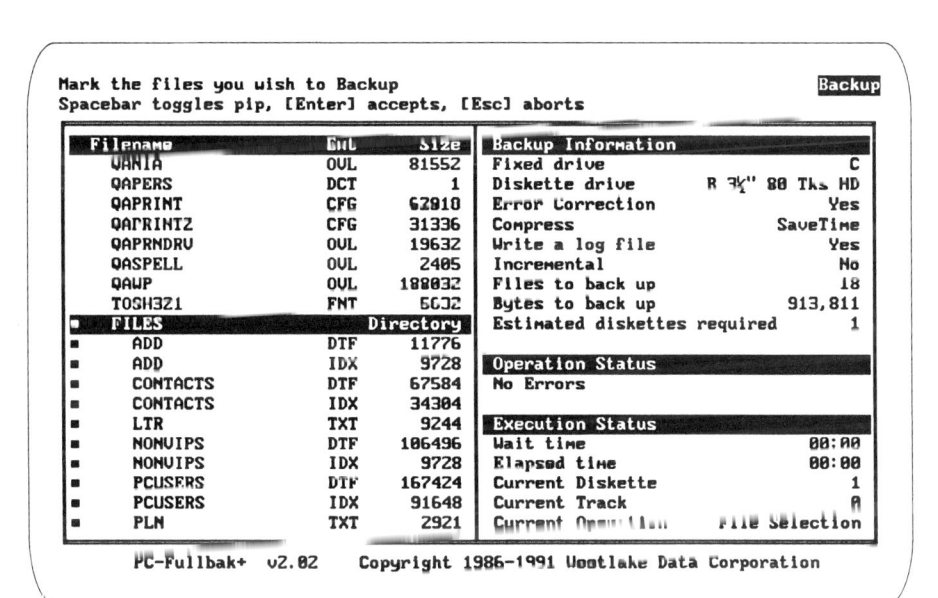

```
Mark the files you wish to Backup                                    Backup
Spacebar toggles pip, [Enter] accepts, [Esc] aborts

 Filename        Ext      Size    Backup Information
 QANTA           OVL     81552    Fixed drive                          C
 QAPERS          DCT         1    Diskette drive        B 3½" 80 Tks HD
 QAPRINT         CFG     62910    Error Correction                   Yes
 QAPRINTZ        CFG     31336    Compress                      SaveTime
 QAPRNDRV        OVL     19632    Write a log file                   Yes
 QASPELL         OVL      2405    Incremental                         No
 QAWP            OVL    188032    Files to back up                    18
 TOSH3Z1         FNT      6032    Bytes to back up               913,811
 FILES                   Directory  Estimated diskettes required       1
 ■  ADD          DTF     11776
 ■  ADD          IDX      9728    Operation Status
 ■  CONTACTS     DTF     67584    No Errors
 ■  CONTACTS     IDX     34304
 ■  LTR          TXT      9244    Execution Status
 ■  NONVIPS      DTF    106496    Wait time                        00:00
 ■  NONVIPS      IDX      9728    Elapsed time                     00:00
 ■  PCUSERS      DTF    167424    Current Diskette                     1
 ■  PCUSERS      IDX     91648    Current Track                        0
 ■  PLN          TXT      2921    Current Operation       File Selection

         PC-Fullbak+  v2.02   Copyright 1986-1991 Westlake Data Corporation
```

Figure PC-10 How you select files for a partial backup (Part 2 of 2)

to display a file listing like the listing you use to back up files. *PC-Fullbak+* calls this the point-and-shoot feature because you can point to and select the directories and files you want.

Unfortunately, if your hard disk fails and all of your files are lost, the FULLBAK.LOG file is lost too. As a result, you won't be able use the point-and-shoot feature to restore your data. Instead, you have to deactivate this feature on the Restore-options screen. Then, you have to set the Path-to-restore and the Restore-subdirectories-also options to enter a file specification for the restore operation.

How to do a full restore   Figure PC-11 shows you how do a full restore of drive D. When you select the Restore function from the main screen, a screen like the one shown in part 1 of figure PC-11 is displayed. After you verify that the appropriate restore options are set, you select the Run function from this screen. Then, a file listing like the one in part 2 of figure PC-11 is displayed. To select all of the files for a full restore, you highlight the backup date you want, and you press the Spacebar. To confirm your selection, the program puts a marker next to each selected file. Also at this screen, the program shows you the number of files and bytes that the operation will restore.

When you press the Enter key to start the restore operation, a screen like the one shown in part 3 of figure PC-11 is displayed. At the top of this screen, the program prompts you for the first diskette from the backup set. As the data from each diskette is restored, the program prompts you for the next diskette in the set. In addition, *PC-Fullbak+* displays the progress of the restore operation. When it completes the restore, the program displays information that summarizes the operation.

How to do a partial restore   Figure PC-12 shows you how to do a partial restore. First, you select the Restore function from the main screen, followed by the Run function from the Restore screen. Then, a screen with a file listing like the one in part 1 of figure PC-12 is displayed.

To select the directories and files you want to restore, you use the Up and Down arrow keys to move to the directories and files you want. And you use the Spacebar to select them. In part 1 of figure PC-12, for example, I selected five files that I wanted restored.

Utility 3: PC-Fullbak+   149

Part 1:

PC-Fullbak+ set to do a restore.

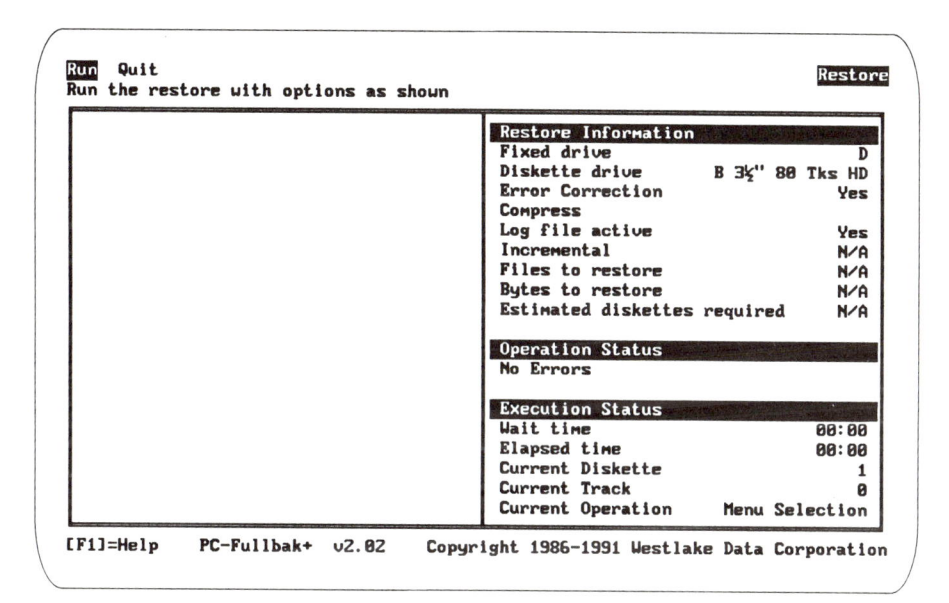

```
 Run  Quit                                                      Restore
 Run the restore with options as shown

                                     ┌─Restore Information──────────────┐
                                     │ Fixed drive                     D│
                                     │ Diskette drive      B 3½" 80 Tks HD│
                                     │ Error Correction              Yes│
                                     │ Compress                         │
                                     │ Log file active               Yes│
                                     │ Incremental                   N/A│
                                     │ Files to restore              N/A│
                                     │ Bytes to restore              N/A│
                                     │ Estimated diskettes required  N/A│
                                     └──────────────────────────────────┘
                                     ┌─Operation Status─────────────────┐
                                     │ No Errors                        │
                                     └──────────────────────────────────┘
                                     ┌─Execution Status─────────────────┐
                                     │ Wait time                  00:00 │
                                     │ Elapsed time               00:00 │
                                     │ Current Diskette               1 │
                                     │ Current Track                  0 │
                                     │ Current Operation   Menu Selection│
                                     └──────────────────────────────────┘
 [F1]=Help     PC-Fullbak+  v2.02   Copyright 1986-1991 Westlake Data Corporation
```

Figure PC-11   How you do a full restore (Part 1 of 3)

Part 2:

First, you highlight the backup date you want to restore; then, you press the Spacebar.

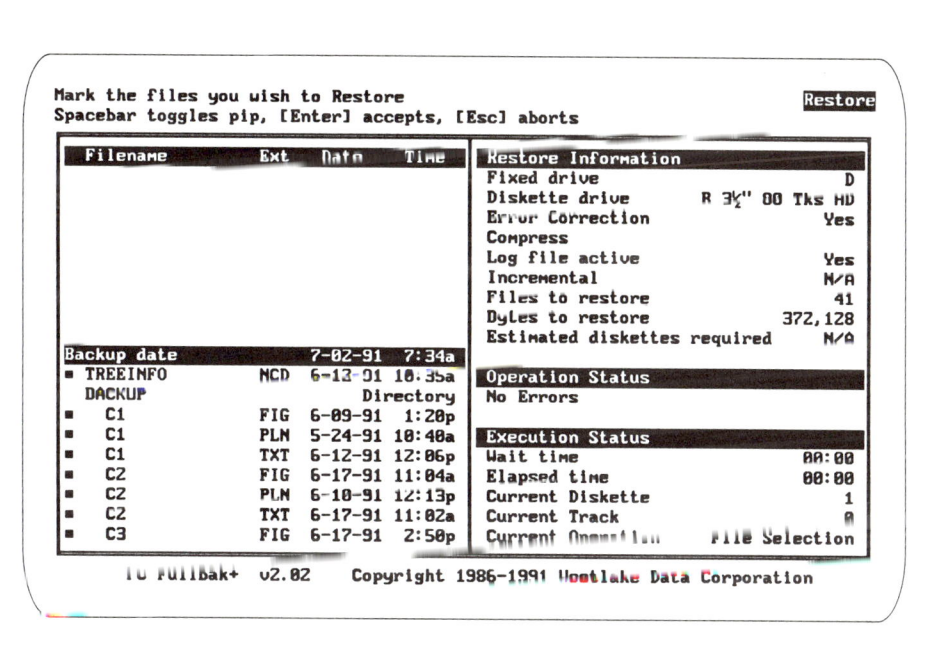

```
 Mark the files you wish to Restore                             Restore
 Spacebar toggles pip, [Enter] accepts, [Esc] aborts

 ┌ Filename      Ext    Date     Time ┐┌─Restore Information──────────────┐
 │                                    ││ Fixed drive                     D│
 │                                    ││ Diskette drive      B 3½" 80 Tks HD│
 │                                    ││ Error Correction              Yes│
 │                                    ││ Compress                         │
 │                                    ││ Log file active               Yes│
 │                                    ││ Incremental                   N/A│
 │                                    ││ Files to restore               41│
 │                                    ││ Bytes to restore          372,128│
 │                                    ││ Estimated diskettes required  N/A│
 │ Backup date          7-02-91  7:34a│└──────────────────────────────────┘
 │ ■ TREEINFO      NCD  6-13-91 10:35a│┌─Operation Status─────────────────┐
 │   DACKUP             Directory     ││ No Errors                        │
 │ ■ C1            FIG  6-09-91  1:20p│└──────────────────────────────────┘
 │ ■ C1            PLN  5-24-91 10:40a│┌─Execution Status─────────────────┐
 │ ■ C1            TXT  6-12-91 12:06p││ Wait time                  00:00 │
 │ ■ C2            FIG  6-17-91 11:04a││ Elapsed time               00:00 │
 │ ■ C2            PLN  6-10-91 12:13p││ Current Diskette               1 │
 │ ■ C2            TXT  6-17-91 11:02a││ Current Track                  0 │
 │ ■ C3            FIG  6-17-91  2:50p││ Current Operation  File Selection│
 └────────────────────────────────────┘└──────────────────────────────────┘
          PC-Fullbak+  v2.02    Copyright 1986-1991 Westlake Data Corporation
```

Figure PC-11   How you do a full restore (Part 2 of 3)

Part 3:

The screen that prompts you for the appropriate diskette and that shows the progress of the restore operation.

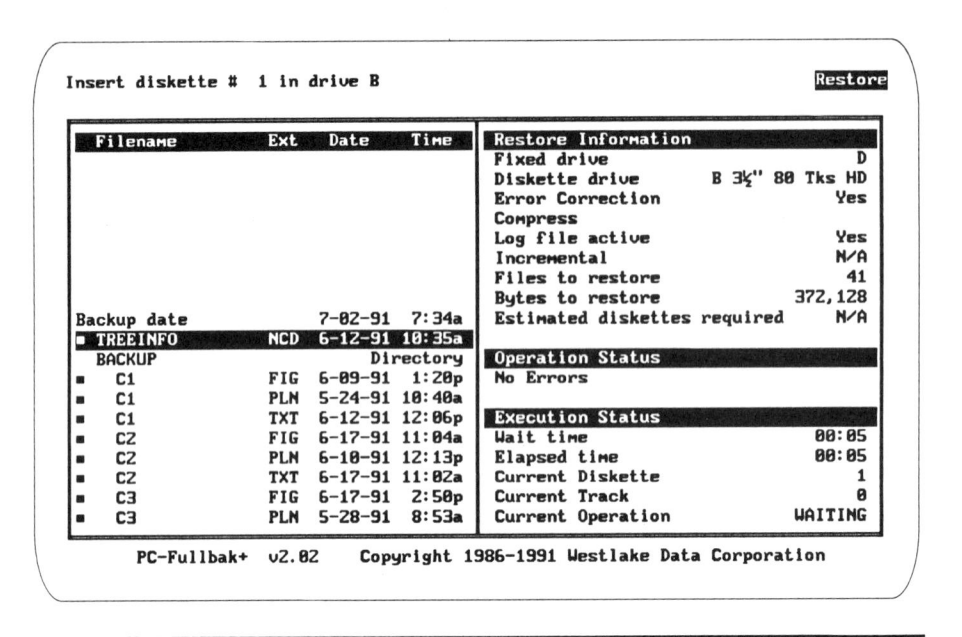

```
Insert diskette #  1 in drive B                                    Restore

 Filename      Ext    Date      Time   Restore Information
                                       Fixed drive                          D
                                       Diskette drive         B 3½" 80 Tks HD
                                       Error Correction                   Yes
                                       Compress
                                       Log file active                    Yes
                                       Incremental                        N/A
                                       Files to restore                    41
                                       Bytes to restore               372,128
 Backup date          7-02-91   7:34a  Estimated diskettes required       N/A
■ TREEINFO      NCD  6-12-91  10:35a
  BACKUP                    Directory  Operation Status
■   C1          FIG  6-09-91   1:20p   No Errors
■   C1          PLN  5-24-91  10:40a
■   C1          TXT  6-12-91  12:06p   Execution Status
■   C2          FIG  6-17-91  11:04a   Wait time                        00:05
■   C2          PLN  6-10-91  12:13p   Elapsed time                     00:05
■   C2          TXT  6-17-91  11:02a   Current Diskette                     1
■   C3          FIG  6-17-91   2:50p   Current Track                        0
■   C3          PLN  5-28-91   8:53a   Current Operation              WAITING

        PC-Fullbak+  v2.02   Copyright 1986-1991 Westlake Data Corporation
```

Figure PC-11 How you do a full restore (Part 3 of 3)

When you press the Enter key to begin the restore operation, a screen like the one in part 2 of figure PC-12 is displayed. At the top of this screen, the program displays a prompt that tells you which diskette to insert from the backup set. Here, for example, the prompt tells you to insert the fourth diskette because that's the diskette that has the selected files. This speeds up the restore operation because you don't have to insert the first backup diskette and continue through the set until you find the diskette that has the files you need.

How to compare a backup

As a rule, you can count on *PC-Fullbak+* to do reliable backups. So you don't need to compare every backup you do. You should, however, compare the first backup you do since the program doesn't perform an automatic compare as part of a setup operation. Then, as you use the utility, you should occasionally compare a backup to make sure that the utility continues to

Utility 3: PC-Fullbak+ **151**

Part 1:

First, you highlight the files that you want to restore from a backup set; then, you press the Spacebar.

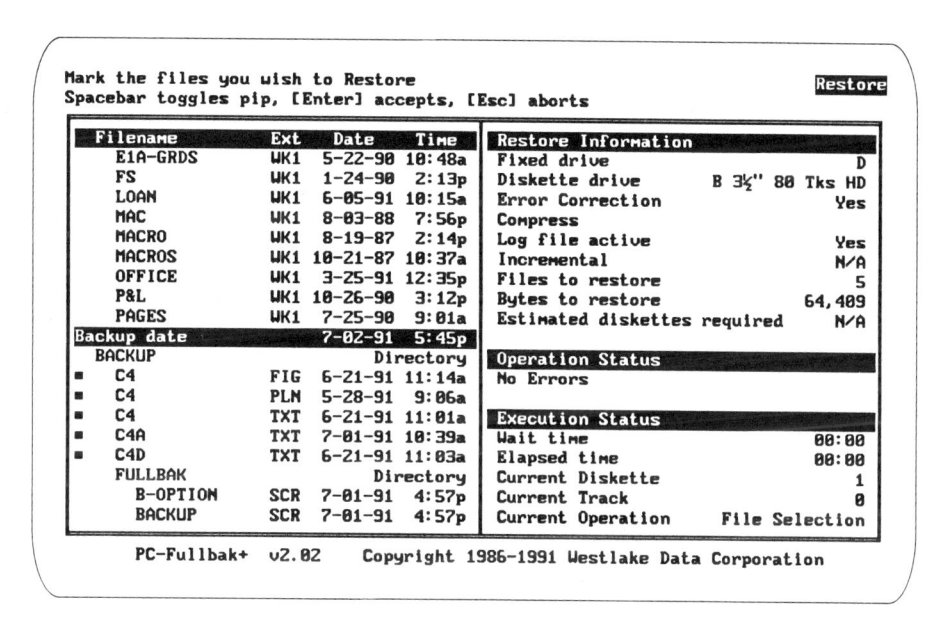

```
Mark the files you wish to Restore                              Restore
Spacebar toggles pip, [Enter] accepts, [Esc] aborts

  Filename      Ext    Date      Time     Restore Information
  E1A-GRDS      WK1   5-22-90  10:48a     Fixed drive                    D
  FS            WK1   1-24-90   2:13p     Diskette drive      B 3½" 80 Tks HD
  LOAN          WK1   6-05-91  10:15a     Error Correction             Yes
  MAC           WK1   8-03-88   7:56p     Compress
  MACRO         WK1   8-19-87   2:14p     Log file active              Yes
  MACROS        WK1  10-21-87  10:37a     Incremental                  N/A
  OFFICE        WK1   3-25-91  12:35p     Files to restore               5
  P&L           WK1  10-26-90   3:12p     Bytes to restore          64,409
  PAGES         WK1   7-25-90   9:01a     Estimated diskettes required N/A
Backup date                 7-02-91   5:45p
  BACKUP                         Directory   Operation Status
■ C4            FIG   6-21-91  11:14a     No Errors
■ C4            PLN   5-28-91   9:06a
■ C4            TXT   6-21-91  11:01a     Execution Status
■ C4A           TXT   7-01-91  10:39a     Wait time                  00:00
■ C4D           TXT   6-21-91  11:03a     Elapsed time               00:00
  FULLBAK                        Directory   Current Diskette             1
    B-OPTION    SCR   7-01-91   4:57p     Current Track                  0
    BACKUP      SCR   7-01-91   4:57p     Current Operation   File Selection

            PC-Fullbak+  v2.02   Copyright 1986-1991 Westlake Data Corporation
```

Figure PC-12 How you do a partial restore (Part 1 of 2)

Part 2:

The screen that prompts you for the appropriate diskette and that shows the progress of the restore operation.

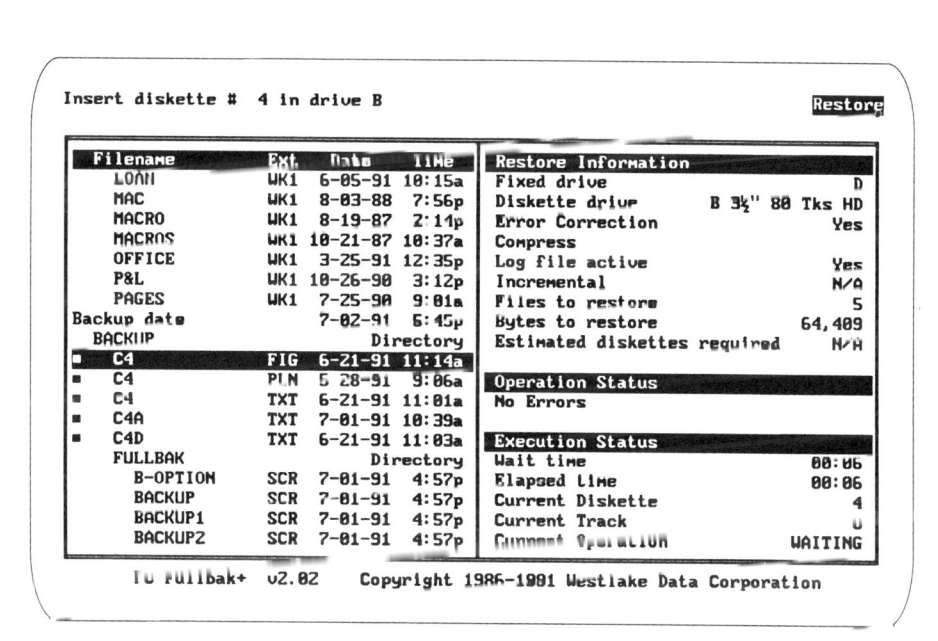

```
Insert diskette #  4 in drive B                                 Restore

  Filename      Ext    Date      Time     Restore Information
  LOAN          WK1   6-05-91  10:15a     Fixed drive                    D
  MAC           WK1   8-03-88   7:56p     Diskette drive      B 3½" 80 Tks HD
  MACRO         WK1   8-19-87   2:14p     Error Correction             Yes
  MACROS        WK1  10-21-87  10:37a     Compress
  OFFICE        WK1   3-25-91  12:35p     Log file active              Yes
  P&L           WK1  10-26-90   3:12p     Incremental                  N/A
  PAGES         WK1   7-25-90   9:01a     Files to restore               5
Backup date                 7-02-91   5:45p     Bytes to restore          64,409
  BACKUP                         Directory   Estimated diskettes required N/A
■ C4            FIG   6-21-91  11:14a
■ C4            PLN   5-28-91   9:06a     Operation Status
■ C4            TXT   6-21-91  11:01a     No Errors
  C4A           TXT   7-01-91  10:39a
■ C4D           TXT   6-21-91  11:03a     Execution Status
  FULLBAK                        Directory   Wait time                  00:06
    B-OPTION    SCR   7-01-91   4:57p     Elapsed time               00:06
    BACKUP      SCR   7-01-91   4:57p     Current Diskette               4
    BACKUP1     SCR   7-01-91   4:57p     Current Track                  0
    BACKUP2     SCR   7-01-91   4:57p     Current Operation        WAITING

            PC-Fullbak+  v2.02   Copyright 1986-1991 Westlake Data Corporation
```

Figure PC-12 How you do a partial restore (Part 2 of 2)

work correctly. This way, you can be confident that your backups will work when you need to restore data from them. The best time to compare a backup is right after you back up, before any changes occur.

To compare a backup, you use the same basic procedure that you use to restore files. First, you select the Compare function from the main screen. Then, you highlight the root directory and press the Spacebar to select all the files. Next, the program prompts you to insert the first diskette from the backup set. The program reads the data from the diskette and compares it to the data on the hard disk. After it reads each diskette, *PC-Fullbak+* prompts you to insert the next diskette until it has compared the data on all the diskettes in the backup set. Finally, the program displays a screen that summarizes the compare operation, and it reports any errors it has found. If it hasn't found any errors, you know that the backup is reliable. If it has found errors, you need to determine how to correct them so you can get a reliable backup set.

How to automate your backups

So far, you've learned how to set options and select functions from various menus to set up and run different types of backups. In some cases, this is the most efficient way to do a backup. However, *PC-Fullbak+* provides several features that you can use to automate your backups. In particular, it provides a menu called FBEZ that you can use for the most common types of backups. In addition, you can use special commands in batch files to run your backups. Since you generally do the same backup operations over and over again, automating your backups can significantly improve your backup procedures.

PC-Fullbak+ also provides another feature that you can use to automate your backups called *script files*. These files work differently from the setup files that most backup utilities provide. Instead of setting all of the options for a backup, you can use these script files to store the names of the files you want selected for a backup operation. That way, you don't have to go through the process of selecting the files for a partial backup operation. Unfortunately, script files don't automatically include the files that you later add to a directory. For most people, this limitation makes using script files more trouble than they're worth. So I won't cover them here.

```
PC-Fullbak+EZ v2.00
Copyright 1988 - 1990 Westlake Data Corporation


              ┌─────────────────────────────────┐
              │  Back up All files              │
              │  Add all New files to backup set│
              │  Compare backup to source       │
              │  Restore backup to source       │
              │  Select source Fixed drive      │
              │  Select Destination             │
              │  Exit to DOS                    │
              └─────────────────────────────────┘



              Fixed drive to back up  : C
              Destination             : B
```

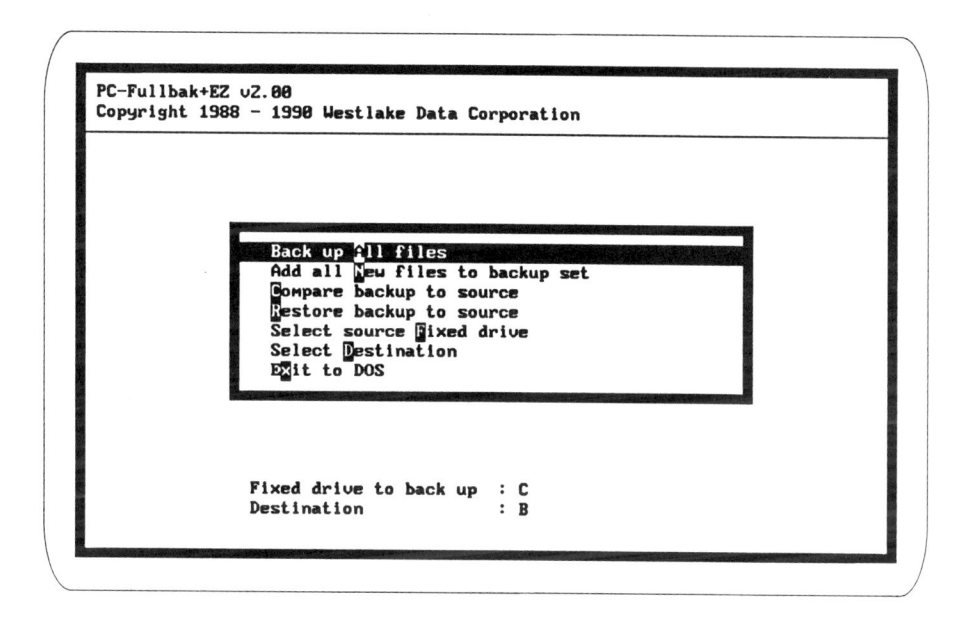

Figure PC-13   The simplified FBEZ menu

How to use the FBEZ menu   Figure PC-13 shows you the *PC-Fullbak+EZ*, or *FBEZ* menu. As you can see, this is a simplified menu that has the most common backup, restore, and compare options on it. If your backup plan calls for just full and appended incremental backups, this menu makes *PC-Fullbak+* much easier to use.

To use the FBEZ menu, first you change to the appropriate drive and the \FULLBAK program directory. Then, you enter the following command at the DOS command prompt and press the Enter key:

    fbez

To use the menu, you can select the function you want by either using the arrow keys and the Enter key, or by pressing the letter that's emphasized in each function. To select the Back-up-all-files function, for example, you press the letter *A*.

The first function on the FBEZ menu, Back-up-all-files, starts a full backup. The Add-all-new-files-to-backup-set function starts an appended incremental backup. As you might expect, the Compare-backup-to-source function starts a full compare. And the Restore-backup-to-source function starts a full restore. The Exit-to-DOS function stops the FBEZ program and returns you to the DOS command prompt.

To specify the hard drive you want to back up, you select the Select-source-fixed-drive function. Each time you do that, the drive that's displayed at the bottom of the screen changes. Similarly, you select the Select-destination function to specify the diskette drive you want to use for a backup.

The main disadvantage of the FBEZ menu is that it only lets you do a full restore. In addition, this menu deactivates the log feature that *PC-Fullbak+* provides. As a result, if you need to do a partial restore, you can't just start *PC-Fullbak+* and use the point-and-shoot feature. Instead, you must activate the Restore options screen. Then, you use the Path-to-restore and the Restore-subdirectories-also options to set the path and file specification for the files you want to restore.

How to use command line options in batch files   *PC-Fullbak+* provides *command line options* that you can include with the FULLBAK command to start the utility. These command line options are presented in figure PC-14. You can use these options to do any operation you can start from the *PC-Fullbak+* menus.

Of course, remembering how to use all of these command line options is difficult. So you probably won't want to use them in place of the *PC-Fullbak+* menu system. But you can put the command line options in batch files. Once you do that, you don't have to remember how to use them. Then, you can just execute the batch file to start your backup instead of using the *PC-Fullbak+* menus to set all the options that are required for that backup operation.

To illustrate, figure PC-15 presents four batch files. These batch files include the commands that are required to change to the appropriate drive and directory to start *PC-Fullbak+*. Also, the batch files for full backups include commands that delete the log file as I recommended earlier. In addition, these batch files include the command line options that are required for full and appended incremental backups. The first batch file does a full backup of drive C. The second batch file does an appended incremental backup of drive C. And so on.

Utility 3: PC-Fullbak+   155

Command syntax

```
FULLBAK file-spec [/switches]
```

Switch	Function
/B	Backup
/P	Append the files to the end of a previous backup set
/SD	Include the subdirectories under the file-spec in the backup
/I	Incremental backup

Typical commands	Description
`FULLBAK C:\*.* /B /SD`	Starts utility and does a full backup of drive C.
`FULLBAK D:\*.* /B /SD /I /P`	Starts the utility and does an appended incremental backup of drive D.
`FULLBAK C:\DATA\*.* /B`	Starts the utility and does a partial backup that includes all of the files in the \DATA directory on drive C.

Figure PC-14 The most useful command line options that you can use with PC-Fullbak+

Is PC-Fullbak+ the right utility for your backups?

Now that you've seen how to use *PC-Fullbak+* for the most common backup and restore operations, you should be able to decide if it's the right utility for you. If you compare this program with the other utilities in this chapter, you'll see that it doesn't have quite as many features. In addition, the standard menu system is harder to use for the most common backup operations.

On the other hand, the FREZ menu is probably the easiest menu system available. And at a price of around $50, *PC-Fullbak+* is an excellent value. So if price is an issue and if you can accept the limitations of the FREZ menu system, you should definitely consider this backup utility.

```
FULL-C.BAT

    C:
    DEL C:\FULLBAK.LOG
    CD \FULLBAK
    FULLBAK C:\*.* /B /SD

INC-C.BAT

    C:
    CD \FULLBAK
    FULLBAK C:\*.* /B /SD /I /P

FULL-D.BAT

    C:
    DEL D:\FULLBAK.LOG
    CD \FULLBAK
    FULLBAK D:\*.* /B /SD

INC-D.BAT

    C:
    CD \FULLBAK
    FULLBAK D:\*.* /B /SD /I /P
```

Figure PC-15 Four batch files that you can use with *PC-Fullbak+* to automate the most common backup operations

Terms

point-and-shoot feature
script file
FBEZ menu
command line option

Utility 4: FastBack Plus

FastBack Plus version 3.0 from *Fifth Generation Systems* is probably the most widely used backup utility. In fact, *FastBack Plus* may already be the backup utility that your company uses. If that's the case, you can be confident that your company has selected a capable backup utility. It's fast, and the latest version (3.0) has at least as many features as any other backup utility.

However, of the four utilities presented in this book, *FastBack Plus* is the hardest to use. In addition, it's the most expensive utility with a price of about $120. So if ease of use and price are important considerations, you'll want to look at one of the other utilities presented in this chapter.

Because *FastBack Plus* is a complicated program, it offers many levels of functions and enhancements. As a result, you may see functions or settings in some of the figures in this chapter that aren't explained. When you do, don't worry about them because they aren't crucial to learning how to do the most common backup, restore, and compare operations.

To start *FastBack Plus* from the DOS command prompt, you change to the appropriate drive and directory. Then, you type the following command and press the Enter key:

fb

Figure FB-1 shows you the main screen that's displayed when you start the utility. At the top of the screen, you can see three menu choices: File, Window, and Help. Later, I'll show you how to use the File and Window menus to set up the program so it works more efficiently. You can select one of these menus by moving the mouse cursor to your choice and clicking the left mouse button. Or you can hold down the Alt key and press the highlighted letter in the menu. For example, you use the Alt+F keystroke combination to select the File menu.

Also in figure FB-1, you can see several functions. The Operation function lets you specify whether you want to do a backup or restore operation. The Files function lets you specify whether you want to do a full, incremental, or partial backup. The Choose-files function lets you select the files you want to back up. The From function lets you specify the hard drive you want to back up. The To function lets you specify the diskette drive you want to back up to. And the Start function lets you start the operation you have selected.

Some of the functions in figure FB-1 have a small arrow to their right, others don't. If the function has an arrow, you select the function by clicking the mouse on the arrow until the option you want appears. If the function doesn't have an arrow, you click the mouse on the function. Then, the program displays the options available for that function. To select an option, you click on it with the mouse, and if necessary, you click on the OK function too.

To select a function using the keyboard, you use the Tab key to move the highlight to the function you want. Then, if the function has an arrow, you use the Up and Down arrow keys to select the option you want. If the function you want doesn't have an arrow, you move the highlight to the function and press the Enter key to display the available options. Then, you use the arrow keys or the Tab key to highlight your selection. To select some options, you must also use the Spacebar to confirm your choice. Next, you either press the Enter key to select the option you want, or you move the highlight to the OK option and then press the Enter key.

If at any point you need help, you can press the F1 key. Then, the program displays a Help screen with information on the function you're using. To exit the Help screen, you press the Esc key.

If you're using an earlier version of *FastBack Plus*, your screen won't look like the one in figure FB-1. Figure FB-2, for example, shows the main screen for version 2.10. Here, the Backup menu has been pulled down, and the Destination function has been selected. Even though the screens look quite different, both versions offer the same basic functions. As a result, you can apply much of what you'll learn in this chapter even if you're using an earlier version of *FastBack Plus*.

On the other hand, version 3.0 provides several features not available in earlier versions. In particular, version 3.0 provides for appended incremental

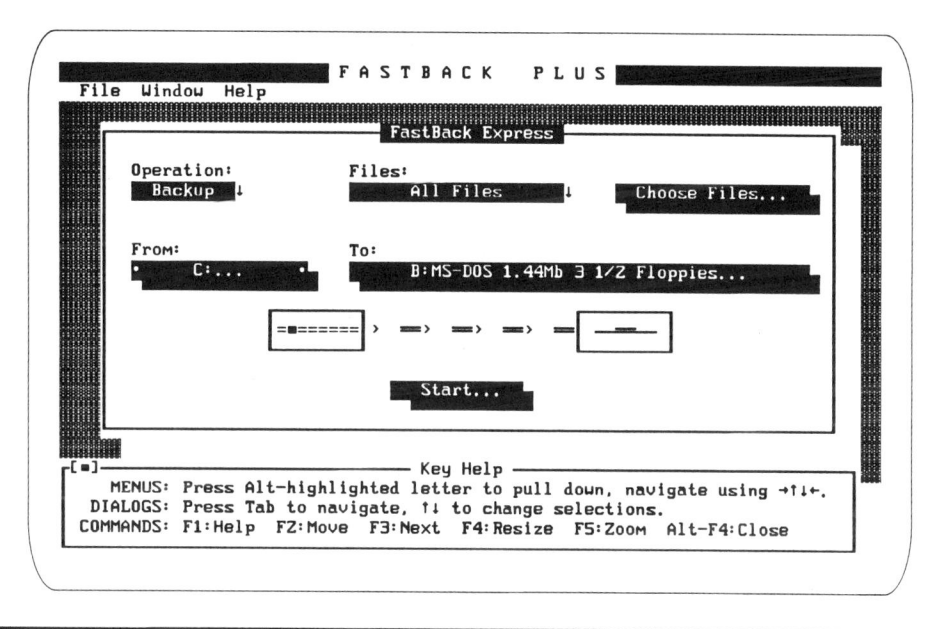

Figure FB-1 The main screen of *FastBack Plus* version 3.0

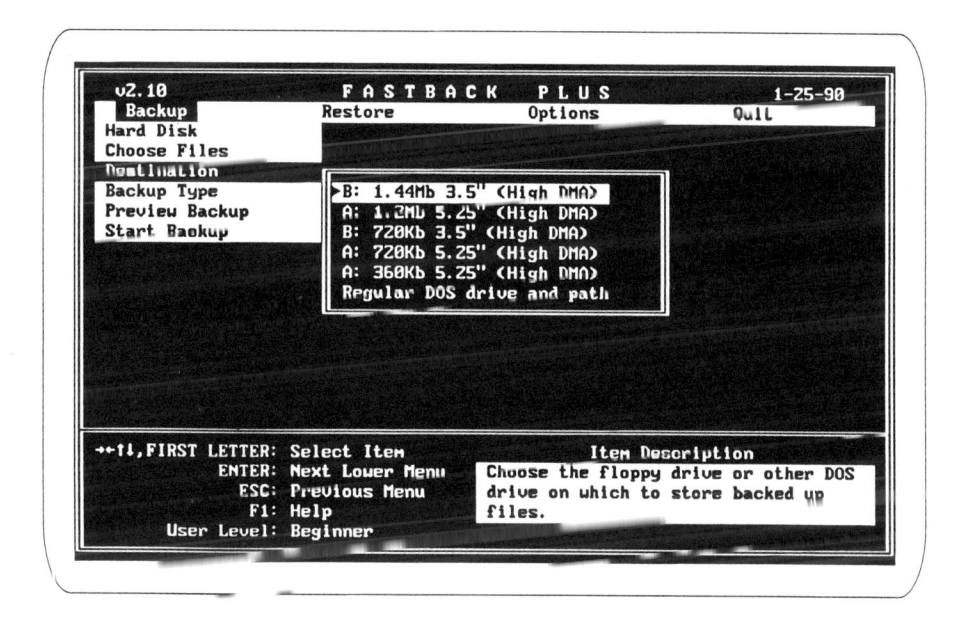

Figure FB-2 The main screen of *FastBack Plus* version 2.10

backups. Since appended incremental backups are more efficient than separate incremental backups, this may be reason enough to upgrade to the latest version of *FastBack Plus*.

How to set up *FastBack Plus*

When you install *FastBack Plus*, it runs a special setup operation. This operation checks your PC hardware and runs a backup test to set up the utility to run at maximum speed. As a result, *FastBack Plus* should work just fine on your PC.

However, you'll probably want to change a couple of options so *FastBack Plus* works more efficiently. For example, I recommend that you change some options so *FastBack Plus* restores files more efficiently than the default settings allow. Then, as you become more familiar with the utility, you may want to change some additional options so *FastBack Plus* works just the way you want it to. You may, for example, want to activate features that offer additional error correction.

Unfortunately, making changes to *FastBack Plus* is hard to do. For instance, if you need to change how it uses your PC hardware, you must use complicated commands that you enter using DOS. As a result, it's easier to simply reinstall the program. And if you want to change some of the options that control the way the program operates, you must use complicated menus. Since I recommend that you change how the program restores files, I'll show you how to use the two menus you need for this purpose: the Window and Options menus.

The Window menu Figure FB-3 shows the Window menu. As you can see, most of the functions on this menu let you control the *windows* that *FastBack Plus* displays. These are the boxes that the program uses to display functions and other information on the screen. Since the default settings for the windows are acceptable, I doubt you'll ever need to change them.

However, you will need to use the Preferences function on this menu. When you select this function, the screen shown in figure FB-4 is displayed. The functions on this screen let you control the sounds that *FastBack Plus* uses, the sensitivity of your mouse, and so on. You may never need to change these settings. But you do need to know how to use the Menu-type

Utility 4: FastBack Plus **161**

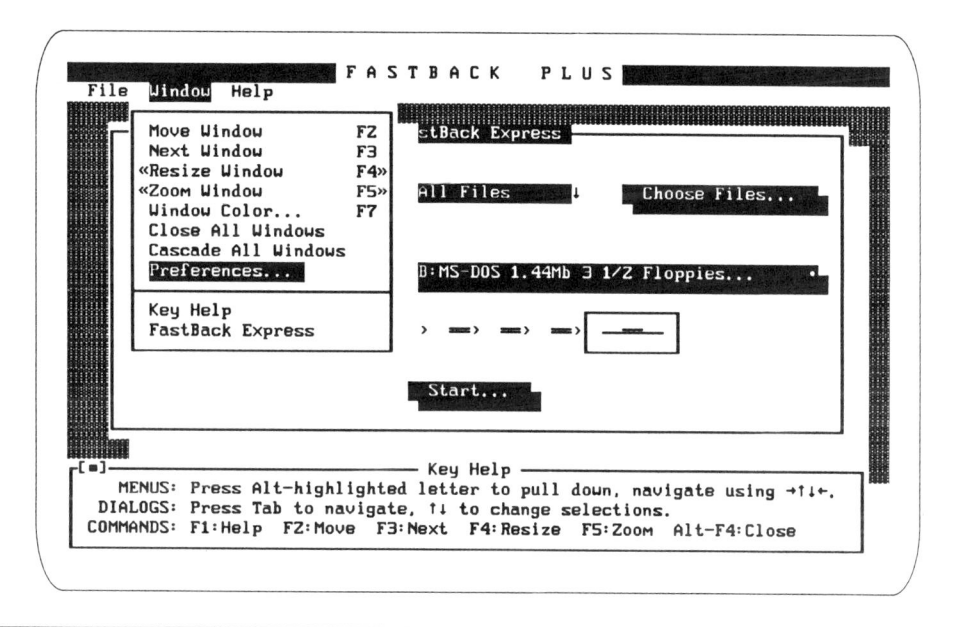

Figure FB-3 The Window menu

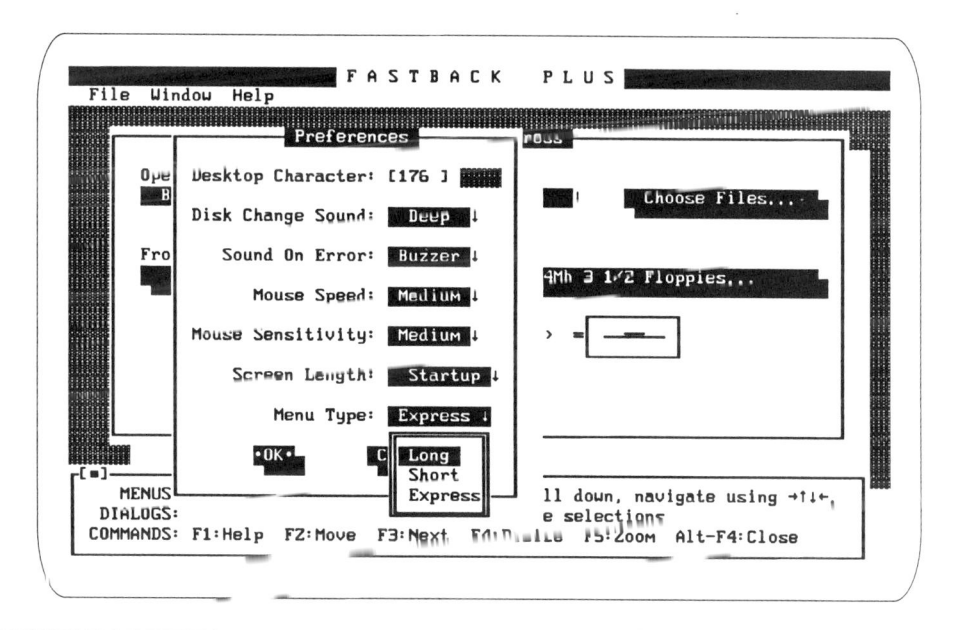

Figure FB-4 The Preferences screen that you access from the Window menu

function. This function lets you control whether *FastBack Plus* uses its Long, Short, or Express menu system. Since the Express menu system is the easiest to use, it's the system that the program uses as the default, and it's the system you've seen so far.

Unfortunately, you need to change to the Long menu system in order to use the Options menu that you need to adjust some other settings. To set up *FastBack Plus* to use the Long menu system, you select the Long option from the Menu-type function shown in figure FB-4. In figure FB-5, you can see the main screen that's displayed under the Long menu system. At the top of the screen, you can see that the Options menu has been added along with several other menus.

The Options menu Figure FB-6 shows you the Options menu. As you can see, the first three functions on this menu are the same ones you access from the Express menu shown in figure FB-1. However, the More-options function shown here is available only when the Long menu system is active. This function takes you to a screen that lets you set several options that affect the operation of *FastBack Plus* including options that affect backup and restore operations.

To illustrate, figure FB-7 shows the Backup-options screen that's displayed when you select the More-options function. Here, the Backup-type option lets you specify the type of backup you want to perform. You can specify a full backup, an incremental backup, or a differential backup, as well as specifying several other options. Since you can specify this information using the Express menu system, you probably won't ever need to use this screen to specify backup type.

The other options shown here are set to the default settings. They control how *FastBack Plus* overwrites files during a backup operation, how it uses diskettes, the level of error correction that's activated, and so on. Since I doubt you'll ever need to change these settings from the defaults, I won't explain them here. Just press the Esc key to exit from the Backup-options screen.

Unlike the default options used to back up files, I recommend that you change two options that are used to restore files. To do that, you must access the Restore-options screen. First, you pull down the Operation menu and select the Restore-files function. Then, you pull down the Options menu and

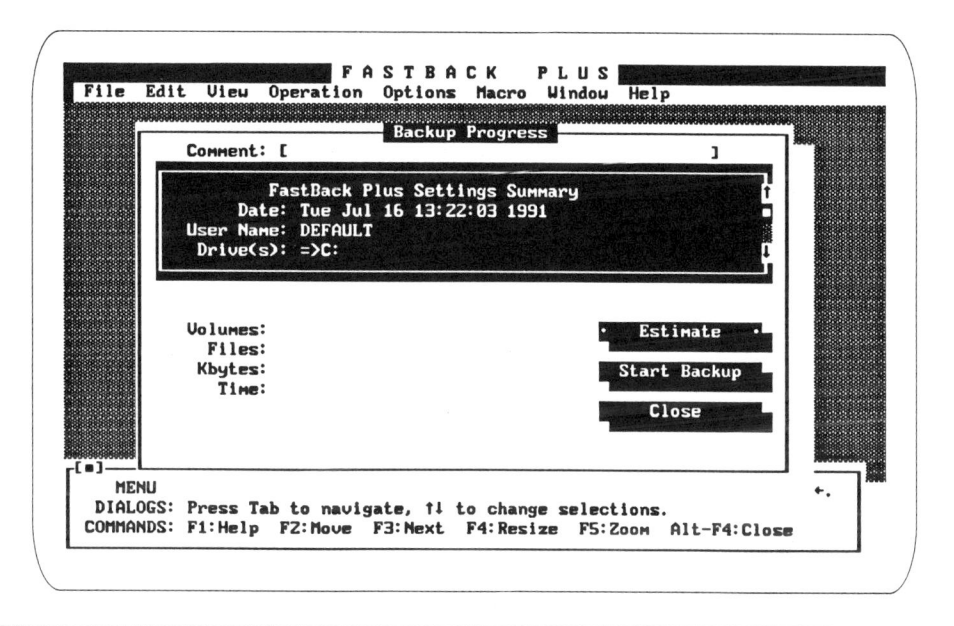

Figure FB-5 The main screen with the Long menu system activated

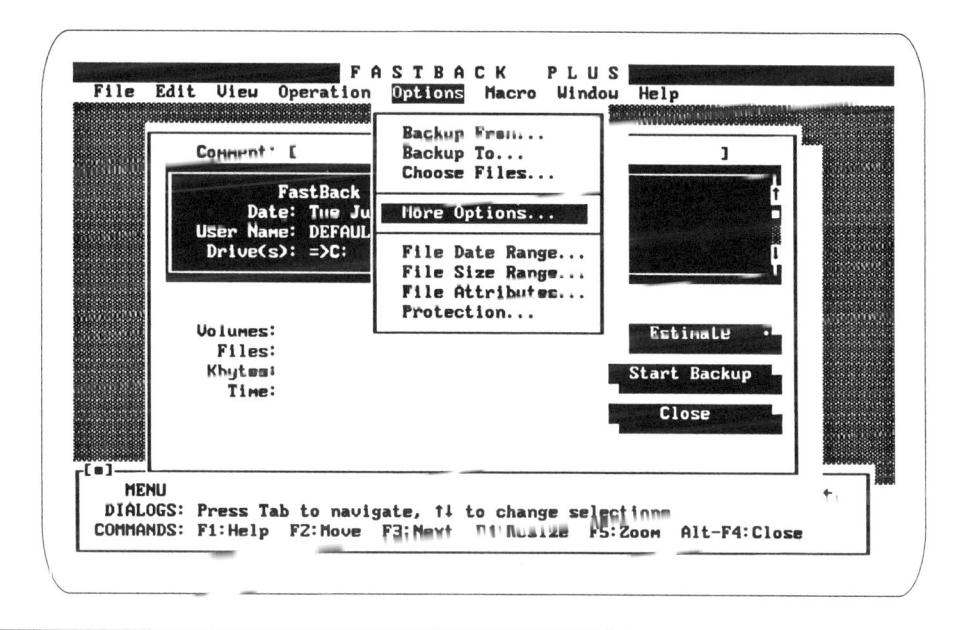

Figure FB-6 The Options menu that's part of the Long menu system

select the More-options function. Now, *FastBack Plus* displays the Restore-options screen shown in figure FB-8.

Most of the options on this screen are set the way you want them. However, you should change the Existing-files option. By default, this option is set to Overwrite-older-only. This setting makes it more difficult to make a mistake when you restore files. But it also makes it more difficult to do some of the most common restore operations. That's why I recommend that you change this option to the Overwrite-always setting shown here.

In addition, you should change the Confirmation option from Off to the Only-on-overwrite setting shown here. This setting causes *FastBack Plus* to ask for confirmation before it overwrites a file on your hard disk. This provides the safeguard that you lose when you change the Existing-files option to Overwrite-always.

After you have changed the restore options to the settings you want, you can return to the Express menu system. To do that, you pull down the Window menu and select the Preferences function. Then, you select the Menu-type function and select the Express menu option. The options you set using the Long menu system remain in effect even after the Express menu system is activated.

How to do a backup

From the main screen of the Express menu, you can specify the type of backup you want to perform; you can select the drive you want to back up; and you can select the drive you want to use for the backup. In short, you can use the Express menu system to specify the options that are required for the most common backup procedures.

How to do a full backup Figure FB-9 shows you how to do a full backup. In part 1, you can see that the Files option is set to All-files; this is what *FastBack Plus* calls a full backup. Since this is the default setting, you shouldn't have to change it. Similarly, the To option should default to the diskette drive you want to use for the backup.

If the From option isn't already set to the hard drive you want to back up, you should change it. When you select the From function, the program displays a list of the hard drives on your system. To select the appropriate hard

Utility 4: FastBack Plus   **165**

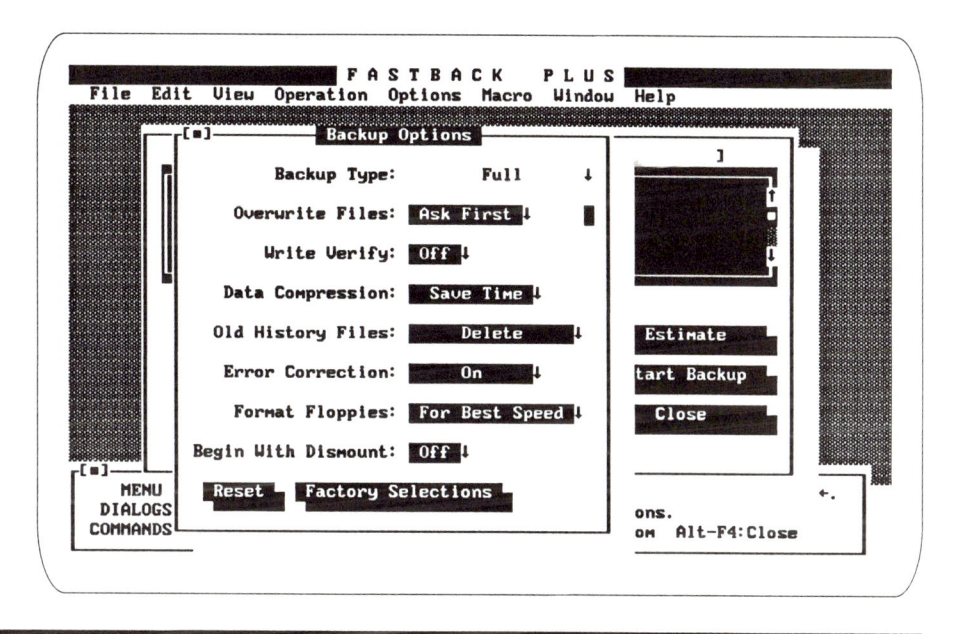

Figure FB-7 The Backup-options screen

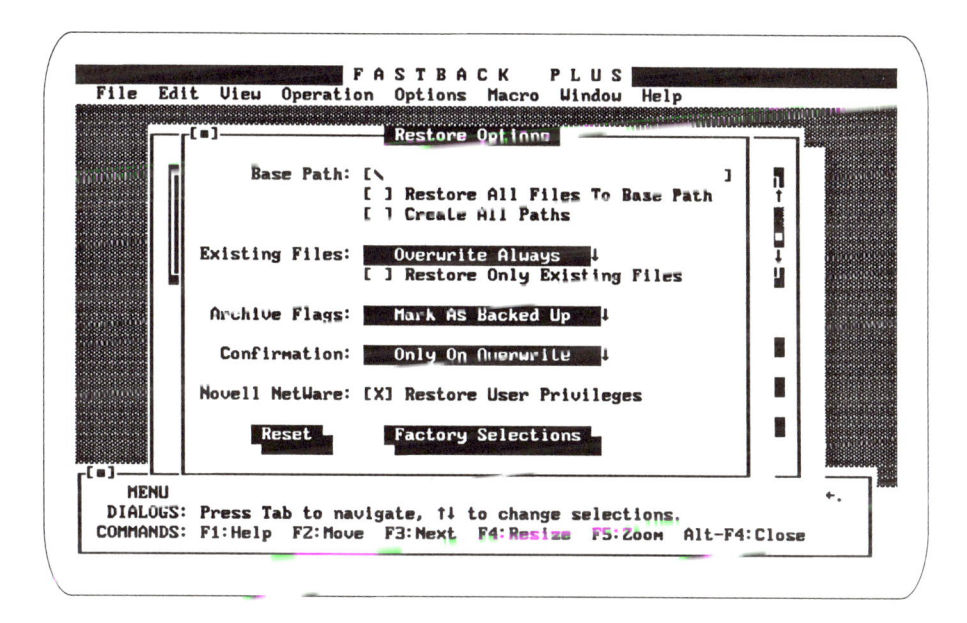

Figure FB-8 The Restore-options screen

drive using a mouse, you click the mouse on the drive you want to back up. *FastBack Plus* puts a marker next to the drive to indicate that it's been selected. To select a hard drive using the keyboard, you use the Up and Down arrow keys to highlight the drive you want, and the Spacebar to select the drive. Either way, when you press the Enter key, the program returns you to the main screen. Then, you select the Start function to start the backup operation.

When you start the backup, the program displays a screen that prompts to insert the first diskette from your backup set. When you do, the program then displays the screen shown in part 2 of figure FB-9. Here, the program tells you if the backup diskette you inserted already has files it. This is usually the case since you generally use the same diskettes for successive backup operations. Since you want to overwrite the existing backup, you select the Erase-all-volumes option at this screen.

Part 3 of figure FB-9 shows the Backup-progress screen that's displayed next. At the top of the screen, you can see the directories and files that are being backed up. And towards the bottom of the screen, you can see additional information about the progress of the operation. Here, for example, the operation has backed up 885 files, has been running over 13 minutes, and is backing up to the ninth diskette. As each diskette is filled, *FastBack Plus* prompts you for the next diskette in the backup set.

When the backup operation is complete, the program displays the screen shown in part 4 of figure FB-9. Here, you can see that the backup used 29 diskettes and took over 23 minutes. To exit from this operation and return to the main screen, you select the Close function.

How to do an appended incremental backup Although you can do appended incremental backups with *FastBack Plus* version 3.0, the way the program refers to diskettes and the way it appends data to them may be confusing. Because of this, it's essential that you know which diskette is the last one in your backup set.

Utility 4: FastBack Plus **167**

Part 1:

Use the main screen to set the functions that are necessary to do a full backup, and then start the operation.

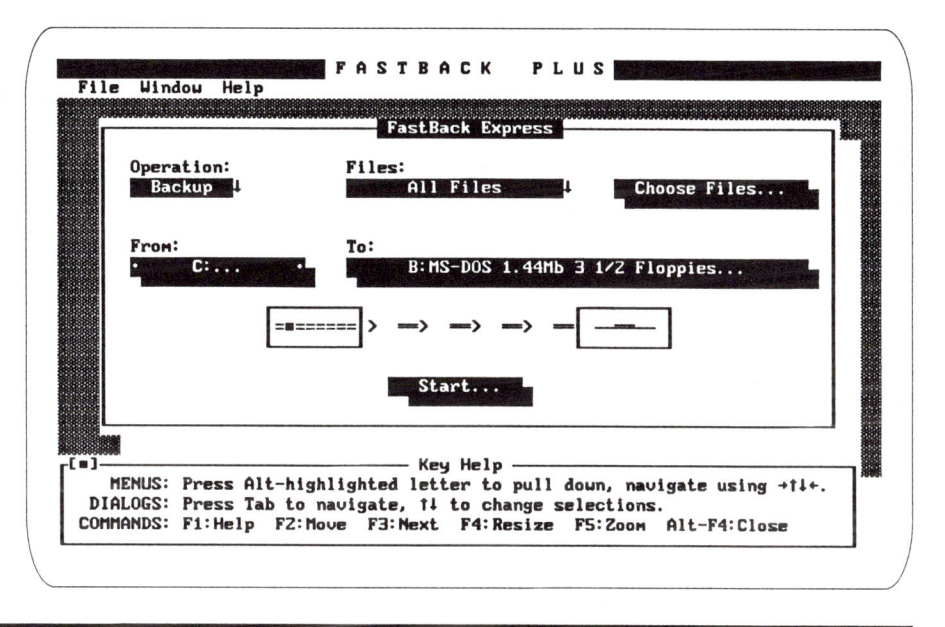

Figure FB-9 How you do a full backup (Part 1 of 4)

Part 2:

Select the Erase-all-volumes option to overwrite the existing files on the backup diskettes.

Figure FB-9 How you do a full backup (Part 2 of 4)

Part 3:

The Backup-progress screen displays the progress of the backup operation.

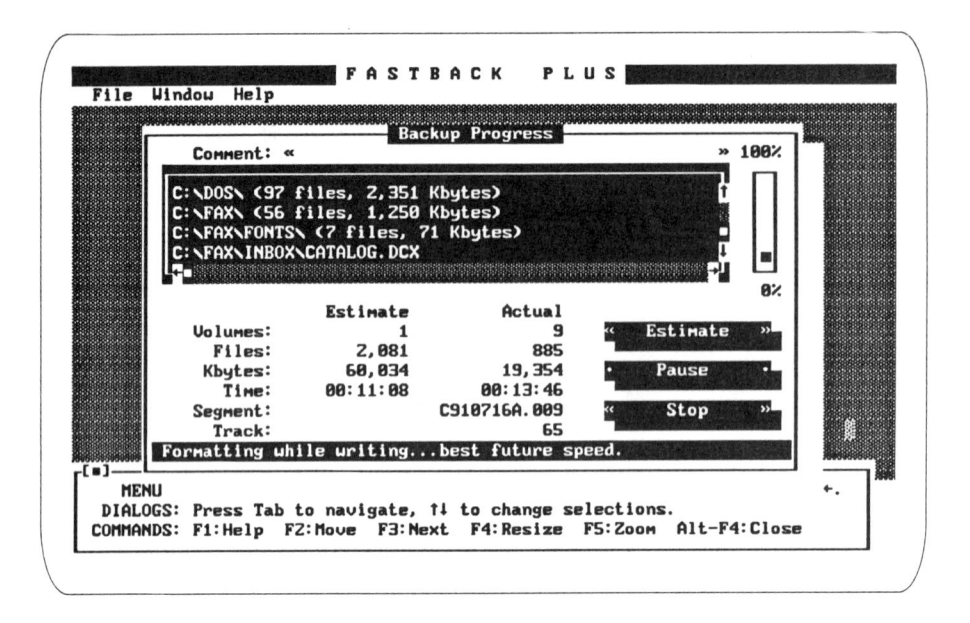

```
┌─────────────────────── FASTBACK   PLUS ────────────────────────┐
│ File  Window  Help                                             │
│              ┌──────────── Backup Progress ────────────┐       │
│              │ Comment: «                           » 100%     │
│              │ ┌──────────────────────────────────┐ ┌─┐        │
│              │ │C:\DOS\ (97 files, 2,351 Kbytes)  │ │ │        │
│              │ │C:\FAX\ (56 files, 1,250 Kbytes)  │ │ │        │
│              │ │C:\FAX\FONTS\ (7 files, 71 Kbytes)│ │■│        │
│              │ │C:\FAX\INBOX\CATALOG.DCX          │ └─┘        │
│              │ └──────────────────────────────────┘  0%        │
│              │           Estimate      Actual                  │
│              │  Volumes:      1             9    « Estimate »  │
│              │    Files:  2,081           885                  │
│              │  Kbytes: 60,034        19,354      • Pause  •   │
│              │    Time: 00:11:08      00:13:46                 │
│              │  Segment:              C910716A.009 «  Stop  »  │
│              │    Track:                   65                  │
│              │ Formatting while writing...best future speed.   │
│              └─────────────────────────────────────────────────┘
│ ┌[■]─────────────────────────────────────────────────────────┐ │
│ │   MENU                                                     │ │
│ │   DIALOGS: Press Tab to navigate, ↑↓ to change selections. │ │
│ │   COMMANDS: F1:Help F2:Move F3:Next F4:Resize F5:Zoom Alt-F4:Close │
└────────────────────────────────────────────────────────────────┘
```

Figure FB-9 How you do a full backup (Part 3 of 4)

Part 4:

The screen that's displayed when a backup operation is complete.

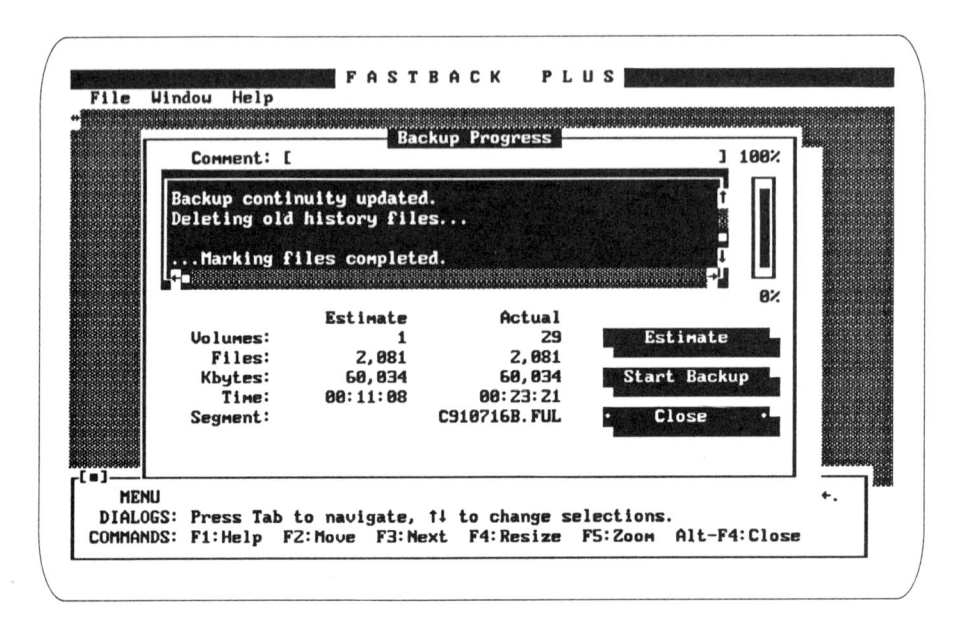

```
┌─────────────────────── FASTBACK   PLUS ────────────────────────┐
│ File  Window  Help                                             │
│              ┌──────────── Backup Progress ────────────┐       │
│              │ Comment: [                           ] 100%     │
│              │ ┌──────────────────────────────────┐ ┌─┐        │
│              │ │Backup continuity updated.        │ │ │        │
│              │ │Deleting old history files...     │ │ │        │
│              │ │                                  │ │■│        │
│              │ │...Marking files completed.       │ └─┘        │
│              │ └──────────────────────────────────┘  0%        │
│              │           Estimate      Actual                  │
│              │  Volumes:      1            29      Estimate    │
│              │    Files:  2,081         2,081                  │
│              │  Kbytes: 60,034         60,034    Start Backup  │
│              │    Time: 00:11:08      00:23:21                 │
│              │  Segment:              C910716B.FUL  • Close •  │
│              └─────────────────────────────────────────────────┘
│ ┌[■]─────────────────────────────────────────────────────────┐ │
│ │   MENU                                                     │ │
│ │   DIALOGS: Press Tab to navigate, ↑↓ to change selections. │ │
│ │   COMMANDS: F1:Help F2:Move F3:Next F4:Resize F5:Zoom Alt-F4:Close │
└────────────────────────────────────────────────────────────────┘
```

Figure FB-9 How you do a full backup (Part 4 of 4)

Utility 4: FastBack Plus **169**

Part 1:

Select the Files function, then select the Only-changed-files option.

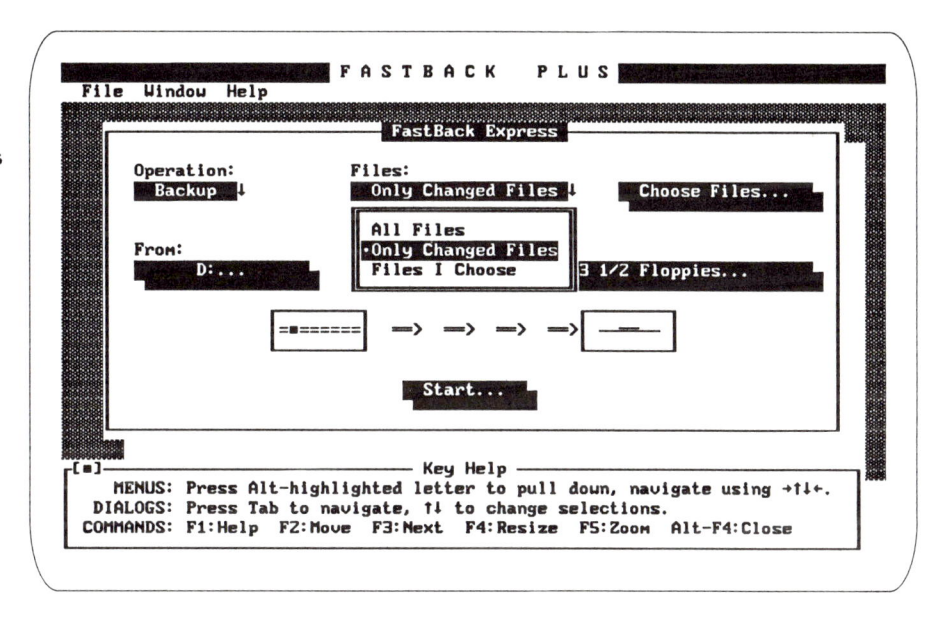

```
┌─────────────────── F A S T B A C K    P L U S ───────────────────┐
│  File  Window  Help                                              │
│ ▓▓▓▓▓▓▓▓▓▓▓▓▓▓▓▓▓▓▓▓▓▓▓▓▓▓▓▓▓▓▓▓▓▓▓▓▓▓▓▓▓▓▓▓▓▓▓▓▓▓▓▓▓▓▓▓▓▓▓▓▓▓▓ │
│              ┌──────────── FastBack Express ────────────┐        │
│              │                                          │        │
│              │  Operation:     Files:                   │        │
│              │   Backup ↓      Only Changed Files ↓   Choose Files... │
│              │                 ┌────────────────────┐   │        │
│              │                 │ All Files          │   │        │
│              │  From:          │•Only Changed Files │   │        │
│              │    D:...        │ Files I Choose     │  3 1/2 Floppies... │
│              │                 └────────────────────┘   │        │
│              │                                          │        │
│              │     [■══════] ═> ═> ═> ═> [────]         │        │
│              │                                          │        │
│              │                  Start...                │        │
│              │                                          │        │
│              └──────────────────────────────────────────┘        │
│ ─[■]──────────────────── Key Help ────────────────────────────── │
│      MENUS: Press Alt-highlighted letter to pull down, navigate using →↑↓←. │
│    DIALOGS: Press Tab to navigate, ↑↓ to change selections.      │
│   COMMANDS: F1:Help  F2:Move  F3:Next  F4:Resize  F5:Zoom  Alt-F4:Close │
└──────────────────────────────────────────────────────────────────┘
```

Figure FB-10 How you do an appended incremental backup (Part 1 of 2)

To do this type of backup, first you select the Files function from the main screen as shown in part 1 of figure FB-10. Then, you select the Only-changed-files option; this is what *FastBack Plus* calls the incremental backup option. Assuming you have already specified the correct From and To options, next you select the Start function to start the backup operation.

Figure FB-10 part 2 shows you the screen that's displayed after you start the backup. Near the bottom of the screen, the program prompts you to insert a diskette. Unfortunately, the way *FastBack Plus* asks for diskettes isn't obvious, so I'll take a moment to explain. In this figure, for example, the following message is displayed:

    Insert volume to receive D910924A.004 in B:

This message is asking you to insert a diskette for a *backup segment*. Here, the segment is identified as D910924A.004. This segment is for a backup set of drive D as indicated by the first letter of the name. The middle portion of the *segment name* identifies the date of the backup (9/24/91). And the

Part 2:

The screen that's displayed at the start of the incremental backup operation.

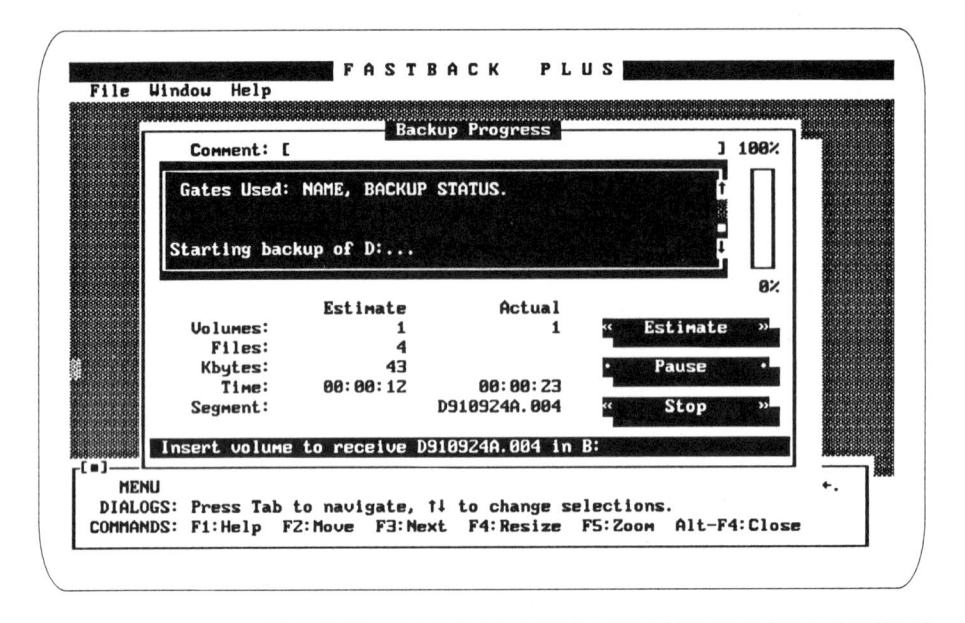

Figure FB-10 How you do an appended incremental backup (Part 2 of 2)

extension, .004, tells you that the program is going to create a fourth segment for the backup set.

When you do a full backup, *FastBack Plus* creates a separate backup segment for each diskette. As a result, the extensions of the segment names correspond to the number of the diskette in the backup set. In other words, segment D910924A.001 is on the first diskette, segment D910924A.002 is on the second diskette, and so on.

When you do an appended incremental backup, though, the segment names don't correspond to the diskette numbers. That's because *FastBack Plus* puts more than one segment on the last diskette for an appended incremental backup. In part 2 of figure FB-10 for example, it looks like you should insert diskette number 4 from your backup set. In this case, however, diskette number 3 was the last one in the set. As a result, you must keep track of which diskette was the last one used by the previous backup operation because it's the first one you insert when you start an appended incremental backup operation.

After you insert the appropriate diskette, *FastBack Plus* does the backup and displays the Backup-progress screen you saw earlier. When the operation is complete, the program displays a screen that summarizes the backup operation. To exit the operation and return to the main screen, you select the Close function.

How to do a partial backup   First, you specify the appropriate From and To options at the main screen. Then, you select the Choose-files function from the main screen as shown in part 1 of figure FB-11. When you do that, the screen shown in part 2 of figure FB-11 is displayed. This is the screen you use to select the files you want to back up.

In figure FB-11 part 2, the screen is divided into three areas. The function area is across the top. The directory and file listing areas are below. To switch between these areas, you can click the mouse on the option you want, or you can press the Tab key to move the highlight to the desired area. If you want to select an entire directory for a backup, you use the directory listing. Otherwise, you select individual files from the file listing. Either way, you can select files or directories by clicking on them with a mouse, or by pressing the Spacebar with the appropriate entry highlighted. When a file or directory has been selected, *FastBack Plus* places a marker next to the selection.

To illustrate, part 3 of figure FB-11 shows you how to select all the files in a directory. First, you move the highlight to the QA\FILES\ directory. Then, you can either click the mouse on the directory or press the Spacebar. When you do, *FastBack Plus* selects all the files in the directory and marks the selected files in the file listing as shown here.

After you have selected the files you want to back up, you select the OK function at the top of the screen. Then, the screen shown in part 4 of figure FB-11 is displayed. As you can see, the Files function now shows that the Files-I-choose option is the current setting. To start the backup operation, you select the Start function. Then, you follow the same procedure you use for other types of backups.

How to restore files

To restore files, you use the same basic procedure that you use to back up files. First, you change the Operation function from Backup to Restore. Then,

172 Chapter 5

Part 1:

Select the Choose-files function.

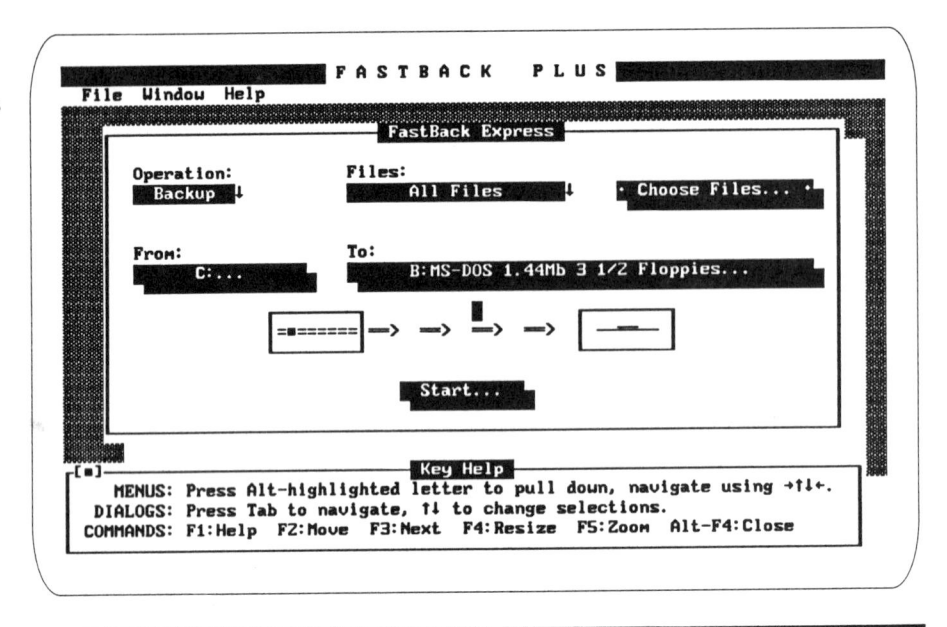

Figure FB-11 How you do a partial backup (Part 1 of 4)

Part 2:

Select the files you want to back up from the Files-to-back-up screen.

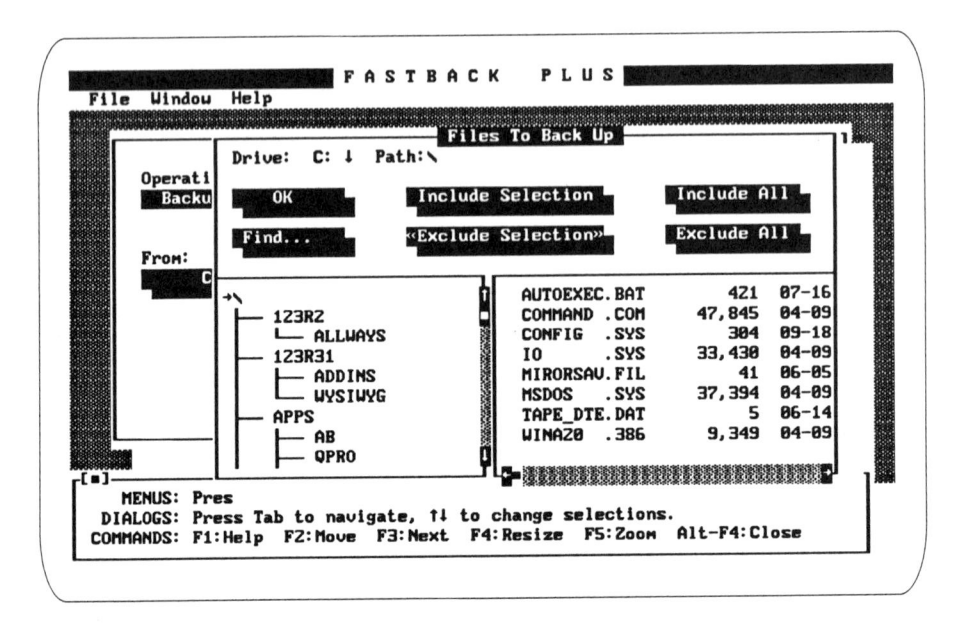

Figure FB-11 How you do a partial backup (Part 2 of 4)

Part 3:

All the files in the \QA\FILES directory have been selected for a partial backup.

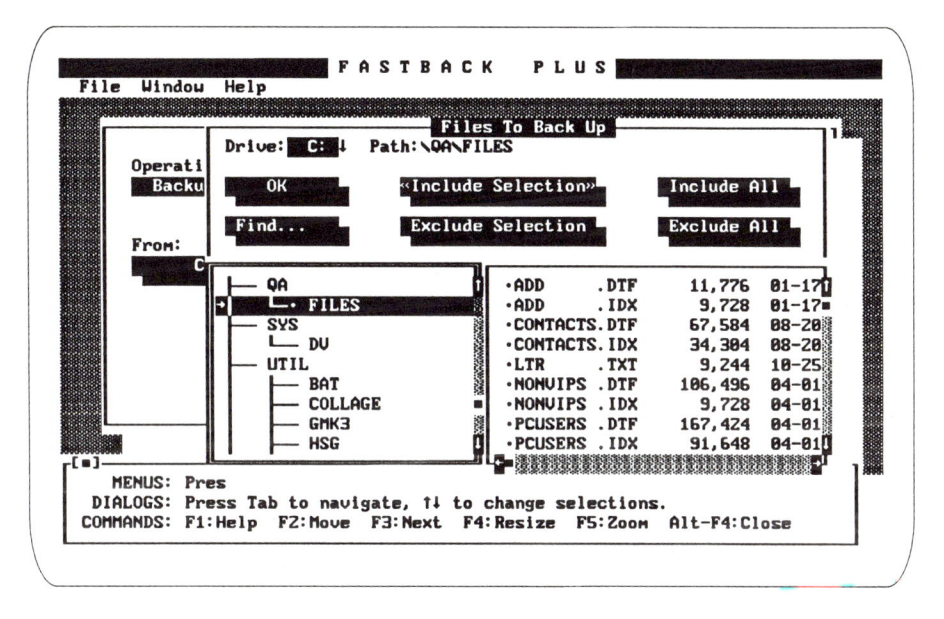

Figure FB-11 How you do a partial backup (Part 3 of 4)

Part 4:

The functions set to do a partial backup based on the selections made in part 3.

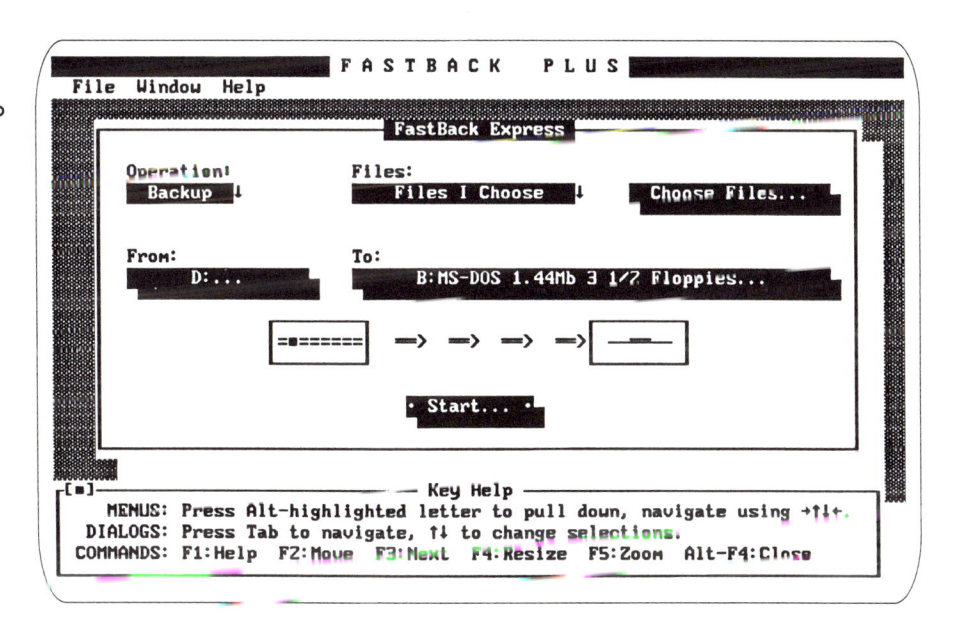

Figure FB-11 How you do a partial backup (Part 4 of 4)

you can specify the drives, directories, and files that are required for a restore operation.

How to do a full restore   Figure FB-12 shows you how to do a full restore. In part 1, all of the functions on the main screen are set for a full restore of drive D. To start the restore operation, you select the Start function.

Then, the screen in part 2 of figure FB-12 is displayed. Here, the program prompts you to insert the first diskette from the appropriate backup set. After you insert the diskette, the program displays a Restore-progress screen that's similar to the Backup-progress screen you're already familiar with.

When the restore operation is complete, the program displays the screen shown in part 3 of figure FB-12. Here, you can see that 888 files were restored in an operation that took about 4-1/2 minutes. To exit the operation and return to the main screen, you select the Close function.

How to do a partial restore   Figure FB-13 shows you how to do a partial restore of drive D. First, you specify the appropriate To and From options as shown in part 1. Then, you set the Files function to Files-I-choose. Next, you select the Choose-files function. *FastBack Plus* then displays a screen like the one shown in part 2 of figure FB-13.

This screen is similar to the one you use to select files for a partial backup. Here, the directories on the backup are displayed in the directory listing, and the files are displayed in the file listing. To select the files you want to restore, you use the same techniques you learned earlier for doing a partial backup. Here, for example, all the files in the \123\WK1 directory have been selected. After you select the files you want, you select the OK function.

Part 3 of figure FB-13 shows the screen that's displayed next. Here, the program prompts you to insert the appropriate diskette. If you can match the segment name of the diskette that the program is prompting you for with the number of a particular diskette in your backup set, you insert that diskette. If, however, you don't know which diskette to insert, you must start with the first diskette in your set and continue through the set until you find the diskette that has the data you want to restore.

This screen also shows you the progress of the restore operation. When the operation is complete, *FastBack Plus* displays a summary of the

Utility 4: FastBack Plus **175**

Part 1:

The functions on the main screen set to do a full restore of drive D.

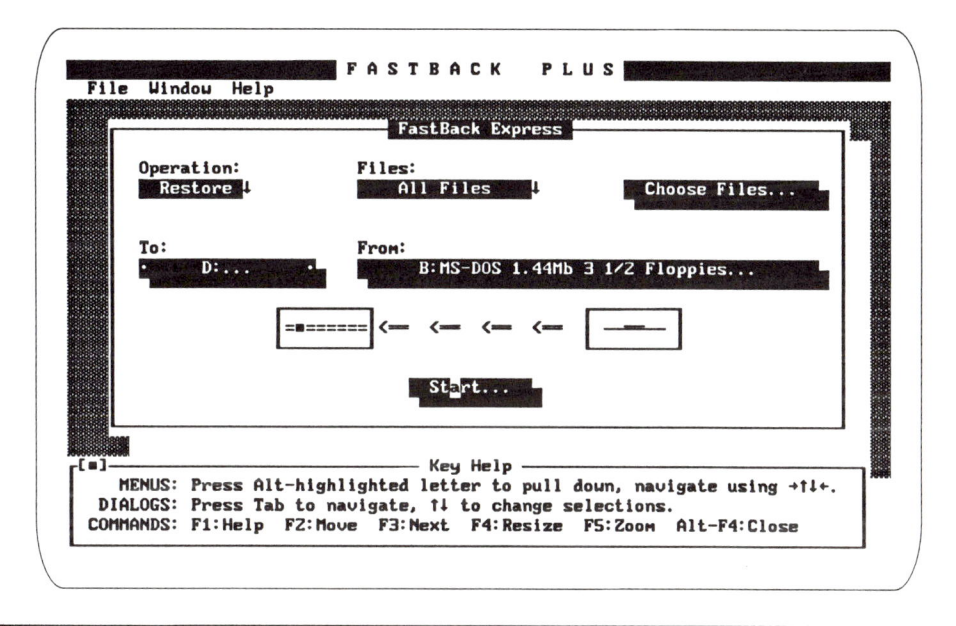

Figure FB-12 How you do a full restore (Part 1 of 3)

Part 2:

The screen that prompts you for diskettes and that shows the progress of the restore operation.

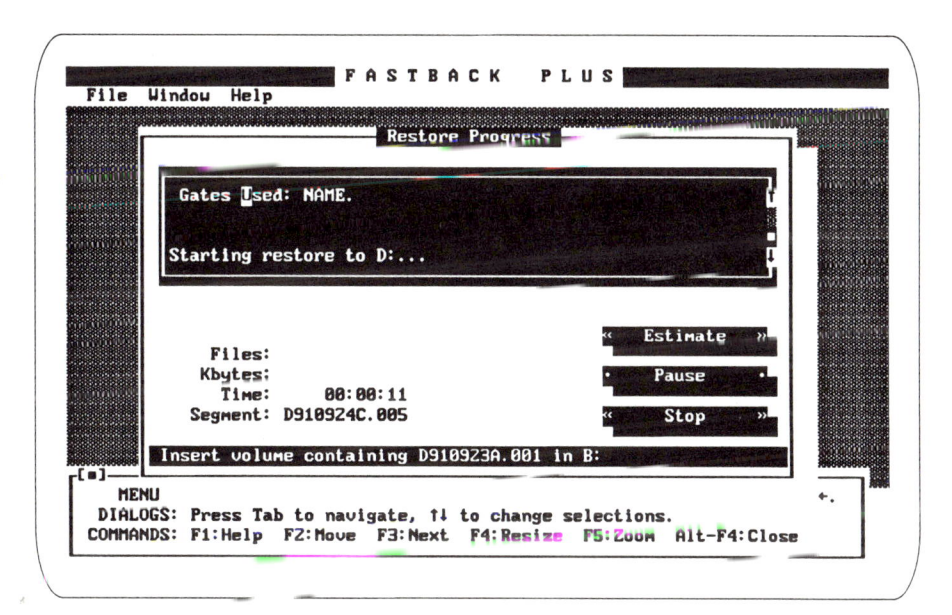

Figure FB-12 How you do a full restore (Part 2 of 3)

Part 3:

The screen that's displayed when the restore operation is complete.

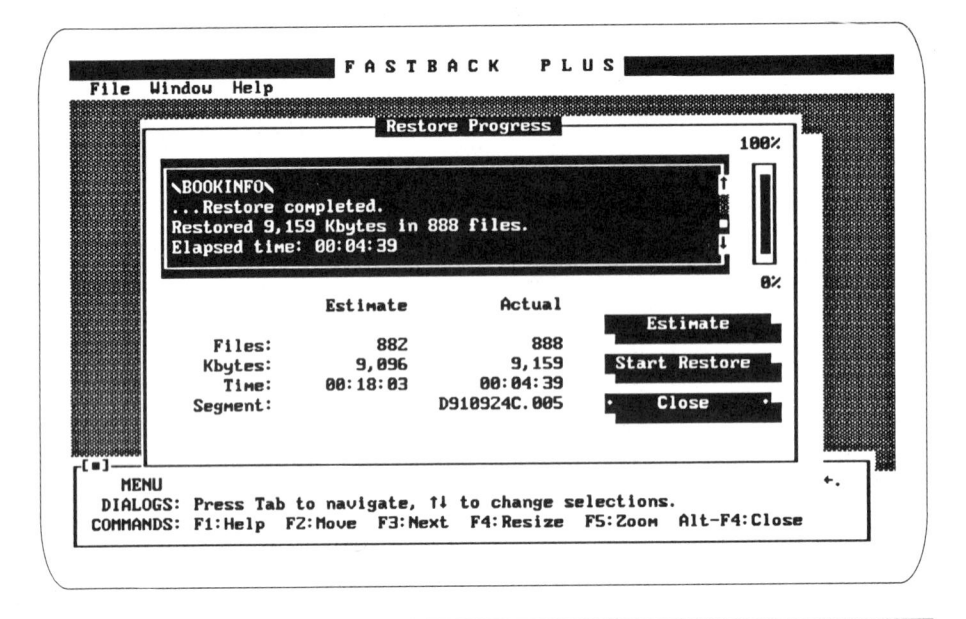

```
┌─────────────────── FASTBACK    PLUS ───────────────────┐
│ File  Window  Help                                      │
│         ┌──────────── Restore Progress ────────────┐    │
│         │ \BOOKINFO\                           ↑ │ 100% │
│         │ ...Restore completed.                  │  ▓  │
│         │ Restored 9,159 Kbytes in 888 files.    │  ▓  │
│         │ Elapsed time: 00:04:39              ↓ │      │
│         │                                        │  0% │
│         │           Estimate      Actual         │      │
│         │   Files:      882         888     ┌─ Estimate ─┐
│         │   Kbytes:   9,096       9,159     │ Start Restore │
│         │   Time:  00:18:03    00:04:39     │    Close      │
│         │   Segment:           D910924C.005 └────────────┘
│         └─────────────────────────────────────────┘
│  MENU                                                   │
│  DIALOGS: Press Tab to navigate, ↑↓ to change selections.│
│  COMMANDS: F1:Help F2:Move F3:Next F4:Resize F5:Zoom Alt-F4:Close │
└─────────────────────────────────────────────────────────┘
```

Figure FB-12   How you do a full restore (Part 3 of 3)

Part 1:

Set the Operation function to Restore and the Files function to Files-I-choose. Then select the Choose-files function.

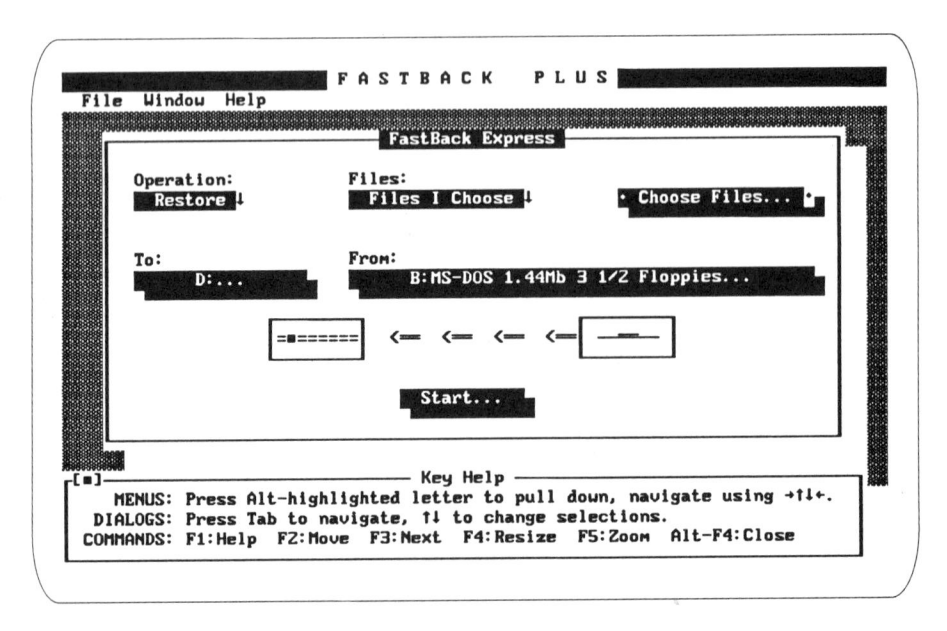

```
┌─────────────────── FASTBACK    PLUS ───────────────────┐
│ File  Window  Help                                      │
│         ┌──────────── FastBack Express ──────────┐     │
│         │ Operation:       Files:                       │
│         │  Restore ↓        Files I Choose ↓   • Choose Files... │
│         │                                               │
│         │ To:              From:                        │
│         │   D:...            B:MS-DOS 1.44Mb 3 1/2 Floppies... │
│         │                                               │
│         │     ▓▓▓▓▓▓▓   ⇐  ⇐  ⇐  ⇐   ┌──────┐          │
│         │                                               │
│         │              Start...                         │
│         └───────────────────────────────────────┘      │
│  ─────────────────── Key Help ───────────────────       │
│  MENUS: Press Alt-highlighted letter to pull down, navigate using →↑↓←.│
│  DIALOGS: Press Tab to navigate, ↑↓ to change selections.│
│  COMMANDS: F1:Help F2:Move F3:Next F4:Resize F5:Zoom Alt-F4:Close │
└─────────────────────────────────────────────────────────┘
```

Figure FB-13   How you do a partial restore (Part 1 of 3)

Utility 4: FastBack Plus   177

Part 2:

Select the files you want to restore, then select the OK function to return to the main screen.

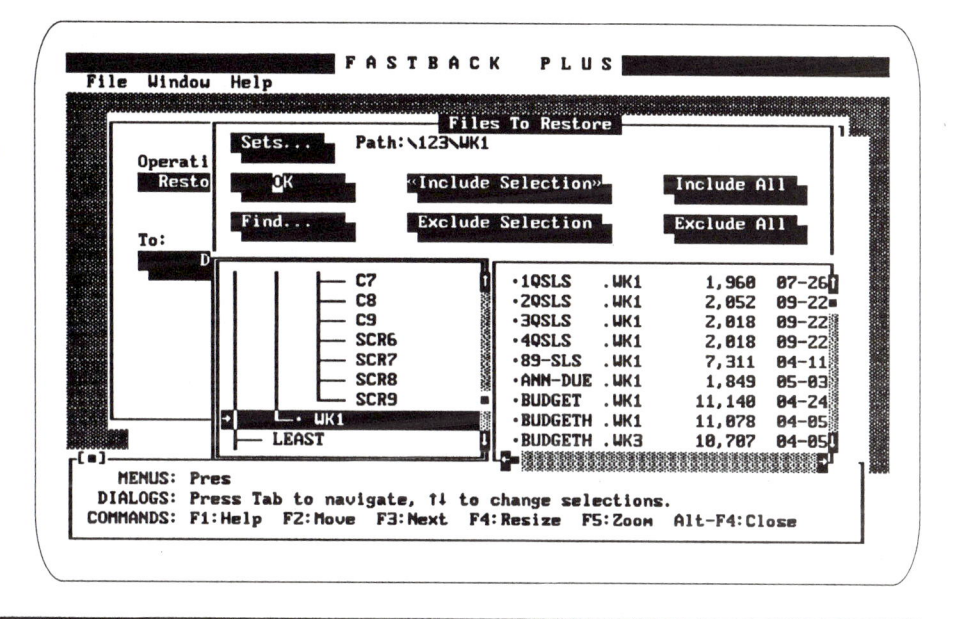

Figure FB-13   How you do a partial restore (Part 2 of 3)

Part 3:

Insert the appropriate diskette as prompted by *FastBack Plus*.

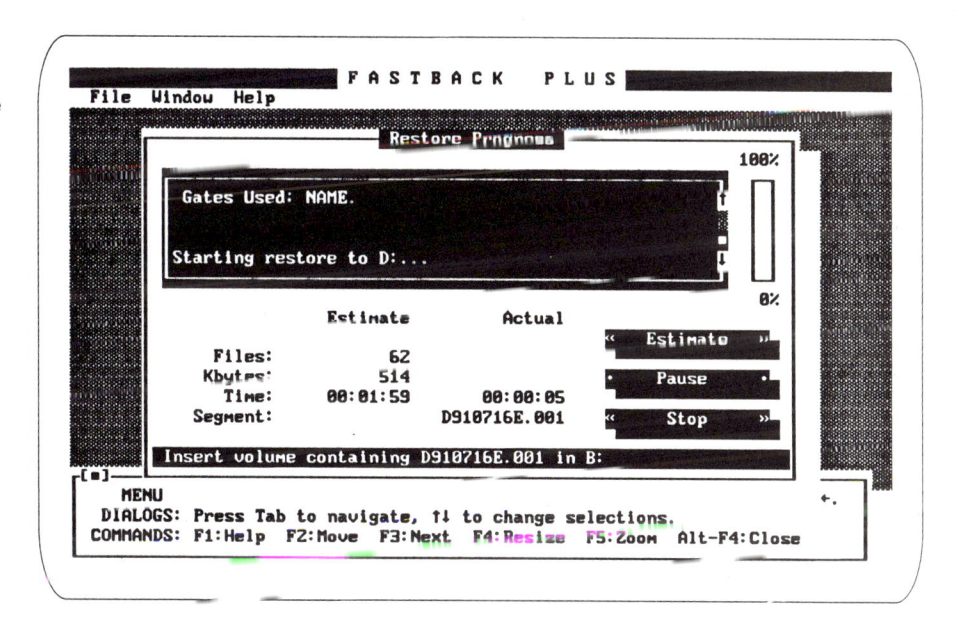

Figure FB-13   How you do a partial restore (Part 3 of 3)

operation. Then, to exit the operation and return to the main screen, you select the Close function.

How to compare a backup

As a rule, you can count on *FastBack Plus* to do reliable backups. So you don't need to compare every backup you do. However, you should occasionally compare a backup to make sure that the utility is working correctly. Then, you can be satisfied that your backups will work when you need to restore data. The best time to do a compare is right after you back up, before any changes occur.

Unfortunately, *FastBack Plus* doesn't let you compare a backup using the Express menu system. Instead, you must use the Long menu system that I showed you earlier. With the Long menu system active, you pull down the Operation menu and select the Compare-files function to display the Compare-progress screen. Now, you can select the Options menu and use it to specify settings including the Compare-to and Compare-from options that are required for the operation.

To start the operation, you select the Start-compare function from the Compare-progress screen. Then, you follow the same basic procedure that you use to back up files. If *FastBack Plus* finds a file on the backup set that doesn't match the file on the hard disk, it alerts you of the condition. Then, you need to determine the cause of the discrepancy and do whatever is necessary to get a reliable backup. If the program doesn't find any errors or discrepancies, you know that the backup is reliable.

How to automate your backups

So far, you've learned to make selections from various screens and menus to do different types of backups. In some cases, this is the most efficient way to do a backup. However, *FastBack Plus* provides several features that you can use to automate your backups. In particular, you can create *setup files* that store all of the settings that are required for a backup. You can also use these setup files in batch files. In addition, *FastBack Plus* lets you add programs called *macros* to a setup file. Although the commands you use in macros are

Part 1:

After you set the functions for the appropriate backup operation, you select the Save-setup function from the File menu.

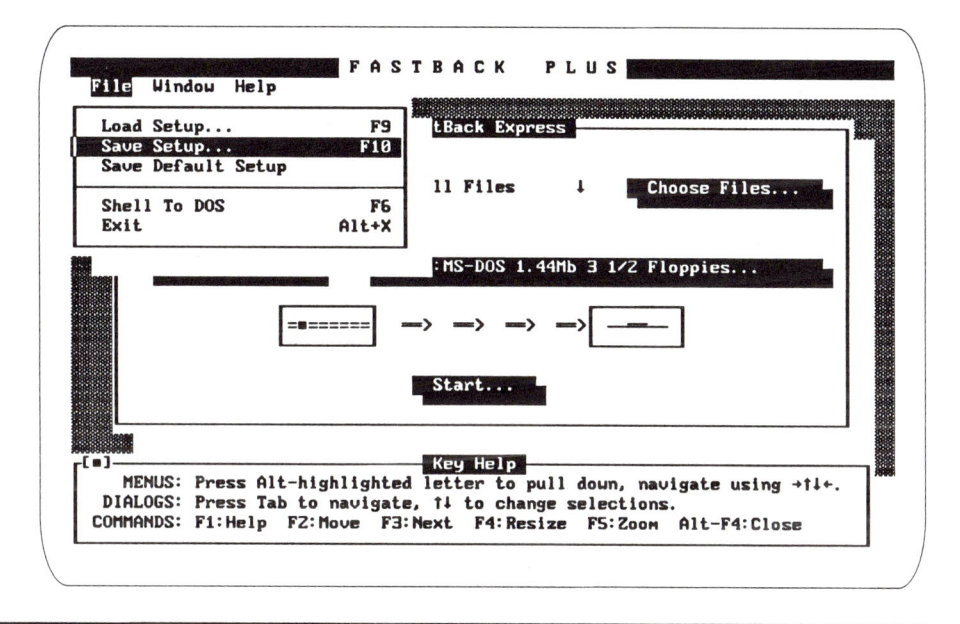

```
┌─────────────────────── FASTBACK     PLUS ───────────────────────┐
│ File  Window  Help                                              │
│ ┌─────────────────────────────┐                                 │
│ │ Load Setup...           F9  │ ┌─ tBack Express ──────────────┐│
│ │ Save Setup...          F10  │ │                              ││
│ │ Save Default Setup          │ │                              ││
│ │                             │ │ 11 Files      ↓  Choose Files...││
│ │ Shell To DOS            F6  │ │                              ││
│ │ Exit                  Alt+X │ └──────────────────────────────┘│
│ └─────────────────────────────┘ ┌:MS-DOS 1.44Mb 3 1/2 Floppies...┐│
│                                 │                              ││
│        ┌────────┐    → → → →   ┌────────┐                       │
│        │=■======│               │   ─    │                       │
│        └────────┘               └────────┘                       │
│                                                                  │
│                         ┌ Start... ┐                             │
│                                                                  │
│ ┌[■]────────────────── Key Help ────────────────────────────────┐│
│ │   MENUS: Press Alt-highlighted letter to pull down, navigate using →↑↓←.││
│ │   DIALOGS: Press Tab to navigate, ↑↓ to change selections.              ││
│ │   COMMANDS: F1:Help F2:Move F3:Next F4:Resize F5:Zoom Alt-F4:Close      ││
│ └────────────────────────────────────────────────────────────────┘│
└──────────────────────────────────────────────────────────────────┘
```

Figure FB-14 How to create a setup file (Part 1 of 2)

rather complicated, I'll show you a simple macro command so you have an idea of how macros work and what they can do.

How to create and use a setup file Figure FB-14 shows you how to create a setup file for an appended incremental backup of drive D. To create a setup file, first you set the functions as if you were going to run the backup operation. Instead of starting the backup, though, you pull down the File menu. Then, you select the Save-setup function as shown in part 1 of figure FB-14. *FastBack Plus* then displays the screen shown in part 2. At this screen, you enter a name for the setup file. Here, for example, I entered the name *inc-d*. After you enter the file name, you select the OK function.

To load the setup file, you pull down the File menu and select the Load-setup function to display a screen like the one in figure FB-15. This screen lists the setup files that have been created. Here, for example, there are five setup files. The DEFAULT.FB file contains the default settings, the FULL-C.FB file contains the settings for a full backup of drive C, the FULL-D.FB contains the settings for a full backup of drive D, and so on. To select one of

180 Chapter 5

Part 2:

At this screen, you enter a name for the setup file.

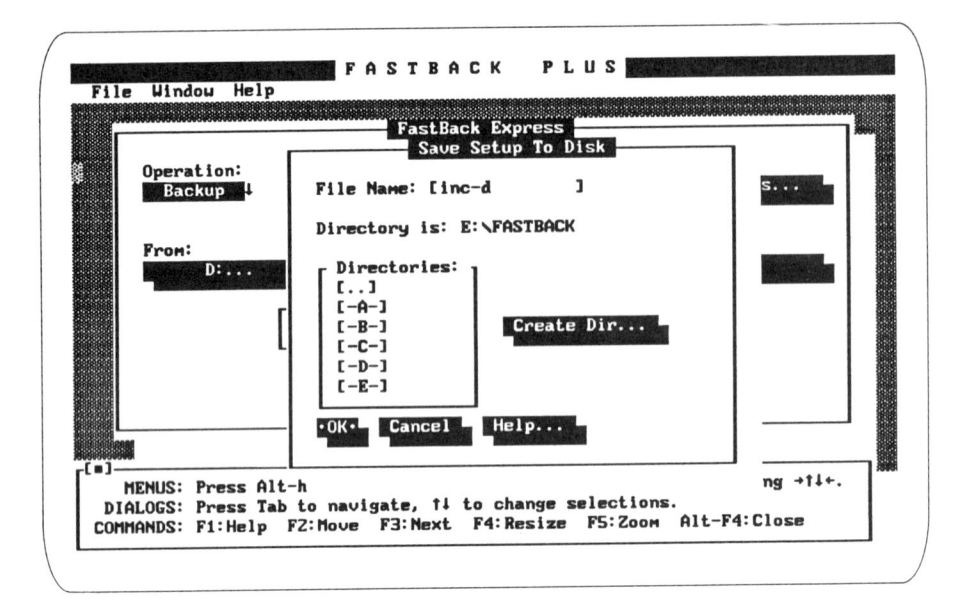

Figure FB-14 How to create a setup file (Part 2 of 2)

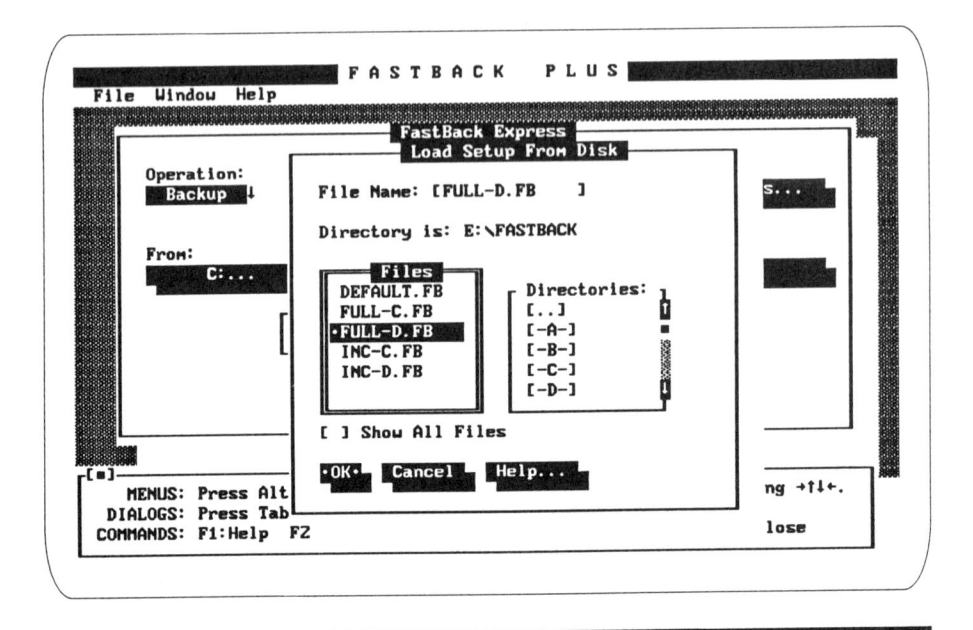

Figure FB-15 The screen you use to load a setup file for a backup operation.

```
FULL-C.BAT

    C:
    CD \FASTBACK
    FB FULL-C.FB

INC-C.BAT

    C:
    CD \FASTBACK
    FB INC-C.FB

FULL-D.BAT

    C:
    CD \FASTBACK
    FB FULL-D.FB

INC-D.BAT

    C:
    CD \FASTBACK
    FB INC-D.FB
```

Figure FB-16 Four batch files that start *FastBack Plus* and load setup files to run backup operations

these files, you click on it with the mouse, or you move the highlight to it and press the Spacebar. When you do that, the program places a marker next to the setup file you selected. Then, you select the OK function. When you do, *FastBack Plus* loads the setup file and returns you to the main screen. Next, you select the Start function to perform the backup operation that was loaded by the setup file.

How to start a setup file from a batch file   Figure FB-16 shows how you can use setup files with batch files. Here, the setup file is included with the commands that start *FastBack Plus*. When you execute one of these batch files, it starts the program and automatically loads the setup file. Then, it displays the main screen. To perform the backup operation, you just select the Start function.

How to add a macro command to a setup file   *FastBack Plus* provides a complicated command language that you can use to program macros. Most of the features provided by this command language are far beyond anything you'll ever want or need to use. You can, however, use this language to add a simple macro command to a setup file to automatically start a backup operation. But before you can add a macro command to a setup file, you have to activate the Long menu system.

To illustrate, figure FB-17 shows you how to add a macro command to a setup file. First, you select the Open function from the File menu as shown in part 1. Then, you specify the setup file you want to modify and select the OK function. *FastBack Plus* then displays the setup file as shown in part 2 of figure FB-17. In this figure, the FULL-C.FB setup file is displayed in a small window.

To enlarge the window so you can see more of the contents of the setup file, you click the mouse on the arrow that's enclosed in brackets by the setup file's name. If you don't have a mouse, you press the Alt+W key combination to activate the Window menu. Then, you press the F5 key (Zoom option) to enlarge the window. *FastBack Plus* then displays the setup file using a full-screen window like the one shown in part 3 of figure FB-17.

At this window, you hold down the Down arrow key to scroll to the end of the file. Then, you move the cursor to the end of the last command line and press the Enter key. Next, you type the following command:

```
StartOperation("Backup")
```

This command causes *FastBack Plus* to start the backup operation automatically after it has loaded the setup file. To save the macro command with the setup file, you select the Save function from the File menu as shown in part 4 of figure FB-17. After you save the command, you can change back to the Express menu system.

If you look back at figure FB-17 part 3, you can see that setup files contain many complicated commands. Aside from macro commands, *FastBack Plus* provides other complex programming techniques. Fortunately, you shouldn't have to use any of these commands or techniques unless you're a PC support person who is setting up the program for someone else to use.

Utility 4: FastBack Plus   183

Part 1:

With the Long menu system active, you select the Open function from the File menu. Then, you select the setup file you want to modify.

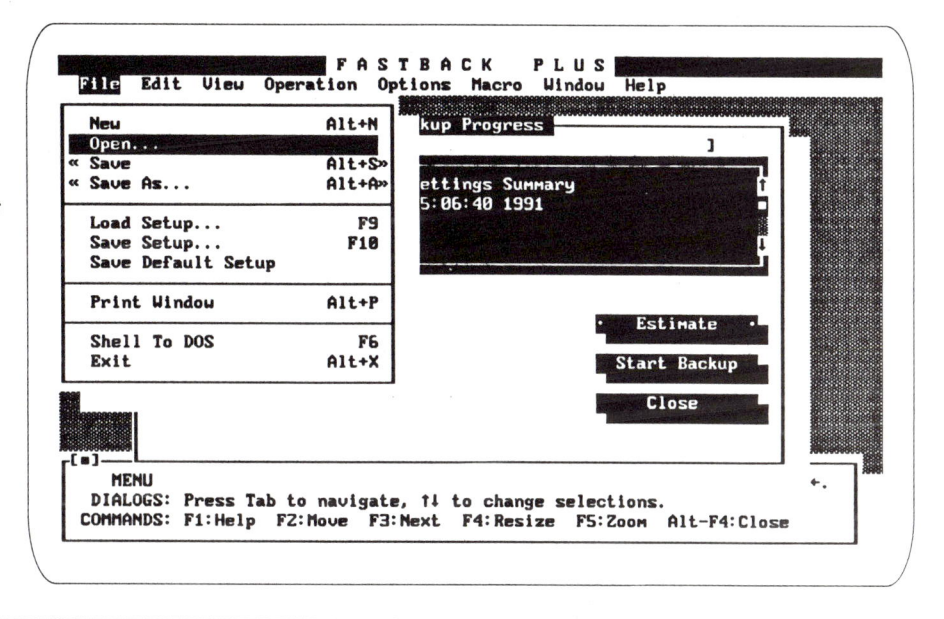

Figure FB-17   How you add a macro command to a setup file (Part 1 of 4)

Part 2:

The window that displays the setup file you selected.

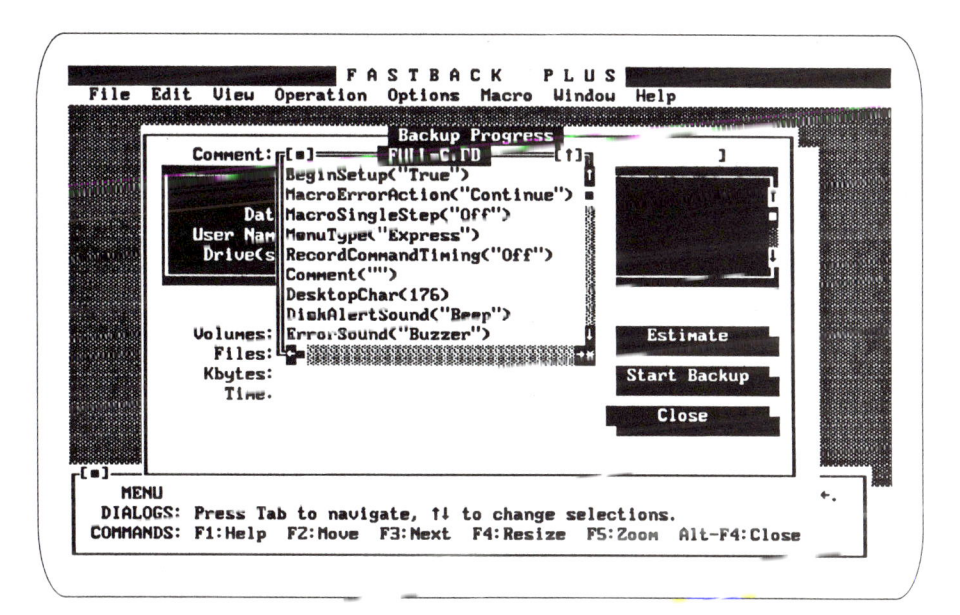

Figure FB-17   How you add a macro command to a setup file (Part 2 of 4)

184 Chapter 5

Part 3:

Scroll to the end of the file and add the macro command.

```
                              FASTBACK    PLUS
     File  Edit  View  Operation  Options  Macro  Window  Help
                                  FULL-C.FB
RestoreArchive("Mark As Backed Up")
RestoreConfirmation("Off")
RestoreOnlyExistingFiles("Off")
CreateAllPaths("Off")
RestoreAllFilesToBasePath("Off")
RestoreNovellObjects("On")
RestoreBasePath("\")
EraseConfirmation("Files")
EraseFloppiesBeforeCopy("Off")
CopySplitLargerThan(1000)
DateRangeEnable("Off")
DateRange("01-01-80","12-31-99")
SizeRangeEnable("Off")
SizeRange(0,"Bytes",2047,"MBytes")
FileAttributeEnable("Off")
FileAttributeGateSet("None")
DMASpeed("High")
SelectWindow("Key Help")
SelectWindow("Express")
EndSetup()
StartOperation("Backup")
```

Figure FB-17 How you add a macro command to a setup file (Part 3 of 4)

Part 4:

Select the Save function from the File menu to save the macro command with the setup file.

```
                              FASTBACK    PLUS
     File  Edit  View  Operation  Options  Macro  Window  Help
                                  FULL-C.FB
  New                    Alt+N    )
  Open...
  Save                   Alt+S
  Save As...             Alt+A

  Load Setup...          F9
  Save Setup...          F10
  Save Default Setup

  Print Window           Alt+P

  Shell To DOS           F6
  Exit                   Alt+X

F
FileAttributeGateSet("None")
DMASpeed("High")
SelectWindow("Key Help")
SelectWindow("Express")
EndSetup()
StartOperation("Backup")
```

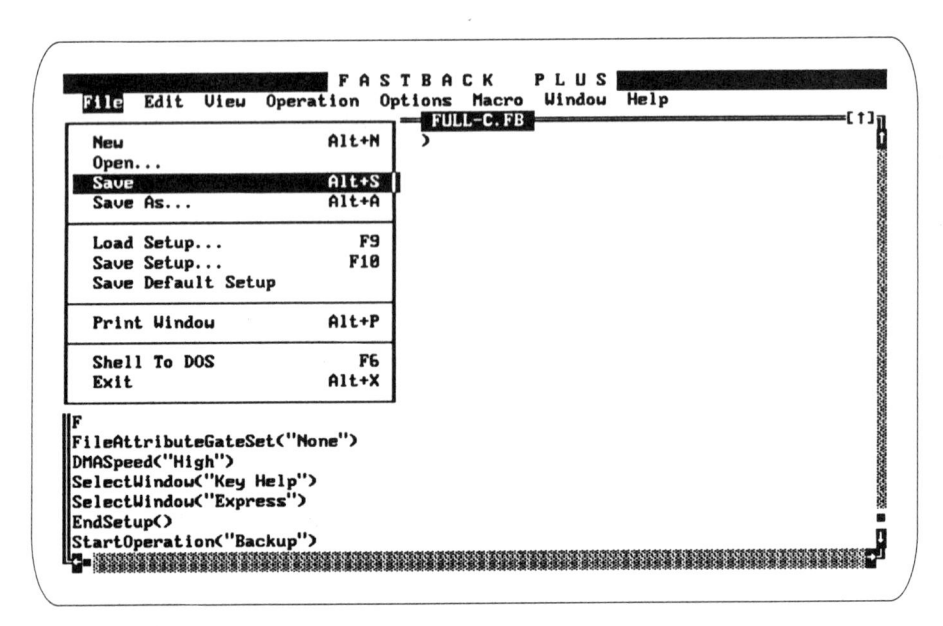

Figure FB-17 How you add a macro command to a setup file (Part 4 of 4)

Is *FastBack Plus* the right backup utility for you?

If you compare *FastBack Plus* with any of the other backup utilities presented in this book, I think you'll agree that's it the most complicated. As a result, it's hard to use. That's why I recommend that you review at least one other utility before you decide on *FastBack Plus*. If you review *Central Point Backup*, for instance, I think you'll agree that it's easier to use. It's also less expensive. In addition, when you get it as part of *PC Tools Deluxe*, you get many utilities that *FastBack Plus* doesn't have for about the same price you'd pay for *FastBack Plus*.

If, on the other hand, your company has already adopted *FastBack Plus*, you can be certain that your company has selected a capable backup utility. And if you limit yourself to the features presented in this chapter, you shouldn't have too much trouble using it. As a result, you'll be able to use *FastBack Plus* to do effective backups of the data on your hard disk.

Terms

window
backup segment
segment name
setup file
macro

Chapter 6

How to use a tape drive to back up a hard disk

In chapter 1, you learned about a special type of hardware called a *tape drive* that you can use to back up a hard disk. This type of drive backs up data to a *tape cartridge* instead of to diskettes. Tape drives are becoming more and more popular for backups for three reasons.

First, tape drives can generally back up data faster than diskette drives. The tape drive in my PC, for example, can back up 40MB of data in under seven minutes. The same operation using diskettes and a backup utility takes over 20 minutes. Being able to do your backups so much faster is a compelling reason for using a backup tape, particularly if your hard drive is larger than 40MB.

Second, using a tape drive is easier than using a diskette drive because you just do a full backup of the entire hard drive. This approach is practical because all the data from the hard drive fits on a single tape. As a result, it's easier to keep track of your backup sets. And it's easier to do your backups because once you start the operation, you don't have to insert a series of diskettes. In other words, you can do *unattended backups*.

Third, backing up to tape is generally considered to be more reliable than backing up to diskettes. In part, that's because tape cartridges are more reliable than diskettes. But it's also because tape drives are better suited for backing up data than diskette drives are.

Today, dozens of manufacturers make many different types of tape drive systems. Unfortunately, it's difficult to know what type of tape drive hardware and software you should use unless you understand a little bit about the different options that are available. That's why I'll start by presenting the most common types of tape drive hardware and software. Then, I'll show you how to do a full backup using a tape drive. By the time you finish this chapter, you'll be able to decide if you should add a tape drive to your PC. In addition, you'll be able to decide which tape hardware and software is appropriate for your backup requirements.

The three most common sizes of tape cartridges

As an overview, figure 6-1 presents the three most common types of tape cartridges. Each tape drive is designed to use a specific size of tape cartridge. In other words, the DC2000 tape cartridges can only be used in a DC2000 drive, and so on. You should also know that these different tape cartridges provide for different storage capacities and different backup speeds. Also, some tapes are more expensive than others, but most cost between $20 and $40 each. Now, I'll briefly present the characteristics of each size.

The DC2000 tape series The *DC2000* is currently the most widely used tape cartridge. About the size of a deck of cards, this tape cartridge can typically store between 40MB and 150MB of data. This range in capacity is due to the tape's length and the amount of file compression that's used. For example, the standard length DC2000 tape can store 40MB of data. Then, if your drive and software provide for file compression, you can typically store 60MB of data on this tape. By comparison, the DC2080 tape can store 80MB of data, and the DC2120 tape can store 120MB of data. If you use file compression, the DC2120 tape can store 150MB of data.

Typically, the lowest priced tape drives use the DC2000 series tapes. You can, for example, buy a DC2000 tape drive that can store up to 60MB on a single tape for as little as $200. In contrast, the higher performance DC2000 drives can cost $800 or more.

The DC600 tape series The *DC600* tapes can provide for higher storage capacities than the DC2000 tapes. Currently, the highest capacity DC600

How to use a tape drive to back up a hard disk   **189**

DC2000 tape series
Capacity: 40MB-150MB

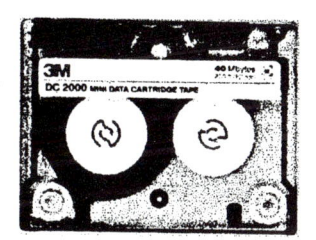

DC600 tape series
Capacity: 60MB-1,000MB

Cassette tape
Capacity: 60-150MB

Figure 6-1   The three most common sizes of tape cartridges and their storage capacities

tapes can store up to 1,000MB. Also, the drives that use the DC600 tapes can do faster backups than the DC2000 drives. As a result, this tape size is often used for backing up the large hard drives that are available today.

However, as you can see in figure 6-1, the DC600 tape cartridge is about twice as big as the DC2000 tape. As a result, the DC600 tapes aren't as convenient to handle and store. Also, the DC600 drives are more expensive. Even the 60MB drives start at about $800.

Cassette tapes A third type of tape drive uses a tape cartridge that looks like an audio cassette. Because *Teac* is the main manufacturer of this type of drive, it's sometimes referred to as a *Teac tape drive*. This tape drive stores 40MB on the standard length tape, and 60MB on the extended length tape. Using file compression features, you can store even more data on these tapes.

Currently, this tape isn't as popular as the DC2000 or DC600 tapes. In part, that's because the drives that use cassette tapes are a bit more expensive than the DC2000 drives. However, the *Teac* drive is faster than the DC2000 drives. In fact, it's about as fast as the DC600 drives. So if speed is important to you, you may want to consider this tape backup system.

Tape formatting standards

Like a diskette or a hard disk, a tape must be formatted before you can use it to store data. Most tape backup programs do this automatically the first time you use a new tape. As a result, you generally don't have to worry about this operation.

You should know, however, that different tape drives use different formats. In fact, most drives have their own proprietary format, but they can also use one of the standard formats. Since you'll probably read about these formatting standards when you go to buy a tape drive, I'll explain them briefly.

The QIC40 and QIC80 formats The *QIC40* and *QIC80* formats are *standard formats* that have been established for the DC2000 size tape. (QIC stands for Quarter Inch Compatibility.) The QIC40 format provides for 40MB of storage on a tape, and the QIC80 format provides for 80MB of storage on a tape. In theory, using a standard format makes it possible for a tape to share data between different makes of tape drives. Using a standard format is also supposed to make it easier for commercial backup utilities like *Central Point Backup* and *PC-Fullbak+* to provide support for a tape drive. Unfortunately, these formats don't always provide for the sharing of data, even though they are supposed to. Furthermore, using these formats reduces the storage capacity and performance of the tape drive system.

Proprietary formats   A *proprietary format* is a format that's used by the software manufacturer to format tapes. Proprietary formats don't follow any established standards. And in some cases, commercial utilities can use their proprietary format even when they support a tape drive that's manufactured by another company. For example, *Central Point Backup* can use its own proprietary format even when you use it with another company's tape drive.

Proprietary formats provide two primary benefits. First, they provide for faster backups. Second, they provide for greater storage capacity on a tape. As a result, you'll probably want to use the proprietary format that's provided by the software you use to back up to your tape drive.

Tape software

When tape drives first became available, there weren't any commercial backup utilities that supported them. So each tape drive was sold with its own backup program. Today, however, most commercial backup utilities support the most popular tape drives. As a result, you have a choice between using the proprietary program that comes with the drive or a commercial backup utility.

Proprietary tape software   The program that comes with a tape drive is often referred to as *proprietary tape software*. This software lets you back up, restore, and compare data. However, proprietary software is usually not as easy to use or as fast as commercial backup utilities.

To illustrate, figure 6-2 shows the main menu of the tape software that's provided with tape drives manufactured by *Mountain Computer*. This program is called *FileSafe*, and it is one of the best proprietary programs on the market. It also provides about as many functions as commercial backup

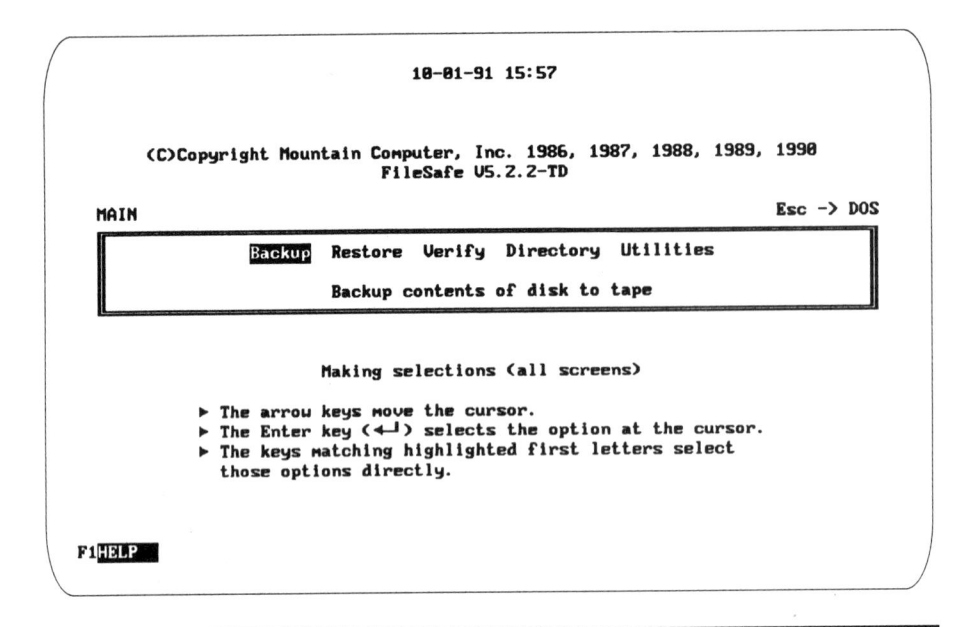

```
                    10-01-91 15:57


        (C)Copyright Mountain Computer, Inc. 1986, 1987, 1988, 1989, 1990
                           FileSafe V5.2.2-TD
   MAIN                                                        Esc -> DOS
   ┌──────────────────────────────────────────────────────────────────┐
   │           Backup  Restore  Verify  Directory  Utilities          │
   │                                                                  │
   │                   Backup contents of disk to tape                │
   └──────────────────────────────────────────────────────────────────┘

                         Making selections (all screens)

             ► The arrow keys move the cursor.
             ► The Enter key (◄┘) selects the option at the cursor.
             ► The keys matching highlighted first letters select
               those options directly.



   F1 HELP
```

Figure 6-2 The main screen of *FileSafe*, a typical proprietary program for tape backups

utilities. But as you will see in a moment, it's harder to use, and it's slower than a commercial backup utility like *Central Point Backup*.

Commercial backup utilities   As I just mentioned, most commercial backup utilities provide support for the most popular tape drives. For instance, all of the backup utilities presented in chapter 5 provide some level of support for tape drives. In fact, *Central Point Backup* supports many different tape drives. As a result, you can often use your backup utility instead of the software that comes with the tape drive. This makes it easier to use your tape drive for backups.

To illustrate, figure 6-3 shows how you can use *Central Point Backup* for a tape backup. Here, the Backup-to function has been set to use a tape drive with a 120MB tape. The Method function has been set to do a full backup and to overwrite the files that already exist on the tape. Other than these two settings, you set the program just the same as you do for diskette backups.

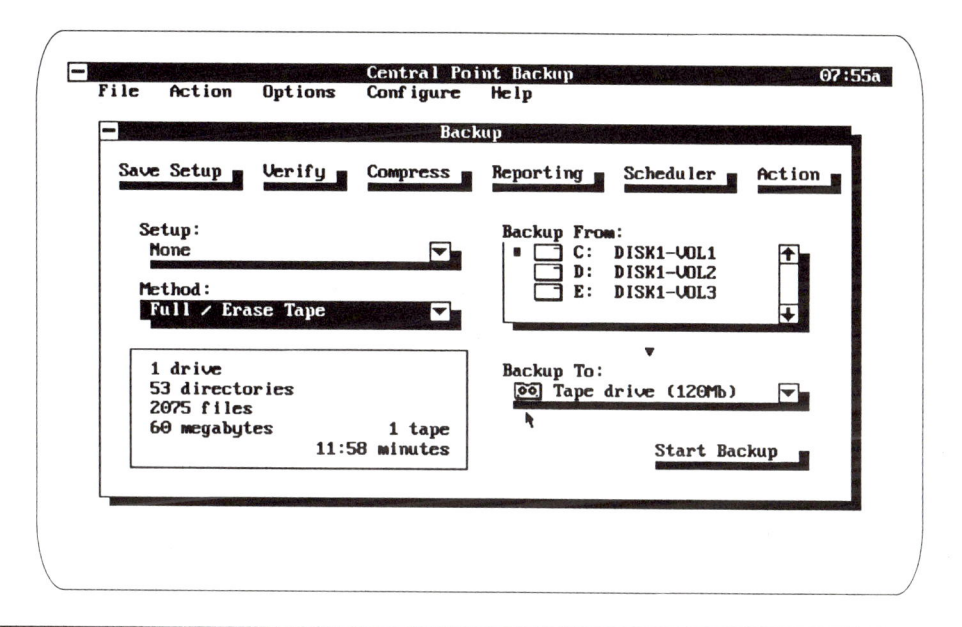

Figure 6-3 *Central Point Backup* set to do a full backup to a tape drive

How to use a tape drive to back up a hard drive

So you'll better understand how a tape backup works, I'll show you how to do a full backup using the *FileSafe* software that comes with *Mountain Computer* tape drives. Since this is a representative program, you'll get a good idea of how you do backups using other proprietary tape software and tape drives.

How to do a full backup   Figure 6-4 shows you how to do a full backup of drive C. In part 1, you can see the screen that's displayed when you select the Backup option from the main screen that you saw earlier in figure 6-2. At the screen shown in part 1, you select the Selective option shown here. This lets you select the files and directories you want to back up.

You're probably wondering why you don't select the Full option to do a full backup instead of the Selective option. The reason is that most proprietary tape software can do two types of backups: *image backups* and *file backups*. An image backup copies all of the data on the hard drive, but this type of

194   Chapter 6

Part 1:

At the Backup screen, you specify the Selective option to do a file backup rather than an image backup.

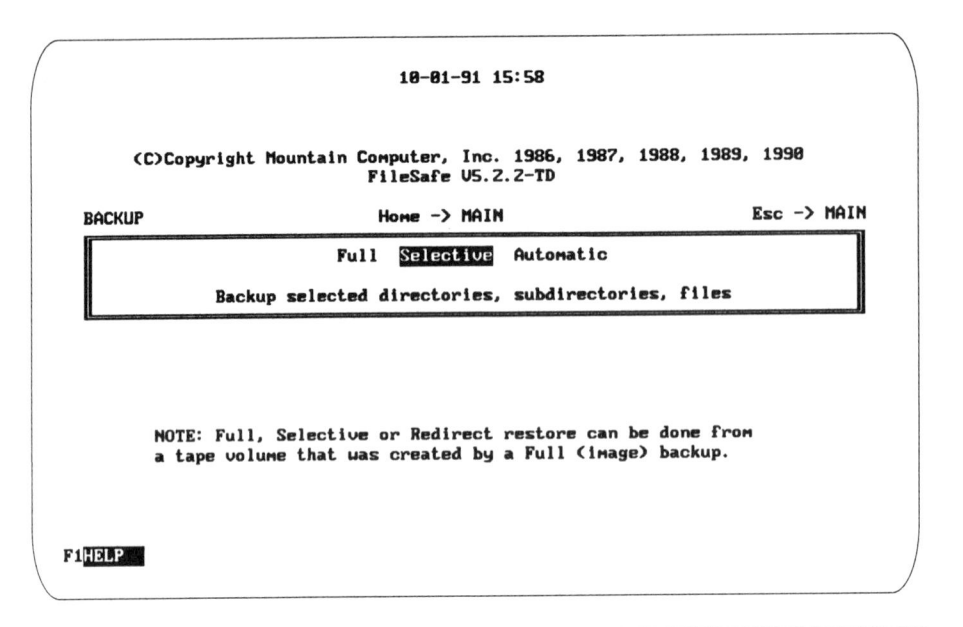

```
                          10-01-91 15:58


           (C)Copyright Mountain Computer, Inc. 1986, 1987, 1988, 1989, 1990
                             FileSafe V5.2.2-TD

   BACKUP                      Home -> MAIN                    Esc -> MAIN

                       Full   Selective   Automatic
              Backup selected directories, subdirectories, files




              NOTE: Full, Selective or Redirect restore can be done from
              a tape volume that was created by a Full (image) backup.



   F1 HELP
```

Figure 6-4   How you use *FileSafe* to do a full backup (Part 1 of 4)

Part 2:

At the Selective-backup screen, you specify the drive you want to back up. Then, you select the Backup-files function.

```
   SELECTIVE BACKUP             Home -> MAIN               Esc -> BACKUP

   Label for tape volume (optional for later searches):

   Description of tape volume (optional):


   Backup files                          Select files


   Options
     Source drive:                  C      Verify:                    No
     Append to end of tape:         No     Password during backup:    No
     Permit restore redirection:    Yes    Hidden file prompt:        No
     Clear Archive attribute:       Yes    System file prompt:        No
     Sort during backup:            Yes    Read-only file prompt:     No


   F1 HELP   F2 JUMP   F3 TOP   F4 BOTTOM
```

Figure 6-4   How you use *FileSafe* to do a full backup (Part 2 of 4)

Part 3:

At this screen, you specify the files you want to back up. Here, the first option is selected so that all the files will be backed up.

```
BACKUP ALL FILES              Home -> MAIN              Esc -> SELECTIVE BACKUP

  Complete backup of files without reference to date and time

  Backup of modified files by archive bit or since  6-14-91 11:58:12

  Archive attribute backup only

  Restricted backup of files dated
          mm-dd-yy hh:mm
    from: 01-01-80 00:00
    to:   10-01-91 15:59

                                              Source drive is C (DISK1-VOL1)


  F1 HELP           F3 TOP    F4 BOTTOM
```

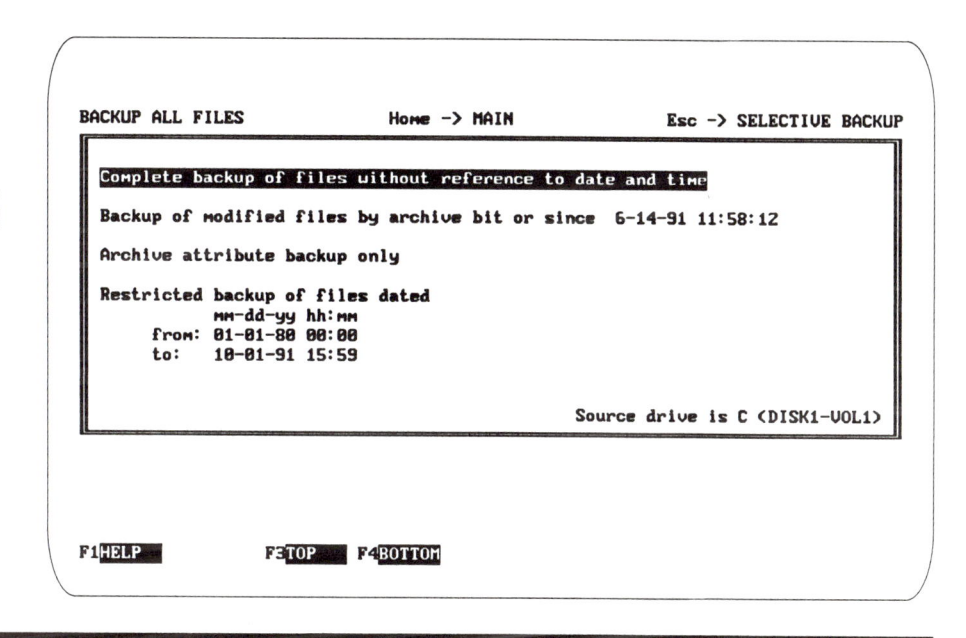

Figure 6-4 How you use *FileSafe* to do a full backup (Part 3 of 4)

Part 4:

The screen that displays the progress of the backup operation.

```
                       EXECUTION: SELECTIVE BACKUP              V5.2.2-TD
  - Volume Information
  Tape #: 1              Source: C (DISK1-VOL1)          10-01-91 15:59:10
  Label: < NONE >
  Desc:  < NONE >
  Tape usage (bytes):   available = 150,321,152    this volume = 63,120,579

  - Current Operation                     - Progress Report
                                          Percent Complete:              9
  Writing file data to tape               Total files to backup:      2069
  Formatting While Writing                Remaining files to backup:  1860
                                          Elapsed Time:  1:10   Buffer: 224k

  - File Display
  <\123R31>




                Ctrl-C or Ctrl-Break to halt operation
```

Figure 6-4 How you use *FileSafe* to do a full backup (Part 4 of 4)

backup doesn't technically distinguish files from one another. As a result, you can only restore the entire backup; you can't restore individual files. This is the type of backup that *FileSafe* does when you select the Full option.

In contrast, a file backup does distinguish one file from another. This makes it possible to do a partial restore. Of course, if you specify all the files and directories during a file backup, you get a full backup. This is the type of backup that *FileSafe* does when you select the Selective option.

After you specify the Selective option, *FileSafe* displays the screen shown in part 2 of figure 6-4. This screen lets you specify several settings for the backup operation. Since you want to do a full backup, you just specify the drive you want to backup. Then, you select the Backup-files option.

Part 3 of figure 6-4 shows you the screen that the program displays next. The options on this screen let you specify which files you want to back up. To do a full backup, you select the Complete-backup-of-files-without-reference-to-date-and-time option. Then, the program starts the backup operation.

In part 4 of figure 6-4, you can see the screen that shows the progress of the backup operation. Here, the program displays information about the tape at the top of the screen. In the middle of the screen, it displays information about the current operation and about the progress of the backup. And at the bottom on the screen, it shows the directory that is currently being backed up.

How to select and install a tape drive

When you select a tape drive, you need to consider three factors. First, you should select a tape drive that has enough storage capacity to back up the largest hard drive on your PC. So if the largest hard drive on your PC is 120MB, you should select a tape drive with a capacity of 120MB or more. That way, you can back up the entire hard drive on one tape. This makes it possible to do unattended backups.

Incidently, if you have a large hard disk that is divided into logical drives, you don't have to get a tape drive that will back up the entire hard disk on one tape. Instead, you need to get a tape that will back up the largest drive that's defined on your hard disk. For example, if you have a 200MB hard disk that's divided into two 100MB drives, you should get a tape drive with a capacity of at least 100MB.

Second, you should select a tape drive that's fast enough for your backup requirements. Generally, a tape drive is rated in terms of the number of megabytes of data that it can back up in a minute. As a result, it's easy to calculate the time required for a given tape drive to back up your hard drive. Then, you can determine if a tape drive you are considering is fast enough for your needs. Of course, speed isn't an important factor if you plan to do unattended backups.

Third, you need to decide between an *internal tape drive* or an *external tape drive*. An internal tape drive installs in your computer just like a diskette drive does. Generally, these drives are cheaper and more convenient to use than the equivalent external drive. To use an internal drive, however, you must have an available drive bay that's accessible from the front of your computer. If you don't, or if you have a computer like some IBM PS/2s that won't accept the tape drive you want, you must buy an external tape drive.

An external tape drive uses a separate case for the drive. Then, a cable attaches the drive to your PC. Often, the external tape drive also has a power cord that plugs into a wall plug. But aside from these physical differences, an external tape drive works just like an internal drive.

When you buy a tape drive, it should come with detailed instructions on how to install the drive. These instructions should show you how to install the drive in your PC's case. And they should show you how to install any cards, cables, or mounting hardware that are required for the drive to operate with your PC.

Usually, the slower tape drives are cabled to the diskette controller card that's already in your PC. Because they use an existing controller card, these drives are easier to install. You just attach a cable from the diskette controller card to the tape drive. And because they use an existing card, they are less expensive than the faster drives. In contrast, the faster tape drives use their own controller cards that you must install in your PC as part of the tape drive installation.

Of course, you can always have a computer technician or consultant install a tape drive for you. Since the job is fairly simple, it shouldn't cost more than $100. The technician or consultant should also be able to help you select an appropriate tape drive for your system and backup requirements.

Is using a backup tape drive the right option for you?

Now that you understand how a tape drive works, you should be able to decide if getting one will improve your backup procedures. If you have much more than 40MB to backup, you should at least consider a tape drive. Because you can back up much faster with a tape drive, you'll cut your backup time to a minimum. Similarly, if you find that using a backup utility and diskettes is too complicated for your needs, you should consider a tape drive. If being able to do unattended backups is an important consideration, then a tape drive is your only option. And if your PC has data on it that is critical to your business, you should consider a tape drive because tape backups are generally more reliable than diskette backups.

With the price of tape drives falling, cost should be less of an issue. For example, you can buy a tape drive that can back up 60MB for about $200. In many cases, this is a small price to pay especially if having a tape drive means the difference between doing regular backups or not doing them.

Terms

tape drive
tape cartridge
unattended backup
DC2000 tape
DC600 tape
cassette tape
Teac tape drive
QIC40 format
QIC80 format
standard format
proprietary format
proprietary tape software
FileSafe
image backup
file backup
internal tape drive
external tape drive

Index

Appended incremental backup, 14, 69, 85-86, 110, 142-144, 146, 166-171
Archive bit, 14, 70, 135
Artisoft, 46
AT, 5-6
Automating backups, 94-97, 122-128, 152, 178-184

Backup command (DOS), 8, 10-11, 13, 33, 55-64, 67
Backup format, 4
Backup log, 36-38
Backup media, 36
Backup options, 26, 27
Backup plan, 25-28, 41
Backup program, 4
Backup requirements, 25-26, 46-50
Backup schedule, 31-32
Backup set, 36, 40
Backup speed, 13-14
Backup techniques, 25-28
Backup types, 12-15
BACKUP.LOG, 58-59, 142
Batch file, 33, 96-97, 98, 124, 126, 154, 156, 181
Bernoulli box, 8
Boot diskette, 40-41

Cassette tape, 189, 190
Catalog file, 114-118
CD drive, 8
Central Point Backup, 13, 66, 67, 74, 75-98, 192-193

Central Point Backup (continued)
   Appended incremental backup, 85-86
   Automating backups, 94-97
   Batch file, 96, 98
   Compare, 94
   Configure menu, 77-78
   CPS format, 79
   Dialog box, 77
   Differential backup, 86
   DMA, 76
   File menu, 80
   File transfer, 86
   Full backup, 81-85
   Full-copy, 86
   History file, 89-90
   Options menu, 78-80
   Partial backup, 86-89
   Restore, 89-93; full 90-91; partial 91-93
   Separate incremental backup, 86
   Setting up, 76-80
   Setup file, 94-96, 98
   Starting, 75
Check-disk command (DOS), 25
CHKDSK (DOS), 25
Commercial backup utilities, 8-10, 11-12, 13, 62-63, 65-185, 192-193
Compare, 94, 120-122, 150, 152, 178
Copying data, 24-25

Data backup, 23-24
Data transfer, 24-25
Date-selected backup, 70, 104

199

DC2000 tape, 188, 189
DC600 tape, 188-190
Dedicated file server network, 44
Differential backup, 70, 86, 110, 112, 135
Direct memory access, see DMA
Directories, 18-20, 23-24
Diskette capacity, 6, 7
Diskette drive, 5-6, 16
Diskless workstations, 44, 45
DMA, 67, 76, 102, 135
Double density, 6, 7

External tape drive, 197

FastBack Plus, 13, 66, 67, 74, 157-185
    Appended incremental backup, 166, 169-171
    Automating backups, 178-184
    Backup segment, 169-170
    Batch file, 181
    Compare, 178
    Express menu system, 162, 164
    Full backup, 164-166
    Long menu system, 162-164, 178
    Macro command, 178, 182-184
    Menu system, 162
    Options menu, 162-164
    Partial backup, 171
    Restore, 174-178; full, 174; partial, 176-178
    Segment name, 169-170
    Setting up, 160-164
    Setup file, 178-184
    Starting, 157-160
    Window menu, 160-162
FBEZ menu, 152-154
FDISK (DOS), 18
File backup, 193, 196
File compression, 68, 104
File extension, 20-21
File name, 20-22
File server, 44, 45

File spec., 16, 17, 18-22
File specification, 16, 17, 18-22
File transfer, 24-25
File-list feature, 136, 148
File-server network, 44-48, 49-50
FileSafe, 191-192, 193-196
Full backup, 12-13, 15, 35, 57-59, 69, 71, 81-85, 108-111, 140-142, 164-166, 193-196
Full restore, 61, 63
FULLBAK.LOG, 142, 146, 148

Hard disk, 6, 16-22, 44
Hardware, 4-8, 26, 27
High capacity, 6, 7
High density, 6, 7

Image backup, 193, 196
Incremental backup, 13-15, 59, 69, 71, 85-86, 110, 113, 135, 142-146, 166, 169-171
Internal tape drive, 197

Kilobyte, 6

LAN, 43
Lantastic, 46
Local area network, 43
Local hard disk, 44, 45
Local resource, 44
Log file, 58
Logical drive, 16-18, 44

Macro, 68, 182-184
Megabyte, 6
Mountain Computer, 191

Netware, 44
Network, 29, 43-51
Network administrator, 45
Network resource, 44
Norton Backup, 13, 66, 67, 74, 99-130

Norton Backup (continued)
   Appended incremental backup, 110
   Automating backups, 122-128
   Backup-options menu, 102-106
   Batch file, 124
   Catalog file, 106, 114-118
   Compare, 120-122
   Confidence test function, 102
   Configure menu, 101-102
   Data compression, 104
   Date-selected backup, 104
   Dialog box, 101
   Differential backup, 110
   DMA, 102
   Full backup, 108-111
   Macro, 123, 124-128
   Options function, 102
   Partial backup, 112
   Preset menu, 128-129
   Program-level function, 101
   Restore, 114-120; full, 118; partial, 118
   Save-changes function, 106
   Separate incremental backup, 110, 113
   Setting up, 100-106
   Setup file, 122-124
   Starting, 99-92
Novell, 44

Optical drive, 8

Partial backup, 59-60, 86-89, 112, 146, 171
Partial restore, 61, 62, 63
Partition, 16
Path, 19-20
PC, 5-6
PC Tools Deluxe, 75, 76, 96
PC-Fullbak+, 13, 66, 67, 74, 131-156
   Appended incremental backup, 142, 144-146
   Automating backups, 152
   Backup-options category, 134-135
   Batch file, 154, 156

PC-Fullbak+ (continued)
   Command line option, 154-155
   Compare, 150, 152
   Compare-options category, 136
   Device-options category, 138
   Differential backup, 135
   DMA, 135
   FBEZ menu, 152-154
   File-list feature, 136, 148
   Full backup, 140-142
   FULLBAK.LOG, 142, 146, 148
   Incremental backup, 135
   List-options category, 136
   Log file, 142
   Options function, 132-134
   Partial backup, 146
   Point-and-shoot feature, 136, 148
   Proprietary format, 138
   Quit function, 139
   Restore, 148-151; full, 148-150; partial, 148, 151
   Restore-options category, 136
   Save function, 139
   Script file, 135, 152
   Setting up, 132-139
   Starting, 131-132
   Video-options category, 138
Peer network, 46, 48-50
Peer-to-peer network, 46
Point-and-shoot feature, 136, 148
Preset menu, 128-129
Program backup, 23-24
PS/2, 5-6

QIC40 format, 190-191
QIC80 format, 190-191

Removable storage, 4
Restore, 4, 10, 60-63, 89-93, 114-120, 118-120, 146-151, 171, 174-178
Restore command (DOS), 10, 60-62

Root directory, 18
Running stand-alone, 44

Schedule, 31-32
Script file, 135, 152
Segment, 169-170
Separate incremental backup, 14, 69, 86, 110, 113
Setup file, 33-35, 68, 94-96, 98, 122-125, 178-184
Source specification, 55, 57
Standard capacity, 6, 7
Subdirectory, 18
Switch (DOS), 56-57
System diskette, 40-41

Tape capacity, 7-8
Tape cartridge, 7, 188-190
Tape drive, 6-8, 9, 187-198
Tape formats, 190-191
Tape software, 191-192
Target specification, 55, 57
Teac drive, 190
Transferring data, 24-25

Unattended backup, 7, 187

Virus, 86

Wildcard, 22, 23, 57, 58
Windows, 97

XT, 5-6

Everything you need to know
to become a more competent, more independent PC user

The Least You Need to Know about DOS

by Patrick Bultema

It seems like every time you get to working on your PC, some "little" problem brings you to a screeching halt. Like you can't start one of your programs because someone else has been using your PC. Or it takes you half an hour to transfer data from one PC to another because the diskette you're using won't work right in both machines. Or you can't find a file that you know is there somewhere. And often, you can't get going again until someone else helps you out.

But you can handle problems like these easily on your own...or avoid them altogether...if you have just a minimum set of DOS skills. That's where this book comes in. Its tightly focused approach will quickly teach you the essential DOS skills you need to become a more competent, more independent PC user:

- how to start your application programs from DOS or a shell, no matter who was using the PC last or what application was being run
- how to manage your directories and files, so you can always find what you're looking for
- how to refer to DOS directories and files from your application programs
- how to transfer data from one PC to another using diskettes
- how to back up the hard disk data on your PC (of course, this is only a small subset of the material in *How to Back Up Your PC*)
- how to change the CONFIG.SYS and AUTOEXEC.BAT files, in case you don't like the way your system starts up or operates
- how to use the DOS 5.0 shell to work more efficiently, in case you have DOS 5.0 installed on your PC
- and nothing more!

So if you're tired of asking for PC help from the PC support group, the "help" line, your colleagues, your friends, or your spouse, this book is for YOU.

14 chapters, 276 pages, $17.95
ISBN 0-911625-61-5

To order by phone, call toll-free 1-800-221-5528 (Weekdays, 8:30 to 5, Pacific Standard Time)

Covers DOS 2.0 through 5.0 for hard disk users

The Only DOS Book You'll Ever Need

by Doug Lowe and Patrick Bultema

This book is for anyone who wants...or needs...to know more about DOS than what's covered in *The Least You Need to Know about DOS* (described on the previous page). So if you don't have anyone to set your PC up for you or to help you solve more technical problems, this book is for you. It's also the ideal book for people who provide support to less technical PC users. As a result, we recommend it for every corporate help desk, for every PC support person, and for the lead technical person in every user department.

Everything in the *Least* book is also in this book, though much of it is in expanded form. So there are chapters on managing files and directories, backing up your hard disk, working with diskettes, using the DOS 5.0 shell, and making changes to the CONFIG.SYS and AUTOEXEC.BAT files. In addition, though, this book covers:

- how to prevent, detect, and recover from disk problems and user errors
- how to improve the performance of your PC without buying new hardware
- the commercial utility programs that actually improve upon DOS (why, for example, should you use DOS to do a function like backup when you can use an inexpensive utility to do it far more efficiently?)
- when and how to install a new version of DOS
- how to partition and format a hard disk
- how to use the DOS 4.0 shell (it isn't nearly as helpful as the DOS 5.0 shell)
- more commands for CONFIG.SYS and AUTOEXEC.BAT
- how to use some of the advanced capabilities of DOS that you'll seldom (if ever) need

So if you want to expand your DOS knowledge...or if you're looking for a resource for PC support...get a copy of *The Only DOS Book You'll Ever Need* TODAY!

27 chapters, 550 pages, $24.95
ISBN 0-911625-58-5

To order by phone, call toll-free 1-800-221-5528 (Weekdays, 8:30 to 5, Pacific Standard Time)

If you're using *Word* without style sheets, you're working too hard...
and you're not getting the word processor you paid for

Get More from *Word* by Using Style Sheets

by Tim Schaldach

When you use style sheets with *Microsoft Word*, you can format long blocks of copy with just a few keystrokes. That's a marked contrast to the way you have to format your documents without style sheets. In fact, *Word* becomes a whole different word processor—a more powerful, flexible one—when you use style sheets.

Unfortunately, at first glance, style sheets can seem to be more trouble than they're worth. And even if you want to know how to use them, the *Word* manuals don't make them easy for you to master.

That's why you need a copy of *Get More from Word by Using Style Sheets*. It explains what you have to gain by using a style sheet with every document you write. Then, it shows you how to use style sheets to quickly format the words, paragraphs, and pages in all your documents.

But that's not all. Some *Word* features are clumsy and almost too difficult to use by themselves. But they're no problem at all when you use them with style sheets. So this book also shows you how to use style sheets with these *Word* features:

- desktop publishing
- the outline feature
- the running head feature
- the footnote feature
- the table of contents generator
- the index generator

So stop working so hard. Get more from *Word* by using style sheets TODAY!

12 chapters, 245 pages, $19.95
ISBN 0-911625-55-0

Note: This book assumes you know the basics of using *Word 4* or *Word 5* on an IBM PC or compatible. Then, in case you ever switch to *Word 5.5*, the last chapter of the book shows you how to use style sheets with *Word 5.5* (the concepts are all the same, so your existing style sheets will still work; it's just the user interface that's different).

To order by phone, call toll-free 1-800-221-5528 (Weekdays, 8:30 to 5, Pacific Standard Time)

You'll never again dread a writing project of any size
with this handbook on technical and business writing

Write Better with a PC

A publisher's guide to business and technical writing by Mike Murach

Have you ever stared helplessly at a blank screen, wondering how to get started on that memo or letter or report you have to write?

If so, I want to tell you about *Write Better with a PC*. Step-by-step, this book shows you how to break your writing projects down into manageable parts that are easy for you to handle. You'll soon be writing with more confidence than ever before... and you'll never again dread a writing project of any size.

No matter how big the writing project is, you'll always know what to do next...and you'll always know you can do it

Writing seems overwhelming when you're staring at the screen, wondering how in the world to get started. So this book tells you exactly what to do first, what to do next, and so on, for any type of business document. You'll find that you can handle each step with ease when you're not worrying about the document as a whole. And you'll see right away why entering the words into the screen is one of the *last* things you do.

But knowing where to start is only half the problem. Sometimes, it's just as hard to know when to *stop* writing. That's especially true when you're using word processing and can easily revise your documents again and again.

But with the writing method in this book, you'll find your documents need less revising to begin with. And when you revise, you won't have to re-think the entire document, wondering if you've said what you should. Instead, you can concentrate on strengthening your paragraphs, sentences, and words—and then you can quit revising, instead of re-working the document again and again.

You'll master the writing and grammar skills you never learned in school

Most business documents fail because they're so poorly written that nobody reads or acts upon them. That's why *Write Better with a PC* also teaches you the language skills you must have to write documents worth reading.

This book doesn't follow the grammar-laden approach that's the norm in school, though. Instead, it focuses first on how to write effective paragraphs because that's where most business writers have trouble. Then, it moves on to sentences, words, and punctuation. I think you'll find this works 100% better for you than the traditional approach that starts with grammar...and usually stops there. So even if you had trouble with these skills in school, you'll master them quite easily using this book. And you'll find yourself making dramatic improvements in your writing right away.

You'll know how to use the right PC software at the right time

There's a lot of software you can use for writing besides word processing; the trick is knowing what to use and when to use it. So *Write Better with a PC* gives you specific software advice for each step in the writing method. For example:

- In chapter 4, "How to Plan What You're Going to Write," you'll learn how an outline processor can help you plan more effectively
- In chapter 5, "How to Write the First Draft," you'll learn how to use spreadsheet and graphics software (as well as word processing) to create visual aids

- In chapter 9, "How to Write Readable Sentences," you'll learn how to use a writing analyzer to test whether your writing's easy to read
- In chapter 15, "When and How to Use Desktop Publishing to Present Your Documents," you'll learn when to use desktop publishing to give your documents a more polished look...and how to do it in a reasonable amount of time

In short, once you finish this book, you'll know what types of software will help you most as you write...and you'll know how and when to use each type.

So why wait to start writing more easily and with more confidence?

See for yourself how quickly you can improve your business writing skills. Get your copy of *Write Better with a PC* today!

15 chapters, 406 pages, $19.95
ISBN 0-911625-51-8

To order by phone, call toll-free 1 800-221-5528 (Weekdays, 8:30 to 5, Pacific Standard Time)

Want to keep a mailing list on your PC?
Here's the book that will help you out

The PC Mailing List Book

by Patrick Bultema

If you use a PC at home or at work, I'll bet you've at least thought about putting a mailing list on it. After all, it seems like such a simple application. You just enter the names and addresses using whatever software you already have (probably your spreadsheet or word processing program). Then, you can easily print out labels, letters, or envelopes whenever you need them.

But if you've ever tried this, you know it's not as simple as it seems. Spreadsheet, and even word processing, programs have some real limitations when it comes to mailing lists. But how do you know what to try instead? And, if you've already got your mailing list entered on your PC, how do you avoid re-doing it from scratch?

That's where *The PC Mailing List Book* comes in. It helps you:

- analyze your mailing list needs so you know what features to look for in an application program (this is the key to having a PC mailing list that's easy to use and maintain)
- evaluate different programs so you can choose one that meets your needs (screen-by-screen examples of 8 popular programs let you compare their mailing-list features and see which programs are easy to use for lists like yours...all without spending a penny on software!)
- create labels, personalized letters, envelopes, address directories, and reports using the program you choose
- set up your mailing lists so they work best, no matter what software you choose
- transfer an existing PC mailing list to another program if you decide to switch software
- avoid mistakes that seem trivial, but that waste time and money...like getting labels jammed in your printer

In short, this book will give you the perspective you need to set up, use, and maintain trouble-free mailing lists on your PC.

7 chapters, 276 pages, $24.95
ISBN 0-911625-53-4

Shows examples using: WordPerfect, Microsoft Word, Professional Write, Q&A, dBase III Plus, Microsoft Works, Address Book Plus, Lotus 1-2-3

To order by phone, call toll-free 1-**800-221-5528** (Weekdays, 8:30 to 5, Pacific Standard Time)

Comment Form

Your opinions count

If you have any comments, criticisms, or suggestions for us, I'm eager to get them. Your opinions today will affect our products of tomorrow. And if you find any errors in this book, typographical or otherwise, please point them out so we can correct them in the next printing.

Thanks for your help.

Mike Murach

Book title: How to Back Up Your PC

Dear Mike: _____

_____
_____
_____
_____
_____
_____
_____
_____
_____
_____

Name _____
Company (if company address) _____
Address _____
City, State, Zip _____

Fold where indicated and tape closed.
No postage necessary if mailed in the U.S.

BUSINESS REPLY MAIL
FIRST-CLASS MAIL   PERMIT NO. 3063   FRESNO, CA

POSTAGE WILL BE PAID BY ADDRESSEE

Mike Murach & Associates, Inc.

4697 W JACQUELYN AVE
FRESNO CA 93722-9888

NO POSTAGE
NECESSARY
IF MAILED
IN THE
UNITED STATES

Order Form

Our Unlimited Guarantee

To our customers who order directly from us: You must be satisfied. Our books must work for you, or you can send them back for a full refund... no questions asked.

Company (if company address) _____
Street address _____
City, State, Zip _____
Daytime telephone number (including area code) _____

Quantity	Code	Title	Price
_____	BACK	How to Back Up Your PC	$ 15.00
_____	LDOS	The Least You Need to Know about DOS	17.95
_____	DOSB	The Only DOS Book You'll Ever Need	24.95
_____	WBPC	Write Better with a PC	19.95
_____	MWSS	Get More from *Word* by Using Style Sheets	19.95
_____	PCML	The PC Mailing List Book	24.95

☐ Bill the appropriate book prices plus UPS shipping and handling charges (and sales tax in California) to my ____ Visa ____ MasterCard:
Card number _____
Valid thru (month/year) _____
Signature _____

☐ Bill me.

☐ Bill my company. P.O.# _____

☐ I want to **SAVE** shipping and handling charges. Here's my check or money order for $_____. California residents, please add sales tax to your total. (Offer valid in the U.S. only.)

To order more quickly,

Call **toll-free** 1-800-221-5528
(Weekdays, 8:30 to 5 Pacific Std. Time)

Fax: 1-209-275-9035

Mike Murach & Associates, Inc.
4697 West Jacquelyn Avenue
Fresno, California 93722-6427
(209) 275-3335

BUSINESS REPLY MAIL
FIRST-CLASS MAIL   PERMIT NO. 3063   FRESNO, CA

POSTAGE WILL BE PAID BY ADDRESSEE

Mike Murach & Associates, Inc.
4697 W JACQUELYN AVE
FRESNO CA 93722-9888

NO POSTAGE
NECESSARY
IF MAILED
IN THE
UNITED STATES